David Potts

THE AUTHOR

An Australian, Ian Grey studied law at the University of Sydney and devoted his free time to history and languages, especially Russian. During World War II, he was sent to Russia, where he served from 1942 to 1944. He was attached to the British Military Mission in Moscow for some months, traveled widely in the Soviet Union, and was a member of one of the first Allied groups to visit Leningrad when the German blockade was lifted. After the war, Mr. Grey was associated with *British Ally*, a Russian-language newspaper published weekly by the British Embassy in Moscow, and with Russian-language broadcasts of the B.B.C.

Throughout his stay in the Soviet Union, the author gathered material on Russia and her history, and in 1960, he published his first book based on his research there, a biography of Peter the Great. His *Catherine the Great* was published two years later.

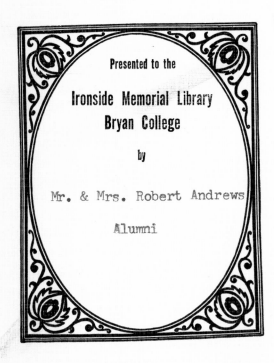

IVAN THE TERRIBLE

Engraving after a contemporary portrait of Ivan the Terrible in the "Book of Titles", Russian State Archives. N. Utkin is the artist.

IVAN

THE

TERRIBLE

by Ian Grey

J. B. LIPPINCOTT COMPANY
Philadelphia and New York

FOR
DAVID

CONTENTS

This vigorous, shrewd and brave monarch was of a very fierce temperament.

Lomonosov

This prince was my forerunner and model. I have always endeavoured to imitate his bravery and the wisdom of his government, but I am far from being his equal. He can be called a tyrant by none but men of weak minds who neither know the circumstances he was in, the nation he governed, nor the greatness of his abilities.

Emperor Peter the Great

PREFACE

No Tsar of Russia has been more widely known by name than Ivan the Terrible. Through history he has exercised a sinister fascination, but he has remained a nebulous figure, seen through a haze of blood and savagery. Most historians have, like Karamzin in the early 19th century, condemned him as a cruel tyrant, perverted by power. But in the Soviet Union he has been recognized as a great Tsar, and as portrayed in Eisenstein's remarkable film, a national hero.

Ivan will always be a source of controversy, as he was in his own day. He was an extraordinarily complex character, extreme in conduct and in speech. His personality was vivid and powerful. He inspired legends and passionate conflicts. His life was tragic. From earliest childhood and throughout his life he suffered terrors, calamities, and personal tragedies which would have unhinged the minds of most men. Fear, betrayals, and desperation made him suspicious and liable to flashing storms of anger, and his punishments were those of his times. Indeed, he revealed many of the symptoms of a manic-depressive. His sense of sin, his obsessive anxiety for his dynasty, and his bouts of inhumanity brought him close to insanity at certain stages in his life. But also he was capable of affection, kindness, generosity, and tolerance, and, where the affairs of the Tsardom were concerned, he remained always the practical and dedicated sovereign.

Ivan was, in fact, one of the most outstanding and truly Russian of the Tsars. An imperious man of great intelligence and ability, he was a natural leader and, as the first crowned Tsar of Russia, he claimed the loyalty and devotion of the mass of his people who saw in him the centre and epitome of the nation.

In the troubled Europe of the 16th century when centralized states were evolving around the persons of their monarchs, Ivan asserted his absolute power and established a strong and united nation. His conquest of the Khanates of Kazan and Astrakhan, which fired the imagination of all Russians, may be said to have brought the nation to birth. But also he laid the foundations of the Russian Empire by opening the way for the colonizing drive eastwards. In the west he struggled to secure access to the Baltic so that Russia would share in trade and free intercourse with the rest of Europe. Furthermore, his reign was a period when the machinery of central government was being created, and it was, in fact, notable for major political, administrative, and ecclesiastical reforms.

To his people Ivan was known as *Grozny* which in Russian means "the Dread" or the Tsar "to be feared" in the sense that the Lord is to be feared. The word *grozny*, as applied to Ivan, perhaps carried something of the meaning of *groza*, a thunderstorm, for his was certainly a stormy temperament. But the word "dread" best reflected their attitude to him which was well stated by the Englishman, Anthony Jenkinson, who wrote, " . . . I think no prince in Christendom is more feared of his own than he is, nor better loved." Ivan's grandfather, Ivan III, was also known at times to his people as *Grozny*, because he, too, was a stern and strong ruler, but historians more often refer to him as "the Great".

The fact that *Grozny* has for so long been rendered as "The Terrible" is not, however, simply a matter of false translation. It derives from the reputation which Ivan had abroad during his reign and which has clung to him through history. But it was a reputation created mainly by the reports and polemics of his enemies, expecially Prince Andrei Kurbsky, whose calumnies, more than any others, have darkened the portraits painted of Ivan and helped obscure his importance as a great national ruler.

I have found Ivan far less terrible than the Tsar of legend. This does not mean that the savageries perpetrated in his reign can be denied or extenuated in any way. It is important, however, that they should be seen and judged by the standards of the time. The bigotry of Philip II of Spain and the barbarities of the Inquisition and of Spanish troops in the Low Countries, the massacre of St Bartholomew's Day in France, the inhumanity of German, Swedish, and Polish troops were all part of the times in which Ivan lived. It was a cruel age and the conduct of Ivan and his people was no worse than that of many of his contemporaries.

In writing this study I have frequently been struck by its contemporary parallels. Mr Khrushchev's comment, made on 10 March 1963, that Stalin was "a deeply sick person, suffering from persecution mania" might be applied to Ivan at certain stages of his reign. But apart from persecutions and executions, other parallels between 16th century Muscovy and 20th century Soviet Russia will impress all who are interested in the Russian people and their history. The

Preface

Oprichniki, the striving westwards, southwards, and eastwards for secure frontiers, the colonizing of the virgin lands, and other events in Ivan's reign seem at times merely the first stages in developments continued in the 20th century. This is, of course, no more than an illustration of the essential continuity of Russia's history, but it is a continuity that is often ignored.

The main sources which I have used are listed in the bibliography. I have also included notes on each chapter, giving the references for quotations and explanatory comments where these seemed necessary. I must acknowledge my indebtedness to the great histories of Karamzin, Solovyev, and Klyuchevsky on which I have relied at every stage of writing this study. Mr J. L. I. Fennell's excellent translation of the correspondence between Ivan and Prince Andrei Kurbsky has been invaluable, for the syntax and vocabulary of 16th-century Russian often require interpretation by the specialist. I have also made every use of the researches of Soviet historians whenever available, for they have been carrying out original work in this field, the results of which are extremely important. The monographs of A. A. Zimin in particular have been of the greatest assistance to me.

I express my gratitude to several friends who have helped me at many points in this work, and especially to Count Alexei Bobrinskoy who read the MS with care, making many valuable comments. To my wife I am yet again, and indeed always, indebted for patience and support.

LONDON,
June 1963.

CHAPTER I

THE RISE OF MOSCOW

THE dramatic growth of Moscow from an insignificant town into the matrix and capital of the nation, revered by Russians and celebrated in their traditional folk poetry, is one of the most fascinating chapters in Russia's history.

The vast region, which was to be united under Moscow's rule, was an expansive plain, largely covered with forests and intersected by great rivers and their tributaries. Maple, birch, and oak mingled with coniferous trees and grew so densely and to such great size that the forests were in places almost impenetrable. Wolves, elks, bears, and wild oxen roamed these forests, which also abounded with sable, fox, beaver, squirrel, and other fur-bearing animals. Hunting was the most lucrative occupation of the people and furs were the main item of trade. The rivers teemed with fish. The soil in the vicinity of Moscow was sandy and not very productive, but the lands to the south, where the trees thinned, were extremely fertile. In the regions of Chernigov and Ryazan, the corn grew so thick and high that horses could not make their way across the fields.

In this country of extremes of climate, the violent upsurge of life in spring and summer offered compensation for the savage cold of winter. Food was not scarce. Game and fish, wild honey and berries were plentiful. Timber for building and heating lay readily at hand. But for the people life was harsh and precarious. Wars between rival princes, raids by Tatars and other enemies, and the scourges of nature, such as forest fires, floods, pestilence, made their lives a cruel struggle against starvation and calamity. But it also developed in them qualities of resourcefulness and stamina which enabled them not only to survive, but also to colonize the great expanses of Asia and to endure as a nation in the hard years ahead of them.

Moscow had begun to rise in the 13th century after the invasion of the Mongols. Occupying an important geographical position between the upper Volga and Oka rivers, the town stood at the very centre of the river system which provided transport and communication over the immense Eurasian plain. This inner position also gave

Moscow greater security from attacks by Tatars and other enemies. As a refuge it attracted people of all ranks from neighbouring principalities, who added to its wealth and power.

Moscow was also fortunate in its princes. They do not emerge from the shadowed distance of history as individuals, but all were careful stewards of their realm, persevering, unscrupulous, and astute in accumulating riches. They acquired new lands by treaty, purchase, and, as a last resort, by force. Within scarcely more than a century, the extent of their principality had grown from some 500 to more than 15,000 square miles.

In this ambitious expansion the princes of Moscow had two important allies, the Golden Horde and the Orthodox Church. The Mongol invasion of the 13th century, the last great western movement of the Eurasian nomads and one of the most shattering and fateful events in history, struck the Russians with its full ferocity. The Mongols burnt towns and villages to the ground, killing most of the inhabitants and carrying off the young people to sell as slaves. The Mongol horde then laid waste parts of Poland–Lithuania, Hungary and Croatia, and suddenly withdrew. They did not renew their conquest westward into Europe, but from Sarai on the lower Volga, which became the capital of the Khanate of the Kipchak or the Golden Horde, the Tatars wielded suzerainty over Russia for some two hundred years.

The Russians recovered only in the following century from the shock and terror of the invasion and from the slaughter and devastation which had brought the national life to a standstill. But early in this century the princes of Moscow had gained from the Khan recognition as Grand Prince, senior to the other Russian princes and intermediary between them and the Horde. Ivan I, called Kalita or Money-Bag (1328–41) also took the title of Grand Prince of Vladimir, which had been the senior principality after the fall of Kiev. He became responsible for the collection and payment of the Khan's tribute from all the principalities, and he and his successors made full use of this office of authority to increase their power.

The support of the Orthodox Church was also an important factor in the rise of Moscow. The church had shared in the terrible sufferings inflicted by the Mongol invasion, but it had recovered quickly, and under the Tatar yoke it had flourished. The Khans were tolerant towards other faiths. At one stage they had shown a leaning towards Christianity so strong that Rome had entertained hopes of their conversion. Even after their adoption of Islam, the Khans continued to show favour to the Orthodox Church. Under their protection the church grew wealthy; its lands attracted peasants; its monasteries and churches multiplied. Every village had its log-built church and the bulbous domes on the horizon marked the spread of Muscovite colonization.

With the permission of the Khan, Ivan Kalita had transferred the seat of the Metropolitan, the head of the Orthodox Church in Russia, from Vladimir to Moscow, which thus became the ecclesiastical capital. Moreover, Metropolitan Peter, revered for his sanctity, was by his own wish buried in Moscow where his tomb became a national shrine.

Under the Tatar yoke the church had comforted the people and fostered their sense of unity and their hopes of casting off the domination of infidels. Successive Metropolitans gave their support to the Grand Princes of Moscow in their policy of uniting all Orthodox Russians under their rule and securing their independence. Already the ecclesiastical capital in the 14th century, Moscow was rapidly becoming the political capital of Russia.

The spread of Moscow's power was also accompanied by an economic revival. After the Mongol invasion the country had gone into a decline. Trade had dwindled. Lands had been abandoned. Towns, with the exceptions of Moscow and Novgorod, had diminished in population and become little more than local centres of administration.

War was the main cause of this general depression. The Mongol onslaughts were followed by forty-five wars, fought between Tatars and Muscovites during the period of the Tatar domination. This was in addition to incessant Tatar raiding. Furthermore, during these two centuries the Russians fought at least forty-one wars with the Lithuanians, thirty with the German Baltic Orders, and some forty-four wars against Swedes, Bulgars, and others. Rivalries between the principalities of Great Russia were so fierce at this time that, despite wars with foreign enemies, the Muscovites fought at least ninety internal wars between 1228 and 1462.[1]

Pestilence, the companion of war, caused further depopulation of the already sparsely settled country. Epidemics in Smolensk and Kiev in the 13th century carried off the inhabitants in thousands. Twenty epidemics were recorded in the years from 1348 to 1448, causing innumerable deaths. The plague which swept through Novgorod in the 1390s was said to have killed 80,000 people.[2]

Gradually during the 15th century the Russians emerged from this dark age in their history. Trade revived as the Tatar hold weakened, and Russian merchants found their way once more to the markets of the Black and Caspian Seas. Industries started up again. Old towns stirred with life and new towns were established, some of them devoted to commerce and industry. In the following century the number of towns was to increase from about 160 to 230.

Perhaps the most significant evidence of the greater security and of the awakening of the new nation was the increase in population. No accurate figures exist and estimates of population of Muscovy towards the end of the 15th century vary from 2·1 million to 9 or 10 million.[3] But land registers and other internal evidence show that by the mid-16th century the central region was far more densely populated than a century earlier. Richard Chancellor, the English seaman who reached Muscovy in 1553, was impressed by the dense settlement that he saw. The lands between Yaroslavl and Moscow were, he remarked, "very well replenished with small villages, which are so well filled with people that it is a wonder to see them".[4]

The rise of Moscow and the political union of Great Russia drew strength from popular support. After decades of hardship the Russians craved the stability and security which a strong centralized state, ruled by the able princes of Moscow, would give them. The peasants in particular longed for peace and security. They bore heavy burdens, tilling the soil, working at cottage industries during the long cold winters, serving in their lord's troop in the incessant fighting, and they suffered most in the raids of Tatars who laid waste the land, destroyed their villages, and carried off their women.

The peasants nevertheless enjoyed certain rights and freedom, especially the freedom to move. They lived in villages and hamlets, working together in patriarchal and, later, territorial communes. On the "black land" which was a vast, but rapidly diminishing, area of land not yet granted to private owners or personally owned by the Grand Prince, although part of his principality, the peasants bought, worked and sold their holdings as though they themselves were the owners. But peasant families sometimes quitted the black lands of their own accord to settle on private estates. Many were tempted by exemptions from tax and other inducements offered by the great landowners, eager to develop their estates. More often they moved in search of greater security.

Peasants on private estates at this time enjoyed considerable independence. Most landowners left the land to be worked by their peasants who in return rendered services or paid a rental in cash or in kind. So long as they met their obligations, they virtually exercised the rights of owner. Peasants were also free to depart from the lands of their lord, but restrictions on the exercise of this right began to appear as early as the 15th century. In the sparsely settled expanses of Muscovy, labour was too valuable to be allowed to come and go freely, and during the following two centuries the peasant became increasingly shackled to the land and to the lord, and the evil institution of serfdom developed.

While the peasants welcomed the formation of the Muscovite state, most princely families felt bitter resentment over what they regarded as their new servitude to the Grand Princes of Moscow. The serving princes were a fairly numerous caste. Originally they had belonged to independent ruling families, but many of these families had become impoverished mainly because of the practice of providing independent princedoms for the sons of each generation. By the 15th century many principalities had been fragmented, and the sons of such families found themselves compelled to seek service in Moscow.

Muscovy herself had escaped this fate, because from the late 14th century each Grand Prince had followed the practice of bequeathing the greatest part of his realm to his eldest son. Certain other principalities had avoided fragmentation in this way. When absorbed into Muscovy their princes had become subordinate to the Grand Prince, but on their patrimonial estates they continued to wield the same authority over their people.

The boyars in Kievan and then in north-east Russia had enjoyed rank and privilege because of their political and especially their military importance to their Grand Prince. On his summons, boyars, who had sworn allegiance to him, assembled at the head of the armed men mustered from their estates. For their service he rewarded them with grants of land and many boyars became wealthy landowners. But the fact of owning land did not by itself bind boyars to serve, whereas the lesser serving men or gentry, holding their land on service tenure, were obliged to answer the summons. For this reason, and because it gave them greater control over landowners, Grand Princes of Moscow increasingly made it their practice to grant land only on service tenure.

In their rise to power the Grand Princes of Moscow had attracted to their service many of the most able boyars in the country. These boyars had given long and loyal service and, indeed, had contributed notably to Moscow's new position. Dmitri Donskoi had said to his boyars ". . . to me you are not to be called boyars, but princes of my realm," and on his deathbed he counselled his heirs to treat them as brothers.[5] But such fraternal relations between the Grand Prince and boyars had not endured.

In the 15th century the old Muscovite boyar families had become merged with the serving princes and the boyars of formerly independent principalities. Of the 200 families in the Muscovite service towards the end of the 16th century, 150 families had entered it only 100 years or so earlier, and of these newcomers the majority were of princely status.[6] Thus the great Muscovite boyar families felt displaced from their former proud position of being the sole trusted advisers of the Grand Prince. Moreover both the boyars and serving princes felt the loss of their freedom. Independent princes had been free to serve any grand prince, and boyars to serve any prince by agreement. But now there was only the Grand Prince of Muscovy and they were compelled to serve him. Some princes and boyars had transferred their allegiance to Lithuania, but this was soon condemned as treason.

A further cause of discontent among the boyars was the growing tendency of the Grand Princes to turn for advice to their lesser serving men, to the gentry who held their land on service tenure, and even to trusted servants and favourites who had no rank or standing. The Boyar Council on which the leading boyars had always served had carried out important legislative, administrative, and judicial functions, sharing in the responsibilities of the prince. Gradually, however, the Boyar Council had been reduced to an advisory body and then to a formality. The decline in the power and prestige of this Council came to symbolize for the boyars the decline in their own position which, they considered, belonged to them by hereditary right. The restoration to the Council of its former powers and responsibilities was to become a matter of furious dispute in the reign of Ivan. But, despite these common discontents, intense rivalries among the boyars prevented the growth of any cohesion among them as a class.

In the 15th century the boyars worked out a complicated hierarchical system, intended to protect their status. This system, called *mestnichestvo*, fixed immutably the order of precedence among noble families, and was applied strictly to official appointments. The *Razryady* or records of appointments were carefully maintained. No serving prince or boyar would accept an appointment lower than any appointment held by his forebears. The system was wholly destructive in its effects. Personal ability, experience, and seniority in service counted for nothing. The position of the family and its individuals in the hierarchy was the sole determining factor. The Grand Prince was completely fettered in an essential exercise of his power, for he could not appoint the most able or suitable men to high office, unless permitted by the system. At the same time it fostered rivalries among families and increased the disunity of the aristocratic class.

The boyars degenerated into an unruly element. If the Grand Prince was weak, they clamoured for power and privilege, each family trying to outdo the others. One of the leading families might assert its primacy and rally others behind it, but then rivals would displace it. Thus the class on which the Grand Princes depended for military leaders and high officers became an unreliable and disruptive force. But it had merely hindered, without halting, the gradual, almost insidious, rise of Moscow which in the late 15th century under the rule of Ivan III gathered a new momentum.

Notes to Chapter I

[1] Jerome Blum, *Lord and Peasant in Russia* (Princeton, 1961), pp. 59–60.
[2] *Ibid.*
[3] *Ibid.*, p. 120.
[4] Richard Hakluyt, *The Principal Navigations, Voyages Traffiques and Discoveries of the English Nation* (London, 1809), pp. 225, 262. Cited as "Hakluyt" in subsequent notes.
[5] V. O. Klyuchevsky, *Course of Russian History* (Moscow, 1956–8), II, p. 158. Cited as "Klyuchevsky" in subsequent notes.
[6] *Ibid.*, p. 140.

CHAPTER II

IVAN III 1462–1505

IVAN III, sometimes called the Great, and the grandfather of Ivan the Terrible, was in many ways the archetype of the long line of Grand Princes who transformed the principality of Moscow. He was immensely ambitious, but cautious. Like a spider he worked methodically from Moscow, spreading his web wider and wider until it covered nearly the whole of the vast area which, he claimed, "since olden times from our ancient forebears has been our patrimony".[1]

Viewed as a whole his reign reveals a pattern, carefully and deliberately wrought in singleminded pursuit of his objectives. His ultimate goal was the creation of a nation, united under the strong rule of the Muscovite autocrat, and embracing not only the upper Volga region, but all the lands occupied by Orthodox Russians.

The course of Ivan III's reign and the chronicles of the time suggest a man who was master of himself, of his principality, and of the policies, at once simple and complex, of which he was principal author. But the man himself hardly emerges from the mists of history.

The only description of him that has survived comes from the Italian traveller, Ambrogio Contarini, who passed through Moscow on his way to Persia. He noted that Ivan "may be thirty-five years of age (he was nearly thirty-seven); he is tall, thin, and handsome".[2] He was also very round-shouldered and in certain chronicles was nicknamed *Gorbaty*, the Hunchback.[3]

Herberstein, the Imperial ambassador, recorded that Ivan was so hostile to women that any woman meeting him by chance fainted with terror.[4] Among his subjects he commanded fear and respect. The Muscovites were a people eager to love and revere their Grand Prince, for on him their fortunes and even their survival depended. But, although Ivan served his country notably, his people did not love him as they were to love his grandson, Ivan the Terrible. On his death the demonstrations of popular grief, which accompanied so many Grand Princes to their tombs, were silent. Even his own son rebelled against him.

Contarini remarked of Ivan that "it is his custom to visit the various parts of his dominions every year".[5] But this was misleading, for Ivan was not a man to delight in travel. He preferred to sit in the Kremlin palace, quietly planning and directing his policies. His son-in-law Stephen of Moldavia often said that he "increased his dominion while sitting at home and sleeping".[6] It was a remark not devoid of malice, but it was true that he seldom led his armies, preferring to entrust them to his commanders. He disliked war as a gamble to be accepted only when diplomacy and other methods had failed. Not dashing brilliance, but foresight, shrewdness, patience, and extraordinary tenacity were the qualities that enabled him to achieve so much.

At the time of Ivan III's accession in 1462 the Russian lands were still divided and vast areas lay under foreign domination. Moscow had brought under her rule the region of the upper Volga and the Oka, except for certain small principalities which were still independent. The city-republics of Pskov and Novgorod, the latter with its dominions extending across the north of Muscovy and to the shores of the White Sea, also remained independent. The Teutonic Order held the Baltic shores and the Swedes ruled over Finland. Western Russia, including White Russia and the Ukraine or Little Russia, formed part of Lithuania–Poland. In the south and east the Tatars of the Crimean and Kazan Khanates dominated the fertile lands and prevented the Russian attempts to settle there. The Golden Horde maintained a precarious existence and, nominally at least, still counted Great Russia as its vassal.

Ivan thus found his realm surrounded by enemies. The Tatars were the immediate danger. The Golden Horde, its power and authority whittled away by internal disputes, had been irreparably weakened by the break-away of the new Khanates of the Crimea, formed about 1420, and of Kazan, set up in 1438. The Tatars of Kazan were within easy striking distance of Moscow and they raided incessantly. In 1469, however, Ivan III mounted a massive campaign against Kazan which capitulated. Unrest in Kazan was to cause him anxiety from time to time, but he did not again have to face serious threats from this quarter.

The Khanates of the Golden Horde and of the Crimea were more distant from Moscow. But their savage and persistent attacks were costly in lives, a burden to Muscovite defences, and disruptive of trade. Moreover, the danger always existed that they might unite against Muscovy. Fortunately for Ivan the bitter enmity between the

Golden Horde and the Crimean Khanate eliminated this danger during his reign, and indeed alliance with Mengli Girei, the Crimean Khan, was to be the foundation of his policy.

The incorporation of the four remaining independent Russian principalities into Muscovy raised no problems comparable with the threats of his foreign enemies. The strong instinctive movement among the Great Russians, which had brought other principalities under Moscow's rule, had influenced Tver, Rostov, Ryazan, and Yaroslavl. Already at the beginning of Ivan's reign their independence was more or less nominal and their eventual subordination could be taken for granted. This did not apply to the city-state of Pskov, which continued to enjoy autonomy until annexed in the reign of Vasily III, or to Novgorod.

Novgorod the Great, despite her extensive empire and her wealth, was vulnerable. She was dependent on Muscovy and Lithuania for food and commerce, and compelled in time of crisis to seek military aid from one or the other. But, while her ties with Lithuania were strong, she was basically dependent on Moscow, and also her people were Russian in race and culture, and Orthodox Christians in religion.

For many years the Novgorodtsi managed to stave off attempts by Lithuania and Muscovy to annex their city and empire. When, however, despite warnings, they persisted in seeking close relations with Lithuania to offset the growing power of Muscovy, Ivan in 1471 declared war and inflicted a severe defeat on the Novgorod army. He did not then formally annex the republic, but was content to allow it nominal independence under close control from Moscow. The Novgorodtsi were soon in a turbulent mood and anti-Muscovite feeling was rampant among them. Ivan's armies advanced on them again and, as he announced exultantly in a message to Moscow, this time he had "subjected his Patrimony, Novgorod the Great, to his entire will and had become sovereign there as in Moscow".[7]

From the outset of his reign Ivan had recognized that his grand objective made war with Lithuania inevitable. The Lithuanians lived in dread of this conflict. On the death of Casimir (June 1492) and the succession of his son, Alexander, as Grand Prince of Lithuania, fear of Muscovite power led them to propose a new peace treaty and, confirming the treaty, marriage between Alexander and Ivan's daughter, Elena. Ivan welcomed these proposals. Negotiating from strength he also demanded recognition of his title as "Ioann, by the grace of God, sovereign of all Russia and Grand Prince. . . ."[8]

Apart from the punctiliousness of all Muscovites in matters of protocol, Ivan attached special importance to this title as a reflection of his policy. The Lithuanians accepted the new title and subsequently in 1494 agreed a treaty which confirmed Ivan's possession of most of the lands seized by the Muscovites in border campaigns.

To Ivan, however, the treaty, like the marriage of his daughter to Alexander in 1495, represented no more than a stage in his preparations. In the spring of 1500 he declared war on Lithuania and within four months he had gained most of his objectives. But his summer campaigns of 1500 and 1501 disappointed him, for he failed to take Smolensk, the key to his whole strategy. In the northwest the Muscovites were engaged against the Teutonic Order which had concluded an alliance with Alexander early in 1501. The Germans won an initial victory, but in November 1501 at Helmed near Dorpat were completely defeated. In 1502 Ivan was again thwarted in his westward drive. But in March 1503 he agreed a six-year truce with Alexander on the expiry of which a permanent peace was to be negotiated. Meantime under the truce Ivan retained, as belonging to Muscovy, all the territories that he had taken from Lithuania. It was an area, comprising most of the lands east of the Dnieper and, in fact, most of pre-Mongol Kievan Rus, except Smolensk and Kiev which remained in Alexander's hands. Ivan was still disappointed over his failure to gain Smolensk, and he planned a new campaign. But before war could break out again, both he and Alexander had died.

Only towards the end of his reign, lasting forty-three years, did Ivan appear to falter in his grasp of affairs. Herberstein reported that he drank heavily, sinking into a stupor after dinner every evening.[9] He had always been moderate, giving the impression of an austere and disciplined character. Contarini, who had seen him several times some twenty years earlier, bore witness to his restraint, especially in drinking, contrary to the general habit of his people.[10] Possibly family rivalries, centred on the claims of his son and grandson to the succession, and the conspiracy of his son Vasily, in 1497, had unnerved him.

Ivan married twice. His first wife, Princess Maria of Tver, bore him a son, Ivan Ivanovich, often called Ivan Molodoi (Ivan the Young), but in 1467 she died. Ivan granted his son the title of Grand Prince and recognized him as his heir. This did not, however, calm the anxiety of his people over the succession and they were further distressed because Ivan himself, although only twenty-seven at the time of his wife's death, showed no haste in seeking another wife.

In February 1469, however, proposals came from an unexpected quarter. Pope Paul II offered Ivan the hand of his ward, Zoe Palaeologa, the niece of the last Byzantine Emperor, Constantine XI, who had died on the walls of Constantinople, fighting against the Turks in 1453. His brother, Thomas Palaeologus, had been Despot of Morea, but had fled before the approaching Turks, finding refuge in Italy where he had died soon afterwards. The Pope had taken his daughter and two sons under his care, appointing Cardinal Bessarion, a Greek scholar and convert to Roman Catholicism, to supervise their education. Zoe was fourteen years old when she went to Rome and she lived there for some ten years.

In proposing this marriage the Pope had two purposes. First, he believed that Zoe, a convert well-schooled in the Catholic faith, would as the wife of the Grand Prince further the cause of Rome in Muscovy and might revive the union of the eastern and western churches, agreed at Florence in 1439.[11] Second, the Pope was anxiously seeking allies against the Ottoman Turks and he believed that Ivan would be a strong and active ally against the infidels. On both counts he miscalculated grievously.

For Ivan this marriage held strong attractions. The prestige of the Byzantine Emperors had always stood high among the Russians, and Byzantium still retained a certain compelling glamour for them, although they saw the just hand of God in the Turkish conquest. Marriage with the niece of the last Emperor would undoubtedly enhance the dignity of the Grand Prince and of his growing principality.

Zoe set out for Muscovy in June 1472, and she probably left Rome without special regrets. She had received an advanced education and had grown up in the exciting, cultured world of an Italy where the Renaissance was about to burst into flower. At the same time she had been an orphan, dependent on charity, and Cardinal Bessarion enjoined on her and her brothers constantly that they should think of themselves as paupers, not as the children of an illustrious family. But Zoe did not forget her imperial origins. She was always to regard herself primarily as a Byzantine princess. Even in 1498, after twenty-six years in Muscovy, when she embroidered an altar-cloth, she added after her name, not the title of Grand Princess of Muscovy, but the title of Princess of Tsargrad, the Russian name for Constantinople.[12]

On 12 November 1472, Zoe Palaeologa entered Moscow. On that day she was received into the Orthodox Church with the name of

Sofia, and married to Ivan. She proved remarkably adaptable. She had come from the warm and colourful Mediterranean coast to the frozen forests and the expanse of Muscovy, from the beautiful highly cultivated city of Rome to primitive snow-covered Moscow, built almost entirely of logs. Everything that met her eye must have contrasted with what she had been accustomed to in Rome, but she quickly settled down and even enjoyed the dignity, power, and independence of her new position. She had her own court, where she was encouraged to receive foreign visitors. Contarini stated that he called on her at the request of Ivan himself, and that "she treated me with great kindness and courtesy, and entreated me earnestly to recommend her to my Illustrious Seignory".[13]

Sofia was described by one visitor who saw her in 1472 as beautiful, but another visitor, present at the same time, considered her distressingly fat.[14] Whether ugly or beautiful, she was undoubtedly an intelligent woman, skilled in intrigue. Among the Russians, even in succeeding generations, she was credited with great, even sinister, powers over Ivan III.[15] Learned and fluent in several languages, she must have seemed exceptional to the illiterate boyars whose wives were ignorant creatures, living closely guarded in seclusion.

Many Russians, while dutifully welcoming her, nevertheless eyed Sofia with suspicion. Orthodox churchmen in particular watched for signs of her adherence to Roman Catholicism, but even they were favourably impressed when they saw her worship in their churches and reverence the ikons. Ivan Molodoi, Ivan III's son by his first marriage, had special reason to be suspicious of his stepmother, for her children might displace him from the succession. Indeed it seems that he might have given vent to his feelings. Contarini recorded in 1476 that Ivan Molodoi "is not in great favour on account of his bad conduct".[16]

In the first four years of marriage Sofia bore three daughters. Contarini thought that she was again pregnant when he saw her in 1476.[17] It was not, however, until three years later that her first son, Vasily, was born. Meanwhile Ivan Molodoi had married Princess Elena Stepanova of Moldavia, who in 1483 gave birth to a son, named Dmitri. In 1490 Ivan Molodoi died. Sofia's son, Vasily, and Elena's son, Dmitri, were as the son and grandson of Ivan III then equally claimants to the throne, for Muscovite law on the succession was far from clear.

Ivan made no haste to declare his choice between his son and grandson, and the rivalry which had grown between Sofia and Elena, the two mothers, became more embittered. Some time in 1497 Vasily, now aged eighteen, learnt that his father was about to proclaim Dmitri his successor with the title of Grand Prince of Vladimir and Moscow. With Sofia's connivance he conspired to make his way to the north and there set up an independent principality. Dmitri was to be murdered. Ivan discovered the plot in time. He had six of his son's supporters beheaded on the ice of the Moskva river. "Evil women" who had visited Sofia with poisonous herbs were arrested, pushed through holes in the ice and drowned. From that time, the chronicler relates, Ivan lived with Sofia "in great vigilance".[18]

With elaborate ceremonial on 4 February 1498 in the Uspensky Cathedral in the Kremlin, the Metropolitan and bishops officiating, Ivan blessed his grandson Dmitri as his heir and successor. But suddenly a year later he publicly bestowed on Vasily the title of Grand Prince of Novgorod and Pskov. This meant that he had forgiven his son, but Dmitri remained the senior as successor to the throne. Sofia and Vasily did not rest until they had supplanted Dmitri. Vasily fled to Vyazma where his father's officers caught up with him and prevailed on him to return. Ivan now took pains to satisfy his son's demands. In April 1502 Dmitri and his mother, Elena, were disgraced and Vasily was proclaimed "Grand Prince of Vladimir and Moscow and Autocrat of all Russia".[19]

During the 1470s the dignity and surroundings of the Grand Prince began to undergo a transformation which continued until the end of Ivan III's reign. His titles became more resounding. His court adopted new and ponderous ceremonials, based on Byzantine models, and he became more remote from his people. Architects were specially summoned from Italy and they built the Uspensky Cathedral, as well as the Granovitaya Palace and a new court of stone in place of the old timbered buildings. Moscow was assuming a dignity worthy of her growing national significance.

Such major changes, because they coincided with the years of Ivan's marriage with Sofia, were attributed to her influence. Always conscious of her imperial background and mindful of the grandeur of Rome where she had spent her most impressionable years, Sofia undoubtedly exercised some influence on her husband. At the same time Ivan's chief purpose in marrying her had been to surround his throne with the aura of Byzantium and he was astute in taking measures to give permanence to this aura.

Ivan's new titles reflected the new importance and power of the throne of Moscow. He had in his relations with some western courts used the title of "Sovereign of All Rus", but after finally discarding the Tatar yoke in 1480 he often referred to himself as "Tsar of All Rus", sometimes adding *Samoderzhets*, the Russian form of the Byzantine title of "Autocrat". Tsar, a Slav contraction of the Latin "Caesar", had at this time none of its later meaning of a ruler, wielding absolute power. It signified only a ruler who owed no allegiance and paid no tribute to any foreign authority. In the past the Russians had usually reserved the title of Tsar for the Byzantine Emperors and the Khans of the Golden Horde. In calling himself "Tsar and Autocrat" Ivan III was at first merely proclaiming that he was the independent sovereign, ruling over the domains listed in his full title. Soon however his title became more pretentious. "Ivan, by the grace of God, Sovereign of All Rus" was an early Muscovite approach to the Byzantine conception of the sovereign as specially sanctified by God in his supreme office. Ivan the Terrible was to develop this idea to the point that the Tsar was divinely appointed and that opposition to his will was sacrilege.

The new titles and ceremonies were not solely exercises in pomp and vanity: they were the expression of the policy and outlook of the ruler of an emerging nation. They reflected Ivan III's grandiose vision of the role of the Grand Prince of Muscovy, who would become Tsar and Autocrat, the national sovereign of all the lands occupied by the Orthodox Russians; he would rule as the heir and successor of the Byzantine Emperors, because the Muscovite Tsar was the sole remaining Orthodox ruler who could take on the mantle of Byzantium.

Vasily succeeded to the throne without dispute in 1505, and Dmitri died on the estate, where he was confined, some three years later. Tall, lean, and stooped Vasily resembled his father in appearance and to some extent in character. He had the same tenacity of purpose and the same ruthlessness in pursuing the policy he had inherited of gathering in the Russian lands. But he could brook no opposition or even unacceptable advice, and was quick to remove those who disagreed with him. He was more ready to act decisively than his father who had often relied on tortuous diplomacy. He was also more devout and, indeed, he appears to have been a more likeable man than his father. He was devoted to his wife and his son, Ivan, who was to succeed him as Ivan IV. Five letters written by Vasily to his wife have survived and they display a warm affection and concern for the well-being of her and the child.[20]

In continuing his father's policy, Vasily did not find that events still favoured him. The Tatars of Kazan menaced Muscovy afresh and the Crimean Khan, Mengli Girei, who had been Ivan III's valuable ally, now became an active enemy. The Golden Horde had ceased to exist and Muscovy's territorial gains from Lithuania had brought her frontiers too close to the Crimea for the liking of the Khan. Moreover, the lands on either side of the Dnieper which he had plundered so profitably when they had been part of Lithuania were no less tempting now that they belonged to Muscovy. Finally personal relations between the Khan and the Grand Prince had deteriorated. Vasily failed to cultivate the Khan's goodwill as his father had done; in particular, he refused to send presents, because he considered this to be paying tribute such as the Grand Princes had paid to the Great Khans of the Golden Horde for so many years. But when in 1521 Mohammed Girei, the son and successor of Mengli Girei, reached the outskirts of Moscow in a large-scale raid, the Muscovites who had crowded into the city seeking refuge were saved only by sending costly presents which induced the Khan to raise his siege and withdraw.

Lithuania was, however, still the chief enemy. The gains of Ivan III had not been confirmed by treaty but only by the instable armistice of 1503; moreover, Smolensk and other Russian regions remained in Lithuanian hands. War broke out between Muscovy and Lithuania in 1508 and again six years later. Vasily succeeded in taking Smolensk, and managed subsequently to hold the town against desperate Lithuanian attempts to recover it. When in 1522 he concluded a new armistice with Sigismund Augustus, he retained Smolensk as well as the lands recovered by his father.

Ivan the Terrible was thus the child of remarkable parentage. His grandfather, Ivan III, the Great, was one of the most able men ever to occupy the Russian throne. His grandmother, Sofia Palaeologa, niece of the last Byzantine Emperor, was a woman of intelligence and character. His father, Vasily III, was a strong and able ruler. Elena Glinskaya, his mother, was a woman of spirit and ability. From these parents he inherited many of his striking qualities.

Notes to Chapter II

[1] Klyuchevsky, pp. 117–18.

[2] A. Contarini, *Travels to Tana and Persia* (London, Hakluyt Society, 1873), p. 163.

[3] S. M. Solovyev, *History of Russia* (Moscow, 1960), Bk. III, Vol. V, p. 9. Cited as "Solovyev" in subsequent notes.

[4] Sigismund von Herberstein, *Notes upon Russia*, Trans. and ed. by R. H. Major (London, Hakluyt Society, 1851–2), I, p. 24.

[5] A. Contarini, *op. cit.*, p. 163.

[6] Sigismund von Herberstein, *loc. cit.*; G. Vernadsky, *A History of Russia. Vol. IV. Russia at the Dawn of the Modern Age* (Yale, 1959), pp. 14, 75.

[7] J. L. I. Fennell, *Ivan the Great of Moscow* (London, 1961), p. 55.

[8] Klyuchevsky, pp. 123–4.

[9] Sigismund von Herberstein, *op. cit.*, pp. 24–5.

[10] A. Contarini, *op. cit.*, pp. 163–5; G. Vernadsky, *op. cit.*, pp. 125–6.

[11] This abortive union of the churches was brought about at the Council of Florence at which the Metropolitan of Moscow, a Greek named Isadore, accepted on behalf of the Russian Orthodox the union of the eastern and western churches and the principle of papal supremacy. The Russians were horrified and on his return Isadore was at once deposed and forced to flee for his life. A declaration of the independence and complete autonomy of the Russian Church followed and a Russian, Iona, Bishop of Ryazan, was elected Metropolitan.

[12] Klyuchevsky, II, p. 121.

[13] A. Contarini, *op. cit.*, p. 164.

[14] LeP. Pierling, *La Russie et le Saint-Siège* (Paris, 1896), I, pp. 150–2.

[15] Sofia's influence on Ivan III and indeed on the course of Russian history has been a matter of dispute among historians. In general her influence has been exaggerated, starting with the enemies of her son and grandson, Vasily III and Ivan IV, who blamed her for their misfortunes. Prince Andrei Kurbsky called her a "Greek sorceress" and even held her guilty of poisoning her stepson, Ivan Molodoi, so that he would not stand in the way of the succession of her own son, Vasily III.

Russian historians in the 18th and 19th centuries ascribed to her a dominating influence. They asserted that Ivan acquired the legal right to the Byzantine succession through his marriage with her, that the marriage gave rise to the theory of Moscow as the third Rome, that she was responsible for the introduction of Byzantine court procedure, that her advice and influence were responsible for the annexation of Novgorod, the discarding of the Mongol yoke, and so forth.

S. M. Solovyev and V. O. Klyuchevsky, the two greatest Russian historians, have discounted many of the theories of their predecessors. But both have acknowledged that she exercised considerable influence in raising the dignity and prestige of the Grand Prince.

Historians in the 20th century have gone further in denying Sofia's influence. Indeed, Mr J. L. I. Fennell has held that Ivan III could have seen in her no more than an "exotic embellishment for his somewhat crude court" and that "there are no signs of Sofia's influence in the creation of a new court ceremonial or of new court ranks and functions". But to deny to her any influence whatsoever is clearly an extreme view.

Professor George Vernadsky, after summarizing the views of the leading historians, has reached the conclusion, which seems the most reasonable to the present writer, that she could hardly have had any serious affect on state affairs, but that she must have influenced the court and prestige of the Grand Prince. He concludes that her "main impact on the course of Russian history was made by the fact of her giving birth to the man who was destined to become father of Ivan the Terrible".

G. Vernadsky, *Russia at the Dawn of the Modern Age* (Yale, 1959), pp. 22–6; V. O. Klyuchevsky, *Course of Russian History* (Moscow, 1957), Vol. II, pp. 120–30; S. M. Solovyev, *History of Russia from Earliest Times* (Moscow, 1960), Bk. III, Vol. 5, pp. 57–64; J. L. I. Fennell, *Ivan the Great of Moscow* (London, 1961), pp. 315–24; K. V. Bazilievich, *External Policy of the Russian Centralized State: Second half of the 15th century* (Moscow, 1952), pp. 83–8.

[16] A. Contarini, *op. cit.*, p. 163. Unfortunately Contarini gave no further information; he wrote, "I might mention other things, but it would take too long."

[17] *Ibid.*

[18] J. L. I. Fennell, *op. cit.*, pp. 336–7.

[19] G. Vernadsky, *op. cit.*, p. 130.

[20] Solovyev, Bk. III, Vol. V, pp. 298–9.

CHAPTER IV

THE REGENCY OF ELENA 1533-8

IVAN's accession was proclaimed at once on the death of his father. The Metropolitan, anxious to prevent an interregnum in which rival princes might muster support for their claims, publicly blessed him as Grand Prince. In the cathedral church of Prechistaya Bogoroditsa before the assembled princes, boyars, churchmen, and people, he made the benediction with the cross and proclaimed loudly:

"God blesses you, Sovereign, Grand Prince Ivan Vasilievich of Vladimir, Moscow, Novgorod, Pskov, Tver, Yugorsk, Perm, Bulgaria, Smolensk, and many other lands, Tsar and Sovereign of All Rus! May good fortune be with the great realm and with the throne of your father!"[1]

The congregation intoned the prayer of long life for their Grand Prince. Princes and boyars brought him rich gifts. Officials of the court were then sent into all parts of the country to administer the oath of allegiance to his subjects.

In accordance with Muscovite law and custom, Ivan's mother, Elena, became regent during his minority. But the people of Moscow were anxious and afraid. Vasily had been a strong energetic ruler who had kept the boyars under control and the enemies of Muscovy at bay, but a three-year-old boy would be at their mercy. As regent Elena commanded no popular support or respect. Many still saw in her a Lithuanian enemy or disliked her for her Western tastes. All were unwilling that power should be at the disposal of a woman so young and inexperienced. All expected trouble and unrest during her regency.

Within five days of the burial of Vasily, news of sedition reached Elena. She had on the intercession of the Metropolitan and the boyars freed Princes Ivan and Andrei Mikhailovich Shuisky, whom Vasily had imprisoned for conspiring against the throne. The Shuisky had immediately begun planning with Prince Yuri, Ivan's uncle, to seize power. In these first months of the regency, Elena's uncle, Prince Mikhail Glinsky, was the strongest influence at court. Counting on his family bonds with Elena and on his experience and ability, Vasily had reposed special trust in him. On his deathbed he had said, "And you, Prince Mikhail Glinsky, must let your blood flow and your body be cut to pieces in the defence of my son, Grand Prince Ivan, of my Grand Princess Elena, and of my son, Prince Yuri."[2] Elena leant heavily on him and he virtually exercised supreme power.

Glinsky saw in the plot of the Shuisky with Prince Yuri a threat to his own position. He gained the support of the Boyar Council and on the advice of the boyars Elena had Yuri arrested and imprisoned.[3] Apparently the Shuisky escaped punishment. But in January 1534 Ivan's other uncle, Prince Andrei Staritsky, was also found to be plotting to seize power. Elena suppressed the conspiracy, and Prince Andrei retired to his estates.

Elena was, however, gaining confidence and she did not lack courage. She knew that her uncle, Mikhail Glinsky, was ambitious and dangerous, and that he resented being subordinate to his own niece and the four-year-old Ivan. In July 1534 she received reports that he was secretly planning to wrest power from her and her son. As though in anticipation of this betrayal, she had come to rely on a forceful and able young noble, named Prince Ovchin-Telepnev-Obolensky, whose sister was nurse to Ivan, and who was soon to become her lover. Supported by Obolensky she had Glinsky arrested and cast into prison, where he died from hunger and the weight of his shackles.

At this time Prince Semeon Belsky and Boyar Ivan Lyatsky, both prominent men, fled to Lithuania. Elena at once ordered the arrest of Ivan Belsky, Semeon's brother, and others on the ground of their complicity. All were probably involved in some plot to seize power.

This acute unrest among princes and boyars, which was so marked in the months following the death of Grand Prince Vasily, was a reaction from the regime of the previous seventy years. Ivan III and Vasily III had kept their boyars under control and had undermined their privileged position. To many boyars the accession of a child meant the relaxation of severe autocratic rule, and they saw the regency as a time to recover the freedom and privileges which they had lost. But they found Elena a strong and determined regent, who actively continued Vasily's policy of establishing a united country under the absolute power of the Grand Prince of Moscow.

In Lithuania, Sigismund Augustus paid close attention to reports of unrest in Moscow. The arrival of such defectors as Semeon Belsky and Ivan Lyatsky seemed to give further proof that Elena's government was weak and instable. The armistice between Muscovy and Lithuania had already expired and, in the summer of 1534, while discussions for a new armistice were taking place, Lithuanian troops invaded and laid waste parts of western Muscovy. But in the autumn of the same year Lithuanian attempts to take Starodub, Chernigov, and Smolensk were repelled with heavy losses. Muscovite resistance during the following two years convinced Sigismund Augustus of the need for peace and in 1537, after heated wrangling, a five-year armistice was agreed.

At this time, however, the Muscovites feared the Tatars of the Crimea and of Kazan far more than they feared the Lithuanians. Saip Girei, the ruthless and able Khan of the Crimea, was seeking to bring the Volga Khanates under his rule and thus to revive the Great Horde of Mamai. It was fortunate for Muscovy that a rival to Saip Girei appeared in Islam Girei, an elder member of the same family, and that the Crimean Tatars were divided between them. But the threat to Muscovy suddenly became more serious when, unexpectedly, Semeon Belsky, who had fled to Lithuania, arrived in the Crimea, seeking to persuade the Turkish Sultan to march with the Tatars and Lithuanians against Muscovy. From such a campaign he hoped to establish himself as ruler of a vast independent principality.

The Muscovite government nevertheless remained in communication with Saip Girei, who sent a steady stream of threats and demands for money and gifts.

"Now it is not as of old that we will march with the Tatar force alone [he declared in one note]. Apart from my own artillery there will be with me 100,000 horsemen from the blessed Khan (i.e. the Sultan) . . . The Kazan lands are part of my dominion and Safa Girei, the Kazan Tsar, is my brother: from this day you are no more to march into the Kazan lands to make war, and if you go there for war, then watch for me in Moscow."[4]

Saip Girei's threats were more than empty bombast. His rival, Islam Girei, had since been murdered, and Saip now wielded great influence in the affairs of Kazan. Safa Girei, his brother, had been installed as Khan and had begun ravaging Muscovite territory. But early in 1537 peace with Lithuania freed the Muscovite army which moved to the east to meet the Tatar threat. Safa Girei then hurriedly withdrew his forces, and Saip Girei became reluctant to risk further invasions.

Elena, guided by Obolensky, thus managed to keep at bay

Muscovy's three most dangerous enemies. Moreover, in 1537 she concluded a treaty with Gustavus Vasa of Sweden, and she also maintained friendly relations with the Austrian Empire. The misgivings of so many Muscovites that her regency would be a time when enemies raided and plundered at will had proved groundless.

In internal affairs, too, Elena's regency had its achievements. The task of building frontier towns and fortresses, launched by Vasily, was continued vigorously. Old towns, damaged or destroyed in Tatar and Lithuanian raids, were restored and many new towns were built. In Moscow on 16 May 1535 the foundations were laid for a new stone wall to be erected by the Italian architect, Peter Friazin, around the quarter known as Kitai Gorod or Middle Town. In the same year Elena also approved the major reform of issuing a new currency which, although it confirmed the devaluation of the coinage of the previous fifty years, was to prove remarkably stable for over a century.

The most serious challenge to Elena and her government came in 1537, towards the end of her regency, from Prince Andrei Staritsky, Ivan's uncle. After his conspiracy had been uncovered in January 1534, he had retired to his principality and had refused to send his boyars, gentry, or troops to serve in the government's military operations against the Lithuanians and Tatars. Summoned to Moscow he had confirmed the oath of allegiance to Ivan which he had sworn in December 1533, but had refused to give the further guarantees of loyalty which Elena demanded.[5]

In 1536 the Khan of Kazan, Safa Girei, was preparing to invade Muscovy. Prince Andrei again refused to send his contingent or come to Moscow himself. Elena treated this refusal as an openly hostile act against the central government. Fearing that other princes and boyars would support him, she decided to summon him again to Moscow and on his arrival to arrest him. At the same time she ordered preparations to be made to meet an armed revolt, led by him. But next Elena received information that he intended fleeing from Staritsa. Hurried preparations were made to capture him. Obolensky and his brother, Nikita, took command of two forces, one to capture Prince Andrei and the other to take his chief Boyar, Feodor Pronsky. Warned of the government plan, however, Prince Andrei escaped from Staritsa and made for Novgorod which had served on many occasions in the past as a base for struggles against Moscow.

Obolensky hastened after him, expecting to fight a decisive battle, but it proved unnecessary. Many of Prince Andrei's men had defected on the march and his army was gravely weakened. Moreover, Novgorod refused him all aid and barred its gates against him. The Novgorodtsi, and particularly the tradesmen and craftsmen, were loyal to the Grand Prince. Makary, their Archbishop, was a convinced supporter of the union of the Russian state under the rule of Moscow and rallied his people to defend the city against the rebels. Prince Andrei recognized the hopelessness of his position and tried to escape to Lithuania, but then surrendered.

Elena dealt severely with these rebels. Prince Andrei was shackled and imprisoned with his wife and son, and died soon afterwards. The boyars and serving gentry who had supported him were imprisoned in one of the Kremlin towers, and many died there. Of the whole population of Novgorod, only thirty citizens had tried to help Prince Andrei, and all were now knouted and hanged. A certain number of Muscovite princes and boyars had joined forces with him, and they were punished. But the revolt had shown convincingly that the people and the serving gentry and even the majority of the boyars were loyal to the Grand Prince.

In spite of her achievements in defending the country against foreign enemies and against rebels, however, Elena remained unpopular. Her relationship with Obolensky was common knowledge and, although immorality and debauchery were widespread in Muscovy at this time, for the Grand Princess herself to take a lover was a matter of fierce disapproval and even contempt. But, apart from her affair with Obolensky, Elena's life appears to have been blameless and even to have deserved respect. She was devout, attending church regularly and making frequent pilgrimages to the Troitsa monastery and other places of special sanctity. She was devoted to her sons and she did not flinch from her responsibilities as regent. But nothing that she would have done would have brought her popular support.

Suddenly at 2 p.m. on 3 April 1538 Elena died. No reports of the time suggested that she had been ill or was in poor health. Herberstein stated that she was poisoned.[6] With a strange and disturbing haste her body was buried in the Voznessensky monastery a few hours after her death.

No display of grief was seen in the city. Boyars and people showed only a cold indifference. It seemed that the Metropolitan did not even perform the customary service for the repose of her soul. Two people alone mourned her death. Grand Prince Ivan, now aged seven, had loved his mother. On learning of her death he burst into tears and threw himself into the arms of Obolensky. But Obolensky, too, was in despair. His high office, his very safety, had depended on Elena. Again the question on the lips of everyone in Moscow was, who would wield power during the minority of the Grand Prince?

Notes to Chapter IV

[1] Solovyev, Bk. III, Vol. VI, pp. 395–6.

[2] *Ibid.*

[3] Prince Yuri died in prison on 26 August 1536 from hunger and the weight of his chains. Karamzin, Bk. II, Vol. VII, cols. 10–12.

[4] Solovyev, Bk. III, Vol. VI, p. 415.

[5] I. I. Smirnov, "The Revolt of Andrei Staritsky 1537" in *Istoricheskie Zapiski*, Vol. 50, pp. 270–2.

[6] Sigismund von Herberstein, *op. cit.*, I, pp. 52–3.

CHAPTER V

THE BOYARS RULE 1538-48

DURING these first years of his childhood Ivan led the calm contented life of a small boy. With his brother, he occupied rich apartments in the Kremlin Palace, secure in the affectionate attention of his nanny, Agrafena Chelyadina, and of the other noble women appointed to look after him. His mother was always near at hand and, even when making an excursion to the Troitsa or some other monastery, she took her sons with her.

The death of his father had probably made no deep impression on him at the time, for he was then only three years old. Obolensky was constantly in attendance on his mother and, always solicitous for his welfare, he must have taken the place of a father. The only interruptions to the quiet routine of the nursery were the formal occasions when, wearing his princely robes of gold, embroidered with pearls and precious stones, he sat on the throne in the audience-chamber to receive foreign ambassadors or to signify approval to some act of state.

The sudden death of Grand Princess Elena shattered this security. The greatest deprivation that a boy of tender years can suffer is the death of his mother; nothing can make up for this loss; no one can bring the same love and companionship to banish his new, bewildering loneliness. But for Ivan, who was a sensitive and affectionate boy, this personal tragedy was infinitely greater, because the years that followed, embracing the formative period of his life, were for him a time of unforgettable terror and neglect.

Elena had no sooner died than the boyars began plotting for power. The court was filled with whispered conspiracies and fears. In the Kremlin Palace with its wide rooms, squat pillars, and numerous stairways, the figures of saints, painted in bright colours, peered on to the mortals below as they plotted secretly and observed each other suspiciously and fearfully. Obolensky, who had had so many allies and friends at court, now found them falling away from him. He became even more attentive to Ivan, hoping that the boy's need for him might help secure his position. Ivan himself clung to Obolensky

43

and to Agrafena, for they represented all the affection and security that remained to him. But the struggle for power went on relentlessly and the wishes of the Grand Prince counted for nothing.

On the seventh day after his mother's death, Ivan had to watch, his cries and tears unheeded, as Obolensky and Agrafena were torn away from him. He was never to see them again. Obolensky was cast into a dungeon where he soon died of hunger. Agrafena was sent away to a nunnery in the frozen forests to the north of Moscow.

The new regent, who had disposed of Obolensky so promptly, was Prince Vasily Shuisky. An able, but cruel and ruthless noble, he had served in Novgorod and, as the city-republic lost the last remnants of its independence, he had transferred his allegiance to Moscow. There in the service of the Grand Prince his family seniority, energy, and ability had brought him to prominence. He had, in fact, been the leader of the Boyar Council in the reign of Vasily and during the regency of Elena, but his position had been merely nominal. He had hated Obolensky because, while conceding to him the senior title, Obolensky had wielded the power and influence. Rumours within the Kremlin even held that Prince Vasily had poisoned Elena so that he could then destroy Obolensky.

Prince Vasily and his brother Prince Ivan Shuisky now dominated the Boyar Council and the state. But they were compelled to share power to some extent with Prince Ivan Belsky who had wide support among other boyars and within the church. One of the first acts of the Shuisky was to release Prince Ivan Belsky, whom Elena had imprisoned. Alone among the boyars, the Belsky faction was strong enough to challenge the Shuisky, and Vasily Shuisky may have hoped to reach some understanding with Ivan Belsky. Among the boyars, however, Vasily's arrogance and abuses of power had aroused such resentment that within six months Ivan Belsky was commanding greater support. The rivalry between the two factions and their numerous supporters increased. But suddenly Shuisky boldly imprisoned Ivan Belsky and exiled his principal officers to distant places. The chief among them, Counsellor Feodor Mishurin, was stripped naked, savagely beaten, and executed.

Within a few days, however, Vasily Shuisky fell ill and died. Prince Ivan Shuisky then seized power and at once showed himself to be more arrogant and vicious than his brother had been. His first thought was vengeance against Belsky and his party. He even dared to depose Metropolitan Daniel and in his place the bishops, obedient to Shuisky's wishes, appointed Ioasaf, Father Superior of the Troitsa monastery.

The church was a most important factor in the struggle of the chief boyar factions for power. The Metropolitan, bishops and the monasteries, which were wealthy landowners, all wielded considerable influence among the people. The Shuisky and to a lesser degree the Belsky competed eagerly for church support and their main means of winning this support was apparently by granting immunities from the payment of taxes and fulfilling various duties to the state. During the eleven years following Elena's death no fewer than 288 deeds, conferring special privileges and immunities, were granted to various monasteries throughout the country.[1]

Within the church itself two factions existed. The Josephans, so called after the renowned abbot of Volokolamsk,[2] maintained that the church needed its wealth and the protection of the state to carry out its great mission among the people. The Trans-Volga Hermits, the other strong party, followed the teachings of Nil Sorski[3] and others that the church must reject luxury and the ownership of lands and peasants so that its priests and monks could dedicate their lives to prayer and meditation. In their pursuit of support among the monasteries, the Shuisky cultivated the goodwill of the abbots and monks of the Simonov, Troitsa, Kirillo-Belozersky monasteries among others, all of them containing important followers of Nil Sorski and the Trans-Volga Hermits. The Josephans, who were the stronger faction, included the Metropolitan Daniel and many monasteries which supported the Belsky party.

Ivan Shuisky, having seized power on the death of his brother, behaved as autocrat. He took what he wanted from the state treasury and had his family name engraved on gold plate belonging to the Grand Princes of Moscow. This plate represented more than riches; it stood for power and prestige, for in Muscovy, as elsewhere in Western Europe, ruling families always amassed gold and silver plate as visible evidence of their dignity.[4] Ivan Shuisky and his followers also preyed on the country, extorting money from landowners and merchants, craftsmen and peasants, and terrorizing all who showed the least resistance.

Towards Grand Prince Ivan, the Shuisky displayed open contempt. Although so young, Ivan burned with anger and hatred, especially towards Ivan Shuisky himself, who seemed to go out of his way to insult him, his throne, and the memory of his parents.

"I will recall one thing [Ivan wrote many years later]. Whilst we were playing childish games in our infancy, Prince Ivan Vasilievich Shuisky sat on a bench, leaning with his elbows on our father's bed and with his leg upon a chair, and he did not even incline his head towards us, either in parental manner or even as to a master, nor was there any element of deference to be found in his attitude towards us. And who can endure such arrogance?" [5]

These and countless other incidents were stored away in the lively memory of this small boy, who brooded on vengeance and on the time when he would be free from fear and be able to assert his rightful power.

Under the Shuisky the law and order established and maintained by Ivan III and Vasily III gave way to anarchy. The rule of violence was aggravated by the numerous robber bands who roamed the land unchecked, murdering and plundering. From Pskov and other districts near the western frontier, hundreds escaped into Lithuania, while others from the central regions made their way to the forests in the north.

The Tatars were always quick to take advantage of any signs of weakness in Moscow. Khan Saip Girei began sending insolent threats and Ivan Shuisky, whose sole concern was to maintain his personal ascendancy, responded by sending an ambassador with gifts to buy peace. The Khan of Kazan demanded annual tribute and sent raiding parties to ravage Muscovy. A chronicler of these times wrote that the Kazan Tatars

"made the blood of Christians flow like water. The defenceless people hid away in the forests and in caves; places where settlements had been became overgrown with wild bushes. Reducing monasteries to dust, the infidels lived and slept in the churches, drank from the sacred vessels, stripped the ikons to make earrings and necklaces for their women. They put burning coals in the boots of the monks and forced them to dance; they defiled the young nuns; those whom they did not take into captivity, they blinded, cut off their ears, noses, their arms and legs . . . I write [concluded the chronicler] not from rumours, but of what I have seen and will never forget." [6]

The Italian architect, Peter Friazin, who had served Grand Prince Vasily, adopted Orthodoxy, married in Moscow, and settled on his Russian estate, received as a reward for his services, fled in

1539, leaving all behind him. In Dorpat, when asked why he had fled, he replied:

"The Grand Prince and Princess are dead. The present Grand Prince is still young, but the boyars do as they wish and they commit great violence. Throughout the land there is justice for no one. The boyars struggle among themselves, and I have come away from great strife and disorder." [7]

Notes to Chapter V

[1] S. M. Kashtanov, "Feudal Immunity in the Years of The Boyar Government 1538–48" in *Istoricheskie Zapiski*, No. 66 (1960), pp. 240–1.

[2] Josef of Volokolamsk was a learned and militant churchman and a strong supporter of the Grand Princes of Moscow in their task of uniting the country under their rule. Josef in 1479 founded in the independent principality of Volokolamsk a monastery which became renowned. At a church assembly held in 1503 he strongly opposed the proposal for the liquidation of the estates of the church, and thus defeated the policy of the Trans-Volga Hermits. Josef was also active in promoting the theory of the divine origin of the Tsar's power.

[3] Nil Sorski took his name from the first hermitage, which he founded, on the river Sor, not far from the Kirillo-Belozersky monastery. Between 1473 and 1489 Nil travelled widely in Palestine, Greece, and Turkey. In his writing and preaching he called on the priesthood to reject luxury and ownership of property, and urged all to lead lives of austerity and prayer. At the church assembly of 1503 he urged the secularization of all church estates, but he was opposed by Josef of Volokolamsk and his proposal was rejected.

[4] C. Oman, *The English Silver in the Kremlin 1557–63*, London, 1961.

[5] J. L. I. Fennell (ed. and trans.), *The Correspondence between Prince A. M. Kurbsky and Tsar Ivan IV of Russia* (Cambridge, 1955), p. 75.

[6] Karamzin, Bk. II, Vol. VIII, col. 35.

[7] Solovyev, Bk. III, Vol. VI, p. 454.

CHAPTER VI

THE TERRORS OF CHILDHOOD

WHILE the Shuisky were in power, Ivan and his brother were completely neglected. No one was responsible for their care and they lived as best they could. Often they were hungry and cold. Food, clothes, and furs were plentiful in the palace, but no one gave any thought to the two young princes. Twenty-five years later Ivan himself was to exclaim: "What sufferings did I not endure through lack of clothing and through hunger!"[1]

More than physical suffering, mental anguish and fear tormented him. He lived in hourly terror of the Shuisky and their boyars. They might seize and maim him, cast him into a dungeon to die of cold and neglect, or simply kill him and his brother and take the throne for themselves. Muscovite and Byzantine history contained many incidents showing the extremes of savagery to which men would go in their lust for power. His own great-grandfather, Vasily the Blind, had had his eyes struck out by his cousin in his struggle for the throne of Moscow. Such events from the past sharpened Ivan's terror for his own life. He was observant and imaginative, and in the solitude of this period of his life his precocious intelligence developed, while the experience and fears of his daily life cut deeply into his mind and character.

Meanwhile the boyars themselves were growing restless. They detested Ivan Shuisky, but were afraid to take any step against him. In July 1540, however, the Metropolitan found the courage to act. He won the support of the Boyar Council and, having gone through the formality of obtaining Ivan's consent, he had Ivan Belsky released from prison. Ivan Shuisky, infuriated by this challenge and swearing vengeance, especially against the Metropolitan whom he had virtually appointed to office, was compelled to recognize the strength of Belsky's support and yielded power to him.

Ivan Belsky was one of the boyars who approved the national policy of Vasily III and Elena, and his rule was a great improvement on that of the Shuisky who were concerned solely for their personal interests. Belsky at once brought the country some relief from

48

oppression and anarchy. He extended clemency to many, even allow-ing his displaced enemies, the Shuisky, to live on their estates in freedom. If this was to prove a mistake, so too was Belsky's action in securing pardon for his infamous brother, Semeon, who was still at the side of the Crimean Khan, planning to bring about a combined Tatar, Turkish, and Lithuanian invasion of Muscovy.

At this time, however, Muscovy was fortunate to have in Ivan Belsky a leader who felt responsibility for the defence and welfare of the country. Khan Saip Girei, convinced that the Muscovites were too divided under a weak government to defend themselves, was actively planning a joint invasion by his Crimean horde with the Kazan horde of his brother, Khan Safa Girei. The plan for joint action failed, but Muscovy was faced with two separate invasions, either of which might reduce the young state to ruins.

In December 1540, Khan Safa Girei advanced from Kazan, but met with strong resistance. When Ivan Shuisky arrived in Vladimir with orders from Ivan Belsky and the Boyar Council to lead the troops assembled there, the Khan at once beat a retreat.

The more serious threat came from the Crimea. Khan Saip Girei with the whole of his horde, supported by a Turkish force, advanced to the Don. Russian scouts sent back word that the Tatar army was so numerous that in the steppes it stretched beyond the horizon.[2] In Moscow everyone made feverish preparations to meet the invading Tatars. Instinctively they looked to their Grand Prince for leader-ship and protection, although he was a mere boy. Ivan himself tear-fully offered prayers in the Uspensky Cathedral that the country might be spared, and in the midst of his fears he felt the burden of the responsibility and hopes which his people placed on him. "We have neither father nor mother, nor power to reason, nor strength in our fingers," he pleaded pathetically in his prayers for divine aid, "but the country demands that we save it."[3]

Ivan then summoned the Boyar Council to advise whether he should remain in Moscow or flee to a safer place. The boyars urged him to stay. Indeed, the ten-year-old Grand Prince had become the focal point of the people, and their attitude to him in this time of national danger showed both the faith and the dependence of all people, from boyars to peasants, on their Prince. All looked to this child as though he could save them by some miracle. But they were far from waiting passively. The Tatar threat united all in a fervour to defend their country, and the boyars even agreed among them-selves to set aside the order of precedence, or *mestnichestvo*, and to serve under the most able among them for the duration of this campaign.

On 30 July 1541 the Khan reached the Oka river. On the opposite bank stood the Muscovite advance force, which he took to be the whole Muscovite army. The Tatars prepared to cross the river, while the Turkish gunners set up a heavy cannonade. The Russians stood firm and at this time their main army began to arrive. Astonished by the size of the defending forces, the Khan turned on Semeon Belsky who was with him and cursed him for leading him to believe that the Muscovites were in no condition to defend themselves. He then ordered the retreat of his horde, for the Khans always avoided pitched battle unless they had an overwhelming superiority.

In Moscow the people gave thanks in all their churches. Their deliverance from the dreaded Tatars, indeed, seemed to them a miracle and in their prayers of thanksgiving they included their Grand Prince. "Sovereign, we conquered by your angelic prayers and your good fortune."[4] He was to them both ruler and talisman.

Once the danger had passed, discords broke out afresh among the boyars. They were incapable of suppressing for long the rivalries between families and individuals or of acting together except in time of extreme danger. They did not seek as a class to destroy or displace the Muscovite autocracy or even to curb its power. The most that they appeared to seek was confirmation of their own privileges and position as a class and with it the right to be consulted in the Boyar Council by the Grand Prince. Such were their limited political objectives, but, locked in internecine feuds, they constantly lost sight even of them.

Ivan Belsky had held the leading position for two years and on the whole he had wielded power wisely. But the very fact that he had been at the head of the state for so long and that both the Metropolitan and Ivan regarded him highly had made him the target of jealousy and resentment at court. Discontented boyars began to go over to Prince Ivan Shuisky who, with the army raised to repel the Tatars now under his command in Vladimir, was preparing to seize power again.

Shuisky had planned to march into Moscow on 3 January (1542). In the early hours before dawn on that day a band of three hundred of his men burst upon the city. They seized Ivan Belsky as well as his chief officers and supporters. They cornered the Metropolitan in his cell and stoned him. He managed to escape and sought refuge in the Kremlin Palace, but Shuisky's men followed him there. In their search for him one group of these men broke into the bed-chamber of the Grand Prince, some three hours before daylight. Awakened by the noise and shouting in his room, Ivan was terrified. He was convinced that these ruffians had come to murder him and his brother. They passed on to other rooms, searching for the old Metropolitan but Ivan remained in a state of terror and collapse as he waited for the dawn, expecting them to return for him at any minute. This was yet another experience which scarred his memory and made fear a permanent part of his nature.

Later on the same day Shuisky entered Moscow without opposition and once again became the most powerful man in the land. Metropolitan Ioasaf, tracked down on 3 January, was nearly murdered and then deposed and sent to the Belozersky monastery. Shuisky now waited for some two months before appointing a successor. The office of Metropolitan commanded great power and influence and, anxious to avoid having another opponent like Ioasaf using such power against him, he acted with caution. Finally his choice fell on the Archbishop of Novgorod, Makary, who had apparently won the favour of the Shuisky when they had been boyars of the city-republic, and it was said by some that this appointment was the reward of an ambitious prelate, seeking greater power and position. Makary's association with the Shuisky and his acceptance of the Metropolitanate at this time are difficult to understand. An ardent upholder of the traditional church policy of supporting the Grand Princes of Moscow in gathering under their strong central rule all the Russian lands, he had rallied the people of Novgorod against Prince Andrei Staritsky and shown loyalty to Ivan and to his mother as regent. He must have recognized that the Shuisky's selfish abuses of power were reducing the country to chaos and destroying the unity in which he believed. But Makary was neither ambitious nor self-seeking; he was a devout and dedicated man of high ideals, and in Moscow he was to use his authority as Metropolitan to protect the Grand Prince and the country.

Ivan Shuisky had hardly seized power, however, when illness forced him to retire to his country estates. Other members of his family, Princes Ivan and Andrei Mikhailovich Shuisky and Prince Feodor Ivanovich Skopin-Shuisky, took his place, and the reign of corruption and violence continued. Andrei Shuisky was now the ringleader of this small group which terrorized the court and the people. He was even more violent, arrogant, and ruthless than his predecessors. He rode roughshod over the Boyar Council and kept all, from Ivan himself down to the humblest peasant, cowed and afraid of what he and his band might do next.

Ivan hated Andrei Shuisky and his hatred was a measure of his fear. Nevertheless he was now, at the age of twelve, growing tall and passing out of boyhood, and he found himself treated differently. He no longer endured the contemptuous neglect of the years immediately after his mother's death, when he was a small child. The Shuisky flattered him and surrounded him with carefree irresponsible youths who could keep him entertained and distracted. At the same time they watched closely that no possible rival won his confidence or his affection.

Ivan spent his time playing wild games in the Kremlin and riding and hunting in the woods of the surrounding countryside. They seemed innocent pastimes, but at the hands of the Shuisky they received a vicious twist. Ivan was encouraged to indulge his taste for cruelty, coarse pleasures, and shameful exploits. Like his father he was a keen huntsman, but this was perverted into a taste for torturing animals. With his companions he had dogs, cats, bears, and other animals carried to the top of the Kremlin walls and the tall towers from which they would cast the unfortunate beasts to the ground below. Another of their jokes was to gallop through the mud and slush of the streets of Moscow, knocking down all, young and old, whom they found in their way. Under the influence of these companions Ivan also had his first tastes of drinking and debauchery.

Such diversions did not, however, absorb Ivan as completely as the Shuisky hoped. He dared to show special favour to Feodor Vorontsov who did not belong to their party. After several attempts to expel Vorontsov from court, the Shuisky resorted to force. On 9 September (1543) the Boyar Council met in the presence of Ivan and the Metropolitan. It was a formal occasion; the boyars wearing their stiff brocaded coats, sewn with pearls and precious stones, and reaching to the ground, sat on their seats on either side of the chamber; Ivan, clad in his full robes, even more richly bejewelled, sat on the throne.

The meeting was proceeding with the ponderous dignity and ceremonial which, since the reign of Ivan the Great, had come to mark the court of Moscow. Suddenly the Shuisky, led by Prince Andrei, burst upon this scene. They shouted abuse and accusations against Vorontsov. They then seized and dragged him into an adjoining room. There they beat him and tore off his clothes. From the cries and shouts it seemed that they were beating him to death.

Ivan sent the Metropolitan and the two Boyars Morozov to beg for his life. They managed to make themselves heard and to quieten the assailants. The Shuisky heard the pleas of the Grand Prince and grudgingly consented to let Vorontsov live, but they dragged him off to prison. Ivan again sent the Metropolitan and the Morozovs to ask the Shuisky on his behalf to exile Vorontsov, if they would not permit him to remain at court or in Moscow. But they heeded Ivan's pleas only after he had sent yet again begging them to show clemency.

This incident, humiliating to Ivan as Grand Prince, hardened his determination to free himself from the tyranny of the Shuisky. He was only thirteen years old and he still lived in terror of being beaten to death or buried in some dungeon or suddenly murdered. But he was approaching the time when he would refuse to be merely the silent and impotent source of power which he himself could not wield. The boyars and even the Metropolitan were afraid of the Shuisky faction, and he could count on no one for support. He was nevertheless growing more conscious of his position and of the power which belonged to him alone. Whether urged by Metropolitan Makary or others or on his own initiative, he reached his decision and with great courage he acted.

On 29 December (1543) Ivan suddenly ordered the arrest of Andrei Shuisky and had him thrown to a pack of hounds which tore him limb from limb. The whole of Moscow was astonished and relieved by this summary despatch of the most feared and hated man in the country. For Ivan, whose order had been executed promptly, it was a striking experience of his power. The hold of the Shuisky on him and on the country had been suddenly and completely broken. From this time, the chroniclers recorded, the boyars began to live in fear of their Grand Prince.[5]

Notes to Chapter VI

[1] J. L. I. Fennell (ed. and trans.), *The Correspondence between Prince A. M. Kurbsky and Tsar Ivan IV of Russia* (Cambridge, 1955), p. 75.

[2] Karamzin, Bk. II, Vol. VIII, col. 39.

[3] *Ibid.*

[4] *Ibid.*, p. 43.

[5] Solovyev, Bk. III, Vol. VI, p. 430.

CHAPTER VII

TSAR, BY THE WILL OF GOD

THE rule of the boyars was still not at an end, but for Ivan it no longer held such terror. After the death of Andrei Shuisky he was treated with careful respect. He might have governed had he wished, but he was too young and disinterested. At this stage he was content to leave such responsibilities to his two uncles, Princes Yuri and Mikhail Vasilievich Glinsky, and to his grandmother, Princess Anna Glinskaya. They remained cautiously in the background, avoiding any appearance of usurping Ivan's authority, but their iniquitous and selfish abuses of power, continuing the evil practices of the Shuisky, quickly antagonized the whole populace.

At the same time, while not ready or willing to take on the burdens of governing, Ivan was eager to assert himself and to win renown as ruler of Muscovy. He was impatient, with the impatience of a precocious fifteen-year-old boy, to carry out some bold undertaking which would make his people love and acclaim him. Nothing could so surely arouse popular enthusiasm and win him praise as a victory over the Tatars, and in April 1545 in what was his first major act as ruler he proclaimed a campaign against Kazan.

In the following month Muscovite troops proceeded, eastwards, some by river-barge and some by land, and they won a number of minor but encouraging victories. More important was the fact that the presence of Muscovite troops caused such alarm among the Tatars that the rivalries, always simmering among them, burst into open conflict. In January Ivan went to Vladimir to be nearer the scene of action. There word reached him that the Khan, Safa Girei, had been forced to flee from Kazan and that many of his Crimean guards had been killed in the internal struggles. The Kazan Tatars sent to beg Ivan to put aside his anger and to make Shig Alei their Khan. In June boyar Prince Dmitri Belsky, the Muscovite commander, rode to Kazan and installed Shig Alei as Khan, but Belsky had no sooner departed than the Tatars rose against their new Khan and restored Safa Girei to power. This was typical of the volatile Tatars; when under strong leadership they were a cruel predatory

54

enemy, but when divided into rival factions they fought bitterly among themselves and were unpredictable. Meanwhile, Ivan was denied the resounding victory of which he dreamt.

At court and among his people at this time Ivan could not resist the temptation to exercise the power which had been beyond his grasp for so long. But he used it capriciously and more for personal gratification. He took advantage now of opportunities to avenge himself on the boyars whom he held guilty as a class for the injustices and miseries of his childhood.

During the years from 1544 to 1546 he had sessions of disgracing and punishing boyars and others for the smallest misdemeanours, and irrespective of their past conduct in opposing or supporting the Shuisky. Feodor Vorontsov, the favourite whom he had saved from being killed by the Shuisky, incurred his displeasure, apparently because he presumed on Ivan's goodwill, and he was summarily executed. Many others were exiled to distant places or cast into prison. One noble, Afanasy Buturlin, charged with insolent speech, presumably made in Ivan's presence, had his tongue cut out in public.

In December 1545, on the intercession of the Metropolitan, Ivan suddenly pardoned his boyars, but this was no more than an uneasy truce. Five months later his suspicions again got the upper hand and he struck at them afresh. Expecting raids by the Crimean Tatars, he had gone with troops to Kolomna, some sixty miles south-east of Moscow. There, while riding with his suite in the countryside, he was halted by a band of Novgorod arquebusiers who presented a petition. Ivan angrily dismissed them. They refused to withdraw and he sent his suite to disperse them. The Novgorodtsi stood their ground. Fighting broke out and six men were killed.

The incident infuriated Ivan and the aggressive stubborn conduct of his Novgorod subjects also disturbed him. He immediately sent Vasily Zakharov, one of his closest counsellors, to investigate and Zakharov reported that three boyars had prompted the Novgorodtsi to behave defiantly and even to threaten the person of the Grand Prince. According to the chronicler of the incident, this report was false, but Ivan, ready always to hold his boyars guilty, at once ordered the execution of the three accused.[1]

The incident was typical of the arbitrary and irresponsible use of power by the sixteen-year-old Grand Prince. But this was how he had seen power exercised by others. Throughout the boyar anarchy, naked force had had free play. During the ascendancy of Belsky, when the Tatar threat had united even the boyars in a popular movement of self-defence, a different temper had reigned, but the moment the Tatars were in retreat the boyars had resumed their rule of corruption and violence. In the absence of any form of guidance, protection, or instruction, Ivan adopted similar methods. Metropolitan Makary was alone among those with whom Ivan had frequent contact in providing a better example.

Makary was a fascinating and at times enigmatic figure at Ivan's court. A man of strong and persuasive personality he seems nevertheless to have effaced himself, and yet his influence permeated the Kremlin. When he arrived in Moscow he was already renowned as a preacher and pastor, and revered as a saintly man. The Russian Orthodox clergy rarely delivered sermons, mainly because in their ignorance and illiteracy they might perpetrate some heresy. But, as Archbishop of Novgorod, Makary had spoken to the people in tales and parables which held them spellbound and were so clear in meaning that he was credited with inspired eloquence and wisdom. As a pastor he cared more effectively than his predecessors for the poor and orphans, and he opened the monasteries more widely to the needy.

Makary was not only a practical man of the church, but also a scholar and historian. He had the idea of assembling in one collection all the lives and teachings of the saints. For this purpose he took as his beginnings the *Mineya-Chetya*, a 9th century Byzantine compilation, arranged in a form to give monthly devotional readings. To it he added the accumulated teachings and history of five centuries of Christianity in Russia. He brought together for this task a group of scholarly collaborators, including the priest, Sylvester, who was later to play an important role. With these assistants he worked on his great collection for ten years in Novgorod and by 1541 it contained more than 13,500 large pages, embracing 1,300 lives of saints and holy writings of every kind. On his appointment to the Metropolitanate in 1542, he took with him to Moscow his band of assistants and the work itself to which he was still adding.

In the first years after Makary's arrival in the capital, Ivan's chief diversions were to ride wildly about the country, visiting monasteries, and indulging his passion for hunting. He was unconcerned about the hardships and discontents of his people as he pursued these pleasures. Indeed, a visit which he and his brother, Yuri, made to Novgorod and Pskov in the autumn of 1546 left bitter memories among the inhabitants. The people of Pskov complained that the

Grand Prince had paid no heed to their local problems, especially the wrongs which they suffered at the hands of the *Nastavnik* or governor, appointed by the Glinsky. In Novgorod, according to local accounts,[2] Ivan even committed thefts in the Cathedral of St Sofia. The people of both cities nursed angry resentment against the Grand Prince and hatred for the Glinsky. In Moscow, too, hatred against the Glinsky was also mounting. Such strong feelings were soon to find expression in popular revolt and demonstrations.

Riding and hunting did not take up all of Ivan's time and energies, or dull his restless searching mind. At some stage in his childhood he had been grounded in grammar and taught in the usual manner of ancient Russia, which meant learning by heart the psalter, pages of the gospels, and the book of hours, and repeating them endlessly by heart. He absorbed these books and was always able in later years to quote freely from the scriptures, sharpening his arguments with apt biblical illustrations. As he grew older he greedily read everything that he found. He studied the Bible, Greek and Roman history, the writings of the holy fathers, and the lives of the Saints, and he remembered all that he read. It is probable also that Makary guided him, and certainly the *Mineya-Chetya* provided him with a wealth of materials of the kind he sought, for he studied with a purpose.

Ivan was keenly aware of the heritage which he had received from his grandfather and father, both of whom he revered. They had conscientiously pursued the policy of gathering in the Russian lands under the rule of Moscow and of increasing the authority and dignity of the Grand Prince. Ivan embraced this policy and with a powerful singlemindedness devoted himself to developing it further. He came to identify himself with his people and with his realm, and to envisage Muscovy as a great nation. At the same time his conception of his power and position grew so that he saw himself as the divinely ordained sovereign on whom the nation centred.

Relations between the Grand Prince and his subjects had up to the 15th century been marked by a simple directness. Neither churchmen nor peasants and townsmen hesitated to speak with a certain man-to-man frankness to their Grand Prince. In 1480 Ivan III, instead of remaining with his troops on the Oka river in readiness to repel a Tatar invasion, had suddenly returned to Moscow. There he had found himself strongly and openly criticized by his subjects who loudly accused him of failing in his duty to defend them. Vassian, the Archbishop of Rostov, did not mince words, but called him a deserter and a coward.[3] A few years later Josef, the renowned abbot of Volokolamsk, had occasion to upbraid Grand Prince Vasily, Ivan's father, for showing too little respect for a man of the church; Vasily humbly removed his hat, stood, and asked his pardon.[4] Such a simple frank attitude, even on the part of a venerable churchman, towards the Grand Prince was soon to become unthinkable.

When towards the end of the 15th century, Ivan III adopted as his cipher the two-headed eagle of the Byzantine Emperors, he symbolized the transformation in the status of the throne which he was effecting. His marriage with Sofia Palaeologa, niece of the last Emperor, was an important stage in this transformation, for this allowed him to stand as the heir and successor of the Byzantine Emperors. It is unlikely that Ivan III himself, realistic and even cynical as he was in pursuing his policy, believed that Sofia could convey to him any legal title.[5] But he was employing symbols, legends, and associations which would uphold his pretensions and win popular credence and support.

In the 15th century the Grand Princes began to trace their genealogies directly from the Roman Emperors. A legend, apparently composed later in Ivan III's reign, related how the Emperor Augustus had divided his empire among his family, granting to his brother, Prus, a kingdom on the banks of the Nieman river, which came to be known as Prussia. It was claimed that Rurik, the Varangian founder of Russia, was descended directly from Prus, and thus he and his successors, the Muscovite autocrats, could trace their family line back to the Roman Emperors. Although bearing all the marks of a fable, Ivan was to quote it with conviction in 1563 in justification of his tsarish title during the negotiations with the ambassadors of Poland.[6]

Another legend, composed about this time, concerning the Kievan Prince, Vladimir Monomakh, became part of the fabric of Russian thought. It related that Vladimir, having been crowned in Kiev, despatched troops to wage war on Constantine Monomachus (1042–54) in Constantinople. But Constantine sent the Greek Metropolitan to Kiev with gifts and his own crown to propose peace so that all Orthodoxy might dwell in harmony "under the combined power of our Tsardom and your mighty autocracy, 'Great Rus' ".[7] Vladimir was then crowned with Constantine's crown and took the name of Monomakh, divinely ordained Tsar of Great Rus. The *Shapka Monomakha* (the cap of Monomachus) was thereafter always used as the coronation crown of the Tsars of Russia.

The significance of this legend lay in the claim of the Muscovite

Grand Prince to be the heir to the Byzantine Emperors in the fullest sense. To his subjects the Emperor had been absolute in both temporal and ecclesiastical spheres. After 1453, when Constantinople fell to the Turks, the succession was claimed for Moscow and Ivan III, her autocrat. In 1504, a Church Council, in defining the Tsar's duties in sixteen chapters, stated that "by nature the Tsar is like any other man, but in power and office he is like the highest God".[8]

In a letter to Vasily III, Ivan's father, a monk of a Pskov monastery, named Philotheus, wrote:

"I wish to add a few words on the present Orthodox Empire of our ruler; he is on earth the sole Emperor (Tsar) of the Christians, the leader of the Apostolic Church which stands no longer in Rome or in Constantinople, but in the blessed city of Moscow. She alone shines in the whole world brighter than the sun. . . . All Christian Empires are fallen and in their stead stands alone the Empire of our ruler in accordance with the prophetical books. Two Romes have fallen, but the third stands, and a fourth there will not be."[9]

This pronouncement by Philotheus at the beginning of the 16th century was probably in advance of the understanding of the Muscovites at the time, but it undoubtedly had a tremendous emotional appeal to a people so devout, whose church imposed the pattern of their daily lives, shaping it with ritual, fasts, and holy days. Their feeling was perhaps more simply expressed by the chronicler who wrote in 1512:

"Constantine's city is fallen, but our Russian land by the help of the Mother of God and the saints grows and is young and exalted. So may it be, O Christ, until the end of time."[10]

Reaching towards this heritage, it was not enough for Ivan III that the source of his power was, in fact, the patrimony received from his father, which he had expanded until it embraced most of the Russian Tsardom which he envisaged. Such power had to rest on the more noble and irrefutable foundations of divine sanction, as suggested by the example of Byzantium. Thus, when the Emperor, Frederick III, offered him the title of king, Ivan III proudly rejected the offer. "We, by the grace of God," he replied, "have been autocrats in our land from the beginning, from our earliest ancestors, and we hold our appointment, as with our ancestors, from God."[11]

Ivan embraced with passionate fervour this process of elevating the Muscovite autocrat so that "in power and office he is like the highest God".[12] A child of his age, he was devout and filled with the strong simple faith of the primitive Christians, which the Orthodox Church inculcated. The idea of his divine appointment to the throne and of his role as absolute ruler and defender of Christendom was one which he could readily accept as part of his faith and of his heritage.

This idea of the divine source of the monarch's power was readily accepted by the people of Muscovy, as it was by most of the peoples of Europe at this time. It was the century of the monarchy when the divine right of kings was passionately proclaimed and obedience to the monarch was a duty readily accepted because the monarch was both the symbol and the source of the unity and security which they craved. Thus, independently Ivan was pursuing a line of development similar to that of several other European monarchies, but he was also rooted to the traditions of Muscovy.

This theory made a special appeal to the furious fear-ridden nature of Ivan. The suspicion of people which his childhood had implanted in him had developed into a morbid mistrust. He saw in everyone an enemy who was plotting to destroy him and through him the young nation, and in the boyars he recognized his greatest enemies. In the unremitting struggle to which he felt himself committed to protect his throne and dynasty and to establish the nation, he searched feverishly for proofs of his absolute power. Even under the regime of the Shuisky, he had never heard anyone question his position; the boyars had humiliated and neglected him as a child, but they had fawned on him as Grand Prince. Nevertheless he sought proofs, perhaps to convince himself of the divine source of his power and perhaps, too, to find in these proofs moral justification for the hatred and bitterness which he felt. Certainly he wanted to prove to his boyars and subjects, and indeed to the world, that his power and position were unassailable.

Reading everything in terms of his own predicament and searching through the scriptures and through history for texts and examples, Ivan identified himself with the great biblical and historical figures. He would rule with the absolute power of Augustus and Theodosius, and like Solomon and David, because he, too, was appointed by God. Brooding over his succession to the throne and the nature of his authority, he clarified his conception of the role of the Muscovite autocrat. Three elements entered into it: first, God was the source of his power; second, Muscovy as the heir of Byzantium was the only surviving representative and defender of Orthodoxy, that is, of

Christendom; third, as the direct heir of Vladimir Monomakh, the Grand Prince of Muscovy was the true all-Russian autocrat. It followed that anyone who dared to oppose him was guilty of treason and of apostasy.

Ivan's father and grandfather, Vasily III and Ivan III, had pointed to these principles, but he developed them further. Already at the age of sixteen he seems to have understood them. But, although he was precocious in intelligence and although stimulated to a fury by his obsession with self-preservation and personal invulnerability, it is difficult to believe that he developed and understood these theories alone and without guidance of any kind. Metropolitan Makary, wise, learned, and himself sharing this conception of the supreme power, must surely have influenced and guided him.

Nevertheless, according to the chronicler, it was Ivan alone who summoned the Metropolitan and then his boyars and dramatically announced that he would be crowned, not as Grand Prince, but as Tsar.[13]

Notes to Chapter VII

[1] Solovyev, Bk. III, Vol. VI, p. 431.

[2] Karamzin, Bk. II, Vol. VIII, col. 54.

[3] Klyuchevsky, II, pp. 136–7.

[4] *Ibid.*

[5] Of Sofia's two brothers, Andrew, the elder, offered to sell his rights to the Byzantine throne to the highest bidder and, in fact, sold them three times, each time to a different person! He visited Moscow twice, once in 1480 and again in 1490. No doubt he offered to sell his rights to Ivan, but apparently Ivan was not interested, for no transaction was recorded. The younger brother Manuel returned to his native country and recognized the authority of the Sultan. Vernadsky, *op. cit.*, pp. 22, 25. See also J. L. I. Fennell, *Ivan the Great of Moscow* (London, 1961), p. 186.

[6] Klyuchevsky, II, p. 124.

[7] *Ibid.*, p. 125.

[8] N. H. Baynes and H. St L. B. Moss (eds.), *Byzantium* (Oxford, 1961), p. 384.

[9] N. Zernov, *The Russians and their Church* (London, 1945), p. 71.

[10] N. H. Baynes and H. St L. B. Moss, *op. cit.*, p. 384.

[11] Klyuchevsky, II, p. 127.

[12] N. H. Baynes and H. St L. B. Moss, *loc. cit.*

[13] Solovyev, Bk. III, Vol. VI, pp. 431–2.

CHAPTER VIII

CORONATION, MARRIAGE, AND THE FIRES OF MOSCOW 1547

ON 13 December 1546 Ivan had a long conversation in private with the Metropolitan, who emerged from this meeting smiling with pleasure. On the following day, after prayers in the Uspensky Cathedral, Makary called together all the boyars and led them into Ivan's presence in the Kremlin Palace. Many among them were anticipating an important announcement, but few expected an announcement as momentous as was made.

After invoking the blessings of the saints and the holy miracle-workers, Ivan stated simply that he had decided to marry.

"At first [he went on to explain, addressing himself to the Metropolitan] I thought of marrying from the family of some king or tsar of a foreign realm. I put that idea from me, however, and I do not wish to marry someone from foreign parts, because I was young when left alone by my father and mother, and if I take to myself a wife from foreign lands and we are not by our customs suited, then our life together will be unhappy; and so I wish to marry within our own realm whom God bless by your blessing."[1]

According to the chronicler, the Metropolitan and the boyars were moved to tears by this pronouncement, delivered with such dignity and maturity by one so young. But then Ivan astonished them all with a further statement. He had decided, he said, that before his marriage he would "assume the titles of our ancestors . . . and of our kinsman, Grand Prince Vladimir Vsevolodovich Monomakh" to the Tsardom and would be crowned.[2] Many of the boyars present were far from pleased by the young autocrat's decision to be crowned. He had already demonstrated his suspicion and hostility towards them, and this development could only mean a strengthening of the autocratic power over them. But with their usual display of humble obedience, they expressed their pleasure and acceptance of his decision.

On 16 January 1547, with the magnificent ceremonial of the Orthodox Church, Ivan was crowned Tsar of all Russia. But this coronation was an exceptional and even unprecedented occasion. Ivan was crowned Tsar, not Grand Prince. His grandfather, Ivan III, had used the title of Tsar of all Russia, but intermittently and without the full significance that Ivan gave to it. Further, this was the first coronation to follow the Byzantine precedents and at which, it was claimed, the regalia used was that which had been received five centuries earlier from the Emperor Constantine Monomachus.[3]

Ivan, having been crowned Tsar, then proceeded to his marriage. Already in the previous December, senior officials of the court had ridden to all parts of the realm with a pronouncement, addressed to princes, boyars, and landowners, which, after reciting the titles and dignities of the autocrat, read:

> "When this message reaches you, those among you who have maiden daughters, should ride forthwith to our representatives in the towns with your daughters for inspection, and not under any circumstances may you hide your daughters. . . ."[4]

There were heads of families who prized the peace and security of life on their estates. They had no wish to be drawn into the savage struggles for position and power which made Moscow a place of real dangers. Direct connexion with the autocrat through marriage would bring a family great eminence and authority, but at a price which many boyars considered too high. This attitude was so widespread that the Tsar's proclamation contained the warning that all who hid their eligible daughters would suffer disgrace and even execution.

The maidens, chosen for their comeliness, piety, and good character, assembled in Moscow for the Tsar's final selection. Vasily III, Ivan's father, had had 1,500 of the most beautiful maidens in the land from whom to choose his first wife, according to Herberstein.[5] Ivan probably made his choice from a similar number, but nothing is known of the occasion nor of the reasons why his choice fell upon Anastasia, daughter of the deceased *Okolnichy*, Roman Yurievich Zakharin-Koshkin, a family of Prussian origin which had migrated to Muscovy in the 14th century, and which was to give Russia the Romanov dynasty.[6] Anastasia's uncle, Mikhail Yurievich, had been a trusted counsellor of Vasily III and this fact may have told in her favour. The boyars were, however, horrified that the Tsar should lower himself by marrying a girl of such humble origins. His grandfather had married a princess of Byzantium, and his father had married the daughter of a family which, while possessing many enemies, was undeniably eminent and noble. But Ivan had chosen a bride whose family was not even of minor princely standing. The boyars felt that this choice was not only unworthy of him, but that it demeaned them, and this was to give rise to resentment and conflict.

Anastasia herself possessed all the womanly virtues, prized among Orthodox Russians, of humility, charity, and devoutness, which made her a gentle and obedient companion. Women in Muscovy were completely subservient to their men, and their lives were hard and often miserable. Herberstein noted that the Muscovites "consider no woman virtuous unless she live shut up at home and be so closely guarded that she go out nowhere".[7] They were not even free to go to church on public occasions. Relegated to the *terem*, their special apartments, the women of noble families led a life of idleness in which the monotony was relieved by spinning and needlework. Their sole function was to bear children, for servants carried out all domestic duties. Among the poorer people the women were not shut away, but they worked so hard that they were no more than beasts of burden. A woman of character might exercise a strong influence within her family, but this was exceptional. The wife of the autocrat was, of course, required to lead an exemplary life.

On 13 February the Metropolitan performed the marriage ceremony in the Uspensky Cathedral.[8] The couple then showed themselves to the people who called out their blessings. Muscovites gave themselves up to celebrations, lasting several days. But Ivan and Anastasia devoutly withdrew and, although the countryside was in the freezing grip of winter, they walked together in stages the forty miles to the Troitsa monastery, where they spent the first week of Lent, praying daily at the tomb of Saint Sergius.

Such piety, deeply felt and sincere, was part of the daily life of all Muscovites, and it was expected of the autocrat. But in this harsh age, not only in Muscovy but throughout Europe, Christian devotion went hand in hand with cruelty and inhumanity. In Ivan this capacity for devoutness, even tenderness, and savagery were combined to an extraordinary degree. He was capable of affection; in fact, the few who managed to set aside his morbid suspicions and to win his trust found a gentle spirit, longing to love and be loved. Anastasia awakened such feelings in him and he was always to treat her with gentle affection and respect. In time she was to bring a calming influence to bear on him. But she could not at once assuage his hatreds or exorcize his mistrust of others. Confronted by hostility or even simple opposition, he at once felt himself to be surrounded by enemies and his fury was unleashed.

At this time, despite the Christian vows enjoined on him as Tsar at his coronation, and the example of Christian piety displayed by his Tsaritsa, Ivan was intoxicated by his new-found power. He was autocrat; nothing could be denied him; no one could gainsay him. He indulged his coarsest tastes for entertainers, drinking bouts, and cruel sports, and he played with power, raising up and striking down whomsoever he wished. The government of the country remained in the hands of the Glinsky who, apart from meeting the least whims of the Tsar, were free to pursue their own interests, preying on boyars and people alike. The *nastavniki* or governors, whom they appointed, ruled corruptly and those who suffered had no redress.

The people of Pskov, like the Novgorodtsi, had a tradition of freedom and independence, and were more ready than the people of central Russia to voice their complaints and to demand justice. Boldly they decided to petition the Tsar about the malpractices of their *nastavnik*, Prince Turuntai-Pronsky.

The seventy citizens of Pskov, chosen to present the petition with accusations and proofs against him, made the journey to Moscow and confronted Ivan in the village of Ostrovka. He refused to hear them. Their presence alone was to him a form of sedition. In a rage he shouted, abused, and condemned them. He had hot wine poured over their heads and some had their hair and their beards singed by fire. He ordered them to strip and to lie naked in the snow. Bewildered and resigned, they obeyed, expecting now to be summarily executed, and this was almost certainly the fate awaiting them. But at this moment messengers galloped into the village with news of a terrible fire in Moscow. Ivan at once mounted his horse and rode away with his suite to the city. The petitioners of Pskov were forgotten and to this they owed their lives.[9]

Fires were frequent in Moscow. The houses, built of logs, were heated in winter by crude stoves and dried out until they were like tinder in the short hot summers. The yards surrounding most houses often helped prevent fires from spreading, but it needed only a wind to carry the sparks and then whole districts were aflame. The city had suffered many major fires, but none within recent years.

Moscow was, however, now growing rapidly. Established as the seat of the Tsar and the principal city of Muscovy, it attracted people from all over the country. Houses sprang up wherever there was space. Richard Chancellor, the English sea captain, considered

Moscow "greater than London . . . but it is rude and standeth without all order".[10] Herberstein wrote that the great number of houses, said to exceed 41,500, was "scarcely credible", while the Kremlin was so large that it not only contained "the very extensive and magnificently built stone palace of the prince", but also spacious timbered houses of the Metropolitan, the leading boyars, and many churches.[11] Within and without the Kremlin and even in the newer suburbs the new huddled with the old dilapidated houses, and the congestion, caused by the rapid growth of the city, made the spreading of fires a far greater hazard.

On 12 April 1547 a serious fire broke out in Kitai Gorod, the middle town and merchant quarter. All the stalls and warehouses of the merchants and traders perished. A tower, used to store gunpowder, exploded, blowing parts of the city wall into the Moskva river. This fire then died down, but no doubt smouldered and a few days later new fires destroyed the district beyond the Yauza river, where the smithies and tanneries were concentrated. Again the fires died down or were dormant with only minor outbreaks, but then after several weeks came the great conflagration, the most devastating fire that Moscow had yet experienced.

A high wind was blowing when on 21 June fire first broke out in the Arbat, a suburb to the west of the Kremlin. The church of Vozdvizhenskoe quickly burnt to the ground. The fire spread rapidly, reducing to ashes the whole of the western part of the city up to the banks of the Moskva river. At this stage the wind changed direction, carrying the fire on to the Kremlin which was soon ablaze. The palace, the treasury, armouries, all the state offices, private houses, the Metropolitan's palace, the cathedrals and churches, all were destroyed. The books and manuscripts, the treasures of the Kremlin, the holy ikons with few exceptions, but including the miracle-working ikon of the virgin of Vladimir, perished. The Uspensky Cathedral with its renowned ikonostasis and gold vessels was partly spared, but the structure of the cathedral was seriously damaged. The great bell of Moscow fell from its burning belfry to fracture on the ground below. Adding to the horror of the people in the smoking inferno, which the whole city had become, were the explosions of gunpowder in the state arsenal.

At the first outbreak of fire Metropolitan Makary had gone to the Uspensky Cathedral to pray for the deliverance of the city. The smoke almost suffocated him, but he managed to escape carrying with him the holy ikon of the Mother of God, painted by the Metropolitan Peter. He was followed by several priests and an archpriest, bearing the ancient church statutes, which had been brought originally from Constantinople. He made his way along the city wall by means of a secret passage, but once again the smoke overwhelmed him. The priests, accompanying him, then lowered him from the Kremlin wall by means of a wooden platform. The rope broke and the Metropolitan fell heavily to the ground. He was almost unconscious as he was carried off to the Novospassky monastery.

Driven by the high wind, the fire had swept across the city. Few buildings had escaped damage and most districts had been reduced to smouldering ruins. At least 1,700 people, not including many children, had lost their lives. For days heavy clouds of smoke hung over the city. The survivors, with singed hair and blackened faces, searched hopelessly among the charred ruins for missing members of their families and traces of their property. Everyone had suffered some loss and, bowed down by personal tragedy, sought consolation that was not to be found. The bewildered sorrowful mood of the people began to turn to resentment, especially towards their autocrat who had completely failed to succour or to consider them in this time of need.

At the outset of the disaster Ivan with his wife, brother, and boyars had ridden away to safety in the village of Vorobiovo, not far from the city. There, watching the pall of smoke rising from Moscow, he remained while fire raged. Apparently he had no thoughts for his people for their sufferings, but he and several boyars gave prompt instructions for the rebuilding of their palaces in the Kremlin.

On the day following the fire, Ivan rode with his suite to the Novospassky monastery to pay his respects to the Metropolitan, who was recovering from exhaustion and the shock of his accident. There Ivan's chaplain, Archpriest Feodor Barmin, Boyar Prince Feodor Skopin-Shuisky, Ivan Chelyadin, and others, known to be hostile to the Glinsky, told him that black magic was responsible for the fires and the burning of Moscow. Sorcerers had torn out the hearts from human corpses, soaked them in water, and then had sprinkled this water on the streets of Moscow; this had caused the fire.

Ivan was astonished, but ready to accept this explanation. Witchcraft, a stubborn and powerful relic of pagan religions, was widely practised in Muscovy and Western Europe in the 16th century, as the innumerable trials and the general persecution of witches bore witness. Fervently believing in the devil, people had no difficulty in accepting the existence of witches as his agents. To a young man of Ivan's temperament, witchcraft was a very real force, a manifestation of the devil's evil influence, to be guarded against by prayer. He at once ordered his boyars to conduct an investigation and the method they adopted in carrying out this investigation suggested that either the charge of witchcraft was invented as part of a careful plan to overthrow the Glinsky or that the boyars seized on a popular rumour to achieve this purpose.

On the fifth day after the fire, without the usual interrogations or assembling of evidence, the boyars called the homeless and desperate people of Moscow to the square in front of the Uspensky Cathedral. There they put to the crowd the question, "Who set fire to Moscow?" Spontaneously they shouted in reply, "Princess Anna Glinskaya with her children made the magic . . ." and they recited the details concerning the use of human hearts. Whether because this explanation was the popular belief or because it had been well planted among them beforehand, the crowd needed no prompting. Moreover, they spoke from a burning hatred of the Glinsky and at the same time, since the Glinsky were of his family and his current favourites, they were censuring their young Tsar, who had thought only of his personal safety.[12]

Prince Yuri Glinsky, Ivan's uncle, was with the boyars on the Kremlin Square and heard the crowd condemn him and his family. He quietly slipped away to seek sanctuary in the Uspensky Cathedral. The boyars, themselves opposed to the Glinsky as much as the people, then sent the angry mob in pursuit of him. They swept into the cathedral and, ignoring the fact that they were on consecrated ground and in a place of special sanctity, they killed him near the altar. They then dragged his corpse from the Kremlin to the place of execution on the Red Square, where they exposed it for all to see.

Their fury unabated, the mob stormed through the city in pursuit of the supporters and attendants of the Glinsky and they killed all whom they found. Three days later, still thirsting for blood, the mob made its way to Vorobiovo. They took up a stand before the Tsar's residence, shouting demands that his grandmother, Princess Anna, and his uncle, Prince Mikhail Glinsky, whom they believed to be hidden there by the Tsar, should be handed over to them.

To Ivan this was treasonable conduct and an affront to him personally, such as he could never tolerate from his own subjects. He showed no fear of the mob and not only refused their demands, but had many of the rioters seized and summarily executed. The rest of the mob, not having expected that their young Tsar would act so severely, took fright and made their escape back to the city. The riot and the talk of black magic had come to an end.

The rule of the Glinsky also ceased at this point. They had, in fact, been overthrown by the party of the Shuisky. The chief supporters of Andrei Shuisky had been exiled or dispersed after his execution, but gradually they had found their way back to Moscow. They no longer dared to act directly and had to achieve their ends in alliance with others, who were close to the Tsar. Thus Feodor Skopin-Shuisky worked with the Tsar's priest, Barmin, and the Tsaritsa's uncle, Grigory Zakharin. But they had succeeded in their purpose of overthrowing the Glinsky. Indeed, Prince Mikhail Glinsky so feared for his safety that he attempted to escape with his friend, Prince Turuntai-Pronsky, to Lithuania. Both men were captured and even pardoned, but never restored to power. At the same time it was notable that Ivan did not entrust power to any of the members of the Shuisky faction.

The riots had made a deep impression on him, not only because of the strength of the popular antagonism towards the Glinsky, but because it was also directed at him. Popular discontent had been stirring throughout his reign, but it had always been concentrated against the boyars who were equally his enemies. It came as a shock to him to find himself coupled with a hated faction in the popular mind, and the shock was salutary.

Notes to Chapter VIII

[1] Solovyev, Bk. III, Vol. VI, pp. 431–2.

[2] *Ibid.*

[3] Ivan III's grandson, Dmitri, had on 4 February 1498 been crowned Grand Prince of Vladimir, Moscow, and All Russia, and on this occasion the *shapka Monomakha* and the great collar (*barmy*) had been used and the Byzantine precedents followed. But Dmitri had never succeeded to the throne, and he had not been crowned Tsar. J. L. I. Fennell, *Ivan the Great of Moscow* (London, 1961), p. 337.

[4] Solovyev, Bk. III, Vol. VI, p. 432.

[5] Sigismund von Herberstein, *op. cit.*, I, p. 50.

[6] Nikita Romanov, the brother of Tsaritsa Anastasia, was the grandfather of Tsar Mikhail, elected to the throne in 1613 and the first of the Romanov dynasty.

[7] Sigismund von Herberstein, *op. cit.*, I, p. 93.

[8] Karamzin, Bk. II, Vol. VIII, col. 59.

[9] *Ibid.*, 59–60.

[10] Hakluyt, I, p. 255.

[11] Sigismund von Herberstein, *op. cit.*, II, p. 5.

[12] Karamzin, Bk. II, Vol. VIII, col. 61.

CHAPTER IX

THE CHOSEN COUNCIL 1547-9

THE events of the first six months of 1547 wrought a striking transformation in the outlook and behaviour of Ivan. His coronation and marriage, both occasions of high ceremonial and sacred vows, and then the terrible fires of Moscow and the uprising against his own kinsmen, the Glinsky, with the implicit censure of himself by the people had all moved him deeply. Directly and indirectly as a result of these experiences, Ivan seemed to become a different man. The youth who, like an animal at bay, had lashed out at his enemies or, like a vicious child, had tortured and executed people, while playing with the power vested in him, suddenly shed his vindictiveness and even his anger, and began to behave as a man of humility, responsibility, and vision. It was a remarkable demonstration of the extremes of his nature. Moderation was unknown to him and, in a constant mental and emotional ferment, he was to swing from one extreme to another throughout his life.

Ivan also showed this lack of restraint in speech. He expressed himself always with a spontaneous and at times passionate eloquence. He felt a constant compulsion both to communicate with others and to explain the torments of mind and spirit which he suffered. A sense of guilt, of his fall from grace, pursued him. He did not hide from himself or from others his acts of wrongdoing, but acknowledged them and prayed devoutly for forgiveness. At the same time he was defending himself before his people and before God and placing the blame for his corruption on the boyars. But now in his changed mood, instead of himself arbitrarily disgracing and executing them, as he had done on occasions in the past, he wanted them judged as guilty men. Soon, however, he was to propose forgiveness for all so that the Tsardom might live in Christian love.

Ivan himself attributed his reformation to the fires of Moscow in the last resort. Addressing a church assembly he explained the impact that the fires had made on him and, dwelling on his troubled mind and repentance, he spoke with the humility of Job:

"It is impossible [he said] either to describe or to relate with the human tongue all the wicked things that I have done through the sins of my youth. At first God humbled me by taking from me my father, your pastor and defender. The boyars and nobles, pretending that they were my wellwishers, were in fact seeking after power for themselves. . . . On the death of my mother, the boyars ruled as despots over the Tsardom. Because of my sins, of my being an orphan, and of my immaturity, many people perished in internecine quarrels, and I grew up in neglect, without instruction, and accustomed to the low cunning of boyar practices, and since that time how greatly have I sinned before God and how many punishments has God sent down on us! More than once we attempted to wreak vengeance on our enemies, but without success. I did not understand that the Lord was punishing me with great punishments, and I did not repent, but myself ground down poor Christians with heavy oppressions. The Lord punished me for my sins by deluge and by plague, and still I did not repent. Then God sent great fires, and terror entered into my soul and trembling into my bones; my soul was subdued; I was moved and acknowledged my sins; asking forgiveness of the clergy I granted forgiveness to the princes and boyars."[1]

This transformation in Ivan seemed so dramatic and sudden that some considered it a miracle. Prince Kurbsky wrote that, after the fires of Moscow and the uprising of the people, God miraculously extended his hand "to give respite to the Christian land" by sending to the Tsar a certain priest, named Sylvester.[2] The historian, Karamzin, writing three centuries later, also believed that a miracle took place. "For the correction of Ivan it was necessary that Moscow be consumed by fire" and then that a remarkable man, Sylvester, should suddenly appear before him.[3] In fact, whether miraculous or not, the change in Ivan was not sudden. It took place gradually over many months, but it was mainly due to the influence of this strange and powerful priest, Sylvester.[4]

Ivan readily succumbed to the influence of others. His attitude towards his fellow-men had been distorted by mistrust and towards his boyars poisoned by hatred and fear. But these emotions, felt so intensely, had brought him a terrible loneliness. Mistrust isolates a man so completely that in the desert of his loneliness he is like a traveller dying of thirst, but his craving is for companionship and affection, and it becomes so overwhelming that he will grasp at any hand. Thus, paradoxically, a man of Ivan's suspicious nature falls all the more readily and completely under the spell of another, once his fears have been allayed and his confidence won. With Ivan, too, his trust once given was unrestrained. It needed a shattering betrayal, a serious threat to his safety, or an encroachment on his tsarish power to destroy his faith, and then his vindictive fury pursued the fallen favourite to the end.

Sylvester did not appear suddenly before Ivan. He had probably come to Moscow from Novgorod, his native city, in 1542, with Metropolitan Makary whom he was assisting in the work of the *Mineya Chetya*. He was a scholar, but he also combined religious fervour with practical ability. He demonstrated this in the 1550s, when he wrote the *Domostroi*, a manual of Christian conduct and housekeeping which was a remarkable work, reflecting the spirit of the time, and it was to serve as a guide for generations of Orthodox Russians to come.[5] In Moscow, Sylvester served as a simple priest of the Blagoveshchensky Cathedral, which the Tsar and his court regularly attended. But, although close to the Metropolitan, he might have remained undistinguished among the numerous priests of the Cathedral had he not been a man of fanaticism, courage, and personality.

A stern and devout priest, Sylvester was like Elijah the Tishbite, the prophet who appeared from out of the wilderness and who served a God that answered by fire. Sylvester, too, had impressed his contemporaries as having made a dramatic appearance after the fires of Moscow and, like Elijah, he was relentless in his hostility to those whom he saw as false prophets. To him Ivan was like Ahab, who had done more to provoke the God of Israel to anger than all the kings before him. Without fear he dedicated himself to the task of reforming the young Tsar and bringing him to repentance.

Apparently Sylvester's ascendancy over Ivan began soon after the fires of Moscow and the popular uprising. This was a time of special isolation for Ivan. His kinsmen, the Glinsky, had failed him and had been cast out as a result of the angry demonstrations of the people of Moscow. His brother, Yuri, towards whom he behaved always as a gentle elder, was mentally retarded and no companion to a man of Ivan's ability and temperament. In his loneliness he turned to certain new men whom he found near at hand, and among them the stern priest was dominant. Within a few months Feodor Barmin, the Tsar's confessor, laid down his office to retire into a monastery, and Sylvester was appointed in his place.[6]

Sylvester began his chosen task of reform by threatening and frightening the young Tsar. Yet again Ivan, whose whole childhood had been spent in a state of terror, had fear as his close companion;

then he had feared for his personal safety and now he feared for his salvation. Sylvester scourged him with tales of miracles and apparitions sent by God to warn and hold him from wickedness which would damn his soul through eternity. He devised terrors to haunt this tense imaginative boy, to tame "his wildness and for the sake of his childish unbridled ways".[7] Prince Kurbsky, who was at this time close to Sylvester and Ivan, wrote subsequently in a letter to the Tsar, "So did he, the venerable one (Sylvester), because of your incurable sickness, apply plasters—now attacking you and abusing you with biting words, cutting as it were with a razor your unholy habits by means of harsh punishments. . . ."[8] Ivan himself, replying to Kurbsky at a time when he had passed beyond the priest's influence, referred to the attempts to "scare me with childish bogies".[9] The attempts were nevertheless successful at the time, for alone and frightened in the Kremlin the Tsar, aged only seventeen, was apparently cowed by the priest's burning admonitions and by his threats and terrors. He put aside his evil practices and, like Ahab, repented.

Sylvester's purpose was, first, to reform the Tsar and then to eradicate certain abuses in the government of the country. In this latter task he had the support of allies. Moreover, Metropolitan Makary, while lacking his fervour and powerful personality, was broader in outlook and probably aided him. Makary had played an important part in Ivan's education and upbringing, supporting him in his conception of the role of the autocrat, perhaps inspiring him with the idea of being crowned Tsar, and encouraging in him a crusading spirit against the infidel Tatars. Since all that added to the strength and unity of Muscovy and to the power of the Orthodox Tsar had Makary's support, he would have encouraged the reforms under discussion among Sylvester and the members of his group.

In secular affairs Makary and Sylvester were in broad agreement, but they were opposed in ecclesiastical matters. Makary belonged to the Josephan party which maintained that the church needed its wealth and the protection of the temporal power to carry out its mission. Sylvester belonged to the Trans-Volga Hermits and condemned the wealth of the church, urging the surrender of its lands and riches, so that it would be cleansed of their corrupting influence. The great issues between the two churchmen concerned the privileges and immunities of the church and the secularization of its lands, and they were soon to come into conflict on these issues in the church council. In the late 1540s, however, it appeared that Makary, although Metropolitan, was overshadowed and wielded far less influence than the simple priest.

Sylvester's closest ally was Alexei Adashev, the practical man of affairs and probably the most sympathetic and attractive person serving at the Tsar's court at this time. Adashev was of a minor gentry family and may have come first into Ivan's company as a child when he was one of his appointed playmates.[10] He next became *batozhnik*, the bearer of a stick with which he cleared people from the path of the Tsar. By June 1547 Adashev had become *postelnichy*, or keeper of the Tsar's bedchamber, a position of considerable influence, for it brought him into daily contact with Ivan and involved the management of his personal treasury.

By this time Adashev had won Ivan's confidence and had proved himself a highly efficient and trustworthy courtier. He was, indeed, a man who succeeded by his abilities and yet remained popular. He possessed both charm and a patent uprightness which brought him the goodwill and friendship of all who knew him. Kurbsky considered him to be like an angel. Later, during the Livonian war, according to Kurbsky, enemy towns were ready to surrender if they could surrender to Adashev, and it was "on account of his goodness".[11]

While by the end of 1547 both Sylvester and Adashev had secured the trust and friendship of Ivan, there is no evidence that they were playing any significant part in the government then or even in the following year. Both men were during this period apparently concentrating on bringing about a change of heart in Ivan, parting him from former associates, and consolidating their positions at court. But they were also discussing and planning reforms in the government, while selecting men, who would make a team, devoted to the task of strengthening and reforming the Muscovite state.

This team, named by Kurbsky the "Chosen Council",[12] was to play a part of tremendous importance during the next few years. It was not an organized body, but an informal group, placed around the Tsar, and it was to provide the government. The full membership of the Chosen Council is not known. It was not the same as the membership of the Boyar Council, the formal council of state, but it may have coincided with the inner council, the more intimate advisory body which the Muscovite Grand Princes had gathered around them. It seems probable that the Chosen Council, begun as a small informal team, gradually merged with the inner council and became the Tsar's cabinet.

Sylvester and Adashev were the leaders in the council but, although he wielded great influence, Sylvester may not have been actually a member, because of his priestly calling.[13] Prince Dmitri Kurlyatev, a trusted adviser of Vasily III, Ivan's father, was a member after 1549 when he was elevated to the rank of boyar.[14] Prince Andrei Kurbsky and Mikhail Morozov were probably also members. Of the others the majority probably came from among the various princely families who had had the experience of governing and bearing responsibility. Certainly Ivan was later to accuse the council of showing bias in favour of the princes and boyars by returning to them the patrimonial lands which his father and grandfather had confiscated.[15] But, made in the heat of anger and disillusion, Ivan's accusations at this later date were sometimes unreliable.

The Chosen Council provided a government of compromise. It depended for some support on the boyar-princely aristocracy, but it was sensitive to the demand for reforms by the serving gentry, and from other classes of the population. The degree of compromise was on the whole small, however, and the trend of the reforms, promoted by the council, was to consolidate the central power of the Tsar, undermine the position of the princely-boyar aristocracy, and elevate the new class of military serving men in their place. Thus, while the majority of the members of the Chosen Council may well have come from princely families, the reforms did not favour their interests, and this pointed to the fact that Sylvester and Adashev and later Ivan himself dominated it.

During the two years 1547–9, Sylvester and Adashev busily formulated their policy and prepared for its introduction. The most important preparation at this time affected the Boyar Council, the membership of which increased from twelve to thirty-two by the end of 1549. Several new boyars were created and appointed to the council, and they included men like Prince Dmitri Kurlyatev, Ivan Sheremetev, and Mikhail Morozov who were all close to Sylvester and Adashev and probably members of the Chosen Council itself. This increase in the size of the Boyar Council had the result of reducing the influence of the dominant boyar families, who had during the minority of Ivan so abused power as to earn the hatred of most Muscovites. To the members of the Chosen Council the disastrous effect of the feuds and struggles among the boyars had been to lead the nation back more than a century to the time when northeast Russia was split into rival warring principalities. They knew that to survive, Muscovy had to be a strong centralized state.

The first task, therefore, in any programme of reform was to foster the serving gentry as a class capable of leading and bearing responsibility, while honouring their duties and allegiance to the Tsar. This oblique assault on the position of the boyars and princes was, however, merely a first step in the programme of reforms which sought to root out corruption, injustice, and inefficiency, and to develop a new administration which would give unity and strength to the vast young nation.

Ivan was in his early twenties during the years 1549–56 when this programme of reforms was launched, and it is most difficult to assess the part he played in it at the beginning. The purposes of the reforms undoubtedly had his wholehearted support. For personal reasons he hated and feared the boyar families, and he was determined to create an absolute autocracy. Moreover, he readily understood the need for a strong centralized Muscovy. Thus, while he probably did not initiate the early reforms of this period, the members of his Chosen Council would have discussed them with him, for they would not have been so presumptuous or incautious as to attempt to proceed without his knowledge or taking his approval for granted. Ivan was a man to be led and guided, never one to be pushed or faced with accomplished deeds which he could be expected to endorse.[16] He never forgot that he was Tsar and the source of all power; failure to respect his person and authority made him flare into anger. Furthermore, he was never a passive character, waiting on the stimulus of others. He possessed a strong creative imagination and ability to act decisively.

With his quick intelligence Ivan understood the proposals of Sylvester, Adashev, and others on the Chosen Council. He embraced their ideas with energy and enthusiasm. As the programme of reforms advanced he took more initiative in formulating and carrying them out. In fact, in the course of the intensive preparation and enactment of these reforms, his abilities were schooled and he became a responsible and experienced monarch.

Notes to Chapter IX

[1] Solovyev, Bk. III, Vol. VI, p. 435.
[2] N. Ustryalov, *Statements of Prince Kurbsky* (St Petersburg, 1833).
[3] Karamzin, Bk. II, Vol. VIII, cols. 60–2.
[4] Russia has a tradition of churchmen, some Metropolitans and Patriarchs, others simple priests, who have by their ability, piety, or simply by over-

powering personality exercised strong influence on the throne and the course of policy. They include Josef of Volokolamsk, Metropolitan Makary, Sylvester in the 16th century, Patriarch Nikon, and Archpriest Avvakum in the 17th century, and Rasputin, who was strictly not a priest, in the 20th century.

[5] Sylvester, *Domostroi*, ed. I. Glazunov (St Petersburg 1911), 3rd ed.

[6] Karamzin, Bk. II, Vol. VIII, note 188.

[7] J. L. I. Fennell (ed.and trans.), *The Correspondence between Prince A. M. Kurbsky and Tsar Ivan IV of Russia* (Cambridge, 1955), p. 141 and note 7.

[8] *Ibid.*, p. 203.

[9] *Ibid.*, p. 141.

[10] *Ibid.*, p. 85.

[11] Adashev's reputation not only spread beyond the frontiers of Muscovy, but it endured. Nearly twenty-five years after his death when a Polish archbishop asked the Russian ambassador what manner of man Boris Godunov was, the ambassador could say nothing better than that he was like Adashev in his goodness. S. F. Platonov, *Ivan the Terrible* (Berlin, 1924), p. 48.

[12] S. V. Bakhrushin, "The Chosen Council of Ivan the Terrible", in *Istoricheskie Zapiski*, Vol. 15 (1945). A. A. Zimin, *Reforms of Ivan the Terrible* (Moscow, 1960). The two Soviet scholars, Bakhrushin and Zimin, have assembled all the available material on the Chosen Council and have contributed their own penetrating research. Their interpretations of the material are, however, somewhat arbitrary in some respects, as for example in their reluctance to concede that the church or individual churchmen, especially Makary, played a significant part in Ivan's reign.

[13] A. A. Zimin and other Soviet historians maintain that Adashev was head of the government at this time. The exclusion of Sylvester on the ground that being a priest he could not be a member of the Chosen Council seems to me unacceptable. The Chosen Council started as an informal group of like-minded men. Sylvester was certainly prominent among them and exercised a strong influence on the group. The Council remained an informal body and there was no reason why Sylvester should have been excluded. It is probable, I think, that Sylvester and Adashev formed a partnership and acted jointly. Ivan himself thought of them together, as partners.

[14] Prince Dmitri Kurlyatev had supported the Shuisky when they had held power during Ivan's minority. He had even taken part in the violent attempt to remove Ivan's favourite, Vorontsov, in 1543. Later he was to merit Ivan's mistrust and he was eventually murdered, probably on Ivan's orders. J. L. I. Fennell, *op. cit.*, p. 89.

[15] J. L. I. Fennell, *op. cit.*, p. 89; S. F. Platonov, *op. cit.*, p. 49.

[16] Ivan was later to accuse Sylvester and Adashev of usurping his power, retaining him merely as a figurehead, while they themselves carried out the reforms of the 1550s. But he made these accusations after the fall of the powerful favourites who, he considered, had betrayed him, and he then used every weapon to explain and justify their disgrace. At the time, however, the internal reforms involved no dispute between Ivan and Sylvester and Adashev; indeed, Ivan supported and promoted them with enthusiasm. J. L. I. Fennel, *op. cit.*, pp. 87–9; A. A. Zimin, *Reforms of Ivan the Terrible* (Moscow, 1960), p. 323.

CHAPTER X

THE FIRST REFORMS 1549–51

ON 27 February 1549 a crowd of people gathered on the Red Square in Moscow. They had come in answer to the Tsar's summons that men chosen from all the towns of Muscovy should assemble in the capital for important affairs of state. They now waited patiently in the cold until, from the gate of the Spassky Tower, the tallest and most handsome of all the Kremlin towers, the Tsar appeared. He came in procession with the Metropolitan and bishops, boyars, army commanders, and members of the serving gentry. All were resplendent in their robes. The crowd stood in awed silence as the Tsar, tall, broad-shouldered, and imperious, reached and mounted the *Lobnoe Mesto*, the Place of Execution, about halfway across the square.

Prayers were conducted and then, turning to the Metropolitan, the Tsar spoke. He referred to his childhood when, bereft of parents, he had been neglected and terrorized by the boyars. He often spoke of his cruel upbringing. It was in part a deliberate appeal to popular sympathy and in part it was because these childhood memories were an obsession. All the failures and sufferings of his life were somehow involved in his mind with the twin facts of early orphanhood and boyar terror.

Stirring with these angry memories, Ivan began denouncing the boyars. They had, he said,

"wished to be all-powerful; in my name they stole honours and rank, enriched themselves through injustices, oppressed the people —and no one forbad them. In my pitiful childhood I seemed deaf and dumb; I did not heed the wailing of the poor, and no accusations came from my lips. You, the boyars, you did what you wished, wicked rebels, unjust judges! What answers will you give us now? How many tears, how much blood, you have made to flow! I am clean of this blood! But you will answer before the heavenly court!"[1]

Ivan paused and bowed to all sides before speaking again:

"Godly people, given into our care by God! I invoke your faith in Him and your love for me: be forgiving! Past evil cannot be

78

undone. I can only save you from future oppression and extortion. Forget what has happened and will not happen again! Put enmity and hatred from you! Let us all join in Christian love! Henceforth I will be your judge and your defender!"[2]

Under Ivan's spell this assembly had become a dramatic, even theatrical, occasion. He always expressed himself vehemently, but a large audience moved him to speak with a burning eloquence. He was often to make such appeals to his people and his powerful personality always dominated the occasion. A lonely man, suspicious of individuals, he needed the support of the masses, and as an astute ruler he appealed to their loyalty. But in his approach to this assembly another factor played a part, and that was his need to confess publicly. Scourged by the threats, terrors, and admonitions of Sylvester, the young Tsar had been brought to repentance and reform. But for him it was never enough to repent in the privacy of the confessional, and repeatedly during his reign he was to confess his sins in public.

For the Muscovites, this was a momentous day. Their Tsar, speaking with such passion and sincerity, had denounced the boyars and had identified himself with the people who like him had suffered at their hands. He had confessed his neglect of them in the past and had promised to be their defender in the future. At the same time he had called on them as Christians to forgive the boyars so that they might all live in Christian harmony. No Grand Prince had ever appealed to them in such terms, expressed concern for the general weal, or promised his protection. Herein lay the first foundations of the strong popular support which he was to have from this time on to the end of his reign.

This gathering was also of constitutional importance, for it was, in fact, the first *Zemsky Sobor* or Assembly of the Land. It was attended by the members of the Boyar and Church Councils, and by serving gentry; it was nevertheless far from being fully representative of the people. No deputies came from the merchant class or the peasantry or from many of the towns and districts, and those who attended had probably been arbitrarily appointed, rather than elected. But this Assembly of the Land was to develop further. Through it Ivan could appeal beyond the boyar-aristocracy to all those serving gentry, the officers and officials on whom he depended to assist him in the government and defence of the Tsardom.[3]

On the following day the people gathered again on the Red Square. The Tsar, accompanied by the Metropolitan and other dignitaries, appeared. At this meeting the first of a series of important reforms in the administration of justice was announced. It was a prompt demonstration of his intention to be the defender of his subjects against injustice and extortion.

Ivan's declaration on the Red Square indeed marked the beginning of a far-reaching reform movement and of the great period of his reign. A new legal code was promulgated, and justice, finance, military service and army organization, and the administration of the state and church in Muscovy underwent fundamental change. The reforms were part of the general movement to create and strengthen a centralized state, equipped with an administration adequate to its needs, and served by a new class of men on whom the Tsar could call for civil and military duties.

This was not, however, only a time of reforms and the creation of a new state machinery. It was also an era of religious and moral resurgence in the church and among the people. Ivan himself was infected with a fervent crusading zeal. He felt that he must now rule the Tsardom so that by example and reform it would become a truly Christian land, a worthy guardian of Orthodoxy.

The genesis of this moral and religious movement had been the teachings of a series of remarkable churchmen. Josef of Volokolamsk, Maxim the Greek,[4] Nil Sorski, Makary, Sylvester, and others had by their learning and example continued to give leadership. The church, as distinct from individual churchmen, also played an important part in encouraging it. The meeting of its assembly in February 1547 had resulted in the canonization of a number of Russian saints. Makary had recorded the lives of these saints in this *Mineya Chetya*, thus making their example and precepts more widely known for others to follow. But the corruption and laxity which had been spreading through the church for many years had become critical by the middle of the 16th century. The need to purge it of abuses had been a stimulus in the religious revival which was to reach its climax in comprehensive reforms.

In both civil and religious fields, however, this movement was more than the work of a few forerunners. Ivan and his Chosen Council and the group of zealous churchmen all gave leadership, but at the same time the movement was broadly rooted in the needs and demands of the people.

For almost a century Muscovy had been expanding, but the internal government had not developed. Ivan had inherited an administration which was no more than a makeshift adaptation of the system which had served the small principality, and it was wholly inadequate for the vast new state. The general ferment of discontent and impatient expectation had become more intense during the boyar anarchy. The popular outbursts after the fires of Moscow had been an open manifestation of the general mood. Among the people, however, were a number of thoughtful and able men, not disposed to violence, who worked out projects of reform, and in doing so reflected popular opinion. Ivan's address to the Assembly in February 1549 encouraged certain of them to submit their proposals to him. Among these reformers, Peresvetov was outstanding.

"Ivashka, son of Semeon Peresvetov",[5] as he described himself, claimed to be a descendant of the Peresvetov who had perished heroically on the field of Kulikovo in 1380 when Dmitri Donskoi had routed the Golden Horde. Peresvetov himself had been born under Lithuanian rule and had had a varied career. He had served with the Polish troops who, in defiance of their king's orders, had taken part in the campaign of Jan Zapolya Ianos to seize the Hungarian crown. Jan Zapolya had had the support of the Turkish Sultan, Suleiman II, and it was probably at this time that Peresvetov gained his first-hand knowledge of the Turkish army. He had later taken service under Ferdinand I, King of Bohemia, and then under Peter, voevoda of Wallachia.

After spending some time in Lithuania, he had in 1538 or 1539 entered the Muscovite service, having obtained a commission to produce shields of a Macedonian pattern, which were of leather with iron hoops around the lower part, and were very suitable for use against the Tatars. But Peresvetov's fortunes did not prosper in Muscovy. As a Lithuanian migrant he may have met with strong prejudice, and he apparently lost the lands which he had been granted. On 8 September 1549 in the court church of Rozhdestvo Bogoroditsy (the Nativity of the Holy Virgin) he presented a petition with some of his writings to Tsar Ivan for the recovery of his estate, but his petition failed. Some two months later he presented his "Great Petition" which contained a lengthy exposition of his political views and proposals for reform, which marked him as a man of broad and penetrating intelligence.

Peresvetov's views were fundamentally the same as those of the Chosen Council and of Ivan himself. He urged the need for a strong autocratic ruler, for the centralization of finance and justice, and the creation of a permanent military force. But his proposals dealt with every aspect of the national life, and in some respects they went far beyond the policies of the Chosen Council.

In his "Great Petition" Peresvetov freely quoted the political wisdom of Peter of Wallachia, and the example of his Turkish hero, whom he called Maklimet Sultan, to support his projects. His great theme was that the Tsar must rule, as the Sultan ruled, without fear or thought of his magnates. With some daring he criticized aspects of Muscovite life, doing so under cover of condemning the Greeks. He inaccurately, but no doubt deliberately, described Constantine Palaeologus as having ascended the throne at the age of three and having come under the dire influence of his magnates, an oblique reference to Ivan's early years. Constantine had failed, however, because guided by his magnates he had neglected military affairs and had allowed injustice to go unchecked throughout his empire.[6]

The need for justice and the reform of the administration of justice were among Peresvetov's recurrent themes, and were probably rooted in unfortunate personal experience. He quoted with approval the dictum of Peter of Wallachia that "God loves not faith, but justice", and himself wrote that "in whatever realm there is justice, there God abides and gives it his great aid and God's wrath is not visited on that realm". His ideal of justice was harsh, but in harmony with Ivan's outlook and, indeed, with the customs of the time. "There cannot be a ruler without terror," he wrote. "Like a steed under the rider without a bridle, so is a realm without terror."[7]

Peresvetov's other recurrent theme was equality, and his ideas were advanced. He condemned all forms of bondage, whether the complete bondage of the slave or the partial bondage of serfdom. All men should be legally free, for only free people could labour and serve zealously. Throughout his writings runs his antagonism towards the boyars. "The magnates of the Russian Tsar themselves grow rich and lazy, and impoverish his realm . . . and do not play the game of death against the foe, and thus betray God and their sovereign." He wrote much in this vein. He praised the Turkish Sultan who said, "Brothers, we are all the children of Adam; who among my men serves truly and stands fiercely against the enemy, he will be my most noble."[8] In these ideas, too, Peresvetov was probably in harmony with the Tsar. But the time was not ripe for the eradication of the boyars who were still rooted in Muscovite life with all the force of tradition and custom.

Peresvetov wrote clearly and with courage. His ideas are of special interest, however, because they were the fruits of the independent thinking of a man who belonged neither to the court nor to the church hierarchy. He was indeed closer to the lower gentry and the ordinary people. In his proposals he was expressing the desires of many Muscovites. They, too, longed for a Tsar who would rule with justice, reform the administration of the country and sternly suppress the great boyars. They, too, wanted efficient military leaders and trained fighting men who would not flee as the boyars and their servitors so often fled, but would stand to defend them, especially against the marauding Tatars. Popular aspiration had probably not reached so far as to embrace Peresvetov's ideas of equality. But in his other proposals he was voicing the general demands of the day. In its legislation of the 1550s Ivan's government was to go some way towards meeting them.

The reform, announced to the Assembly in February 1549, imposed restrictions on the *nastavniki* or governors and freed the serving gentry from their jurisdiction. It also gave to "Christians" the right to petition against injustice.[9] A special Petitions Office was established with Adashev, probably aided by Sylvester, in charge. This office received petitions and delivered judgments in the Tsar's name. It served as a high court of appeal and at the same time supervised the general administration of justice throughout the country.

Ivan took special interest in this reform and was genuinely concerned to protect the poor and the humble. When appointing Adashev in charge of petitions, he said:

"Alexei, you are not of noble birth or rich, but you are a man of goodwill. I am raising you to a high position, not at your wish, but to comfort my soul, which reaches out to those poor people; relieve me of my sadness for the suffering people whom God has entrusted to me! Do not fear the powerful or the famous, when they, despoiling honour, behave unjustly. But do not let yourself be deceived by the lying fears of the poor man when he denounces the rich out of envy! Investigate all plaints carefully, and report the truth to me, fearing only the judge in heaven!"[10]

The administration of justice was one of the main subjects dealt with in the *Sudebnik*, or legal code, promulgated in June 1550.[11] The practical ideas embodied in it had been clarified by Sylvester, Adashev, and others on the Council during the previous two or three years. It was, however, the preparation for the 1549–50 campaign against Kazan that brought to a head the urgent need for changes.

During the advance against Kazan, Ivan himself discussed with his army commanders certain of the military reforms. There is also evidence that in June–July, after his return to Moscow from this campaign, he convened an Assembly of the Land which was attended by many military men. This Assembly approved the revision of the law contained in the *Sudebnik* and a proposal to curtail the rules governing precedence among the boyars, and the institution of a permanent force of arquebusiers, or *streltsi*.[12]

The *Sudebnik* itself was more than a revision of the earlier code, issued by Ivan's grandfather in 1497. Of its ninety-nine articles, thirty-seven were new and others, adopted from the earlier code, were substantially rewritten.[13] Many of the innovations, especially concerning land tenure, local government, and military affairs, were merely the first steps in reforms which were soon to be developed further.

The administration of justice was mainly in the hands of the *nastavniki* or governors. The rich patrimonial estates, still held by a few of the princes and senior boyars, and the vast land holdings of the monasteries continued to be administered as more or less independent units within which the word of the landlord was law and in domestic matters the officials of the Tsar exercised virtually no authority. The rest of the country was divided into *uezdi* or regions which were subdivided into districts. A governor was appointed in the Tsar's name for each district, where he was solely responsible for justice and general administration. Moreover, his office being unpaid, he had the right to collect revenues for his maintenance. This was the pernicious system of *kormlenie*, which meant literally "feeding", whereby officials lived off the people.

The system gave rise to widespread extortion and corruption. The governor and his staff were wholly concerned with how much they could wring from their unfortunate people. Furthermore, while in his district the governor could not be challenged and his decisions were subject to no appeal. As soon as he departed, groups of citizens would often set out for Moscow to petition, usually in vain, for justice.

The *kormlenie* system was not only grossly inefficient, but it also aroused general discontent, and was the source of much of the popular hatred felt for the boyars, who directly or indirectly through associates administered most of the districts. The *Sudebnik* did not abolish "feeding" or the governors, but subjected them to restraints and to close surveillance both locally and by the central government. Special clerks were appointed to warn governors and advise the local people on the limits to the taxes and levies that might be raised. The sheriffs and locally elected officials who in some districts had been recognized and granted wide judicial and administrative powers were recognized now in all districts. Not long afterwards Ivan carried this reform to its conclusion by a law permitting each district throughout the country to elect its officials and assume full responsibility for local administration, justice, and taxes.

The *Sudebnik* also introduced new provisions concerning land tenure. The laws and customs governing land ownership in Muscovy were exceedingly complex. In the main they were directed to protecting the patrimonial estates of the boyar-aristocracy and the extensive ecclesiastical lands. But inexorably the pressure of the demand for land to provide estates for the growing class of serving gentry whittled away the old privileges and protection.[14]

By the 1550s the lack of land from which to create new service estates for the gentry had become critical. This was demonstrated by the frustration of Ivan's project to settle 1,000 chosen men on estates near Moscow. As proclaimed on 3 October 1550, Ivan's plan was to form a special guard of the best men among the gentry. Many in this class held several separate estates in different parts of the country and such lands as they possessed in the central region were too small to support them and their servitors. The new ukaz proposed to grant additional lands to the chosen men to enable them to settle near the capital. These "Thousanders" would be listed in the "Thousand's Book". They would hold themselves in readiness for administrative, diplomatic, and military service, and they were to form the "regiments of the Tsar and Grand Prince". In all 1,078 men were chosen to form "The Thousand" and they were to be considered the flower of the gentry. It would seem, however, that despite these detailed preparations, even down to the selection of the men, the project was never realized, because the government could not provide the necessary lands in the Moscow region. It was no doubt this frustration of his plans that led Ivan to order the preparation of a register of land, a kind of Doomsday Book, which was to give him a clear understanding of the land-holding in his realm.[15]

The patrimonial lands of the boyars and princes and the ecclesiastical lands offered a solution to the land shortage. Ivan's grandfather and father had cast covetous eyes on church lands and at this time his government was actively considering their secularization. Sylvester believed on religious and political grounds that the church should divest itself of all its estates and wealth, and he was not a man to nurse beliefs without action. Adashev and other members of the government strongly supported this policy.

On 15 September Ivan received the Metropolitan in audience to discuss this question. Makary, apparently aware of the government's plan, delivered a lengthy prepared speech defending the rights of the church and of monasteries to own property. But Ivan remained unmoved by his arguments and soon after this meeting imposed several new restrictions on the landowning rights of monasteries. They were minor restrictions, but enough to show that the Tsar stood firm.

The struggle between the church and the Tsar and his government then gave rise to the great church assembly, known as the *Stoglavny Sobor* or the *Stoglav*, which was to prove as important to the Orthodox Church as the Council of Trent, meeting at this time, was to be for the Church of Rome.[16]

Preparation for the *Stoglav* began in December 1550. This took the form of drafting questions which the Tsar would put to the assembly and which would serve as its agenda. Sylvester was the author of most, if not all, of these sixty-nine questions. They involved a searching investigation into every aspect of church affairs, and they virtually outlined the programme of reform.[17]

In the Tsar's Kremlin Palace in January 1551 gathered the Metropolitan, nine Bishops, Archimandrites, and Abbots, all heavily bearded and wearing rich vestments. The leading boyars and serving gentry of the Tsardom were also present. It was an imposing assembly of all the highest churchmen and nobles. Ivan came before them. He was now just twenty-one years old, grown tall and striking in appearance. He was not awed by the authority, gravity, and venerable age of most of those present; they were his subjects. Strongly conscious of his position as Tsar and of his own pre-eminence, he was apparently composed, as though confident in his power to dominate the audience.

Ivan addressed them with force and eloquence. He referred again to his orphanhood and to the sufferings which had befallen him and his people during the anarchy of those days. "Then," he said, "my soul was struck with terror and my bones trembled; my spirit was subdued, my heart was touched. Now I hate evil and love virtue." He turned to the Metropolitan and the Bishops. "From you," he said, "I demand zealous instruction, you pastors of Christians, teachers of Tsars and nobles, you worthy Bishops of the Church! Do not spare me in my crimes! Boldly reproach my weakness! Proclaim loudly the word of God and my soul will live!"[18]

Ivan then spoke of his sincere desire to bring order and well-being to his realm, using all the means and talents given him. To this end he had introduced new laws to secure better administration, and he submitted to the church assembly for their examination and approval the *Sudebnik* and his decrees, dealing with the governors and local government. To Ivan there was nothing strange in his calling on the church to affirm this civil legislation. He considered his power and position to rest on the twin pillars of church and state, over both of which he ruled as supreme autocrat. He now needed them to work together for the welfare of the people and the country.

During the previous century, however, corruption, laxity, and abuses had come to infect every part of the church and, as in Western Europe at this time, the cry for "Reform of the church in head and members" had been growing in strength. But the Orthodox hierarchy recognized the need to cleanse the church of abuses, and at the *Stoglav* the Tsar's questions met with an immediate response. Nevertheless, while Makary and the Josephan Bishops, who were predominant in the church councils, were anxious to effect reforms for their own sake, they were conscious of pressure from Sylvester and others of the Trans-Volga Hermits whose policy of extreme reforms included secularization of church lands. They saw prompt reform as a first defence against the extremists.

The Tsar's questions were blunt and specific in their criticisms of the faults of the church. Priests were given to drunkenness and sloth; they were usually illiterate; they failed to conduct services properly, omitted parts of the liturgy, and allowed their congregations to misbehave; they exacted excessive fees for celebrating marriages and other ceremonies. The ecclesiastical courts were corrupt. Errors had crept into translations of the church manuals and should be corrected.

The conduct of the monasteries was the subject of serious indictment. Many monks were allowed to take vows, although not interested in the "savings of souls", but "in bodily ease" and debauchery. Archimandrites and abbots often failed to enforce discipline and themselves lived worldly, idle lives, neglecting their monasteries and estates.[19] Then, in the form of questions, two important proposals were put to the *Stoglav*. It was proposed that the exemption from the jurisdiction of the Tsar's courts for all but the most serious crimes, enjoyed by priests and monks, should be abolished. The next proposal was crucial, for it suggested that it was improper for monasteries to acquire lands and benefit by special privileges, such as tax exemptions. The possession of estates and wealth did harm to monastic life and the *Stoglav* should consider whether it would not be beneficial for monasteries to be deprived of their financial profits.

The need for some state organization to purchase the freedom of the numerous Muscovite prisoners in the hands of the Tatars of Kazan and the Crimea was submitted for the assembly's consideration. The problem was primarily one of providing funds for the purpose, and the church was expected to make some practical suggestions. Another question complained that the poor and the aged were dying of neglect, and it was clearly implied that the church was failing in its duty to provide funds and care for the unfortunate.

A final group of questions called for stricter enforcement of the church bans against shaving beards, giving false oaths, and swearing. *Skomorokhi* and *guselniki*, the strolling players and musicians beloved of the people, but condemned by the church, should be suppressed with greater vigour. They fell into the same category as magicians, fortune-tellers, and lying prophets, whom strict Orthodox churchmen, like Sylvester, abhorred.

Of the great assembly of churchmen and boyars whom Ivan addressed, only ten men belonged to the council which deliberated and returned answers to his questions. They were Metropolitan Makary and nine Archbishops and Bishops. It was significant that of these ten men nine were known to belong to the Josephan faction and therefore likely to oppose any extreme reforms put forward by Sylvester. Nevertheless, they were in agreement with many of the proposals to which they responded with prompt and effective action.[20]

The abuses and laxity were obvious and the assembly provided for stricter enforcement of the laws of the church. They devoted close attention to the suitability and selection of priests and monks, and decreed that special educational institutes should be established in Moscow and in a number of towns to educate priests and deacons. Monastic discipline was to be strictly enforced and the administration of monasteries supervised. Offences against morality among priests and other crimes were to be punished with the utmost severity, for they constituted a "reproach to our Orthodox Christian faith".[21] Shaving of beards, the toleration of *skormorokhi* and *guselniki* at wedding feasts and other occasions, and the reading of heretical books were condemned. The aged and suffering were to be cared for and accommodated in special homes. The fund to purchase the freedom of prisoners in Tatar's hands should, the church council recommended, be collected throughout the country which meant that churches and monasteries, normally exempt from such levies, would contribute.

To the question which threatened the wealth and privilege of the church, however, the *Stoglav* returned unequivocal replies. They rejected the suggestion that priests and monks should be tried in the Tsar's courts for all crimes. They boldly reasserted the Josephan stand against any attempts to deprive the churches and monasteries of their estates and riches, and went so far as to denounce those who coveted the wealth of the church as "ravishers and robbers".[22]

Makary, as Metropolitan, had presided over the meetings of the *Stoglav* and from the text of the hundred chapters it was clear that he himself had drafted them or that they had been drafted under his direct supervision.[23] It was thus on the crucial point of secularization a victory over Sylvester, who had drafted the questions. At the same time it meant that the policy of Ivan and his government had suffered defeat at the hands of the church council.

Ivan detested opposition and could not bear to be thwarted in his plans. He made an attempt to have the *Stoglav*'s rulings reviewed by submitting them to three learned monks of the Troitsa monastery. The three monks were known opponents of the Josephans, but their comments did not influence the final decisions of the *Stoglav* which concluded its work in May 1551.[24]

Ivan and his Chosen Council nevertheless continued their pressure against the Josephans. In May and June he made changes among the church hierarchy which strengthened the position of the Trans-Volga Hermits in the councils of the church. Then followed a series of measures restricting the landowning privileges of ecclesiastical bodies. On 11 May 1551 a decree prohibited their purchase of patrimonial lands without the Tsar's special consent. The *Sudebnik* confirmed by the *Stoglav* had forbidden all further grants of tax-exemption, but this was followed on 17–18 May by an examination of all previous charters of exemption and their subsequent cancellation. Nevertheless, although desperate for land to increase and strengthen the serving gentry, Ivan was not prepared to provoke a major conflict by confiscating ecclesiastical lands. He needed the support of the church and he was to obtain land by other methods.

Ivan the Terrible

Notes to Chapter X

[1] Karamzin, Bk. II, Vol. VIII, col. 64.
[2] *Ibid.*, cols. 64–5.
[3] Klyuchevsky, II, pp. 373–7.
[4] Maxim Grek was born in Greece and studied in Italy. He was invited to Russia in 1518 by Grand Prince Vasily to translate the church books. Learned and eloquent, he gathered around him in Moscow a circle of boyars with whom he discussed not only church matters, but also the internal policies of the Grand Prince. In many of his opinions he was close to the Trans-Volga Hermits. He strongly opposed the owning of property and wealth by the church, and he criticized the living of the priesthood. He also spoke against the oppression of the peasantry by ecclesiastical landlords and against "feeding". In 1525 he was exiled to the Josef Volokolamsk monastery, and six years later after a further trial he was sent to the Tverskoi Otroch monastery.
[5] A. A. Zimin and D. S. Likhachev, eds., *The Works of I. Peresvetov* (Moscow–Leningrad, 1956), p. 163.
[6] *Ibid.*, pp. 165–6, 190.
[7] *Ibid.*, p. 189.
[8] *Ibid.*, pp. 158–9.
[9] A. A. Zimin, *The Reforms of Ivan the Terrible* (Moscow, 1960), p. 326.
[10] Karamzin, Bk. II, Vol. VIII, col. 65.
[11] A. A. Zimin considers that the *Sudebnik* was drafted and issued in June 1550, but it may have been in the spring or the autumn of that year. A. A. Zimin, *op. cit.*, pp. 348–9.
[12] *Ibid.*, pp. 349–50.
[13] An article, No. 100, was added subsequently. *Ibid.*, pp. 415–6.
[14] In the 16th century boyars in increasing numbers were compelled to sell their hereditary estates to meet debts incurred through the expense of providing troops for various campaigns, through mismanagement, and through high living. Such boyars and their heirs had the right to buy back their estates compulsorily within forty years of sale. Article 45 of the *Sudebnik* abolished this right for both the boyar and his heirs, if they had signed the deed of sale; heirs who had not signed retained the right of compulsory re-purchase. The new article was clearly designed to protect members of the gentry. A. A. Zimin, *op. cit.*, pp. 350–1.
[15] Historians have assumed that this project to settle "the thousand" chosen men from the gentry on *pomestii* or estates held on service tenure was carried out. A. A. Zimin gives evidence to show that no estates were in fact granted because of the land shortage and the scheme was never realized. A. A. Zimin, *op. cit.*, pp. 366–71. Later with the establishment of the Oprichnina Ivan was to achieve the settlement of chosen men on estates near Moscow. He managed then by removing boyars from their hereditary lands. See pp. 164–7.
[16] The assembly took its name from its report, containing its decisions, set out in *Sto* (one hundred) *glav* (chapters).
[17] Karamzin gives 23 February 1551 as the date of this meeting. A. A. Zimin, however, gives evidence that the *Stoglav* met during January and February, and that the work on the editing of the report started on 23

February. Karamzin, Bk. II, Vol. VIII, col. 68; A. A. Zimin, *op. cit.*, p. 378.

18 Karamzin, *loc. cit.*
19 A. A. Zimin, *op. cit.*, p. 380.
20 *Ibid.*, pp. 382–3.
21 *Ibid.*, p. 384.
22 *Ibid.*, p. 385.
23 *Ibid.*, p. 386.
24 *Ibid.*, p. 387.

CHAPTER XI

THE CONQUEST OF KAZAN 1551-2

THE Tatars had long been the scourge of the Muscovites. Nomads of Turkish race, they were short, powerfully built men with sunken, slant eyes, swarthy skin; many wore black beards and shaven heads. They were magnificent riders, living on their small swift horses, and both men and horses were capable of amazing feats of endurance. The sight of these Tatars, riding to attack, inspired terror. They appeared unexpectedly, striking with ferocity, killing, plundering, and abducting, and then vanished as swiftly.

Over the years their savage and persistent raiding had laid waste the land and taken a heavy toll of the people. For a distance of some 150 miles to the east and south of Moscow, no village or peasant hut remained standing, and the land lay uncultivated. People in thousands had lost their lives or been taken captive. In 1551 alone the number of Muscovites held prisoner in the Kazan Khanate was said to be 100,000.[1] The slave-markets of the Mediterranean were amply supplied with fair-headed Slavs, carried off in Tatar raids.

The Muscovites had nevertheless come to fear the Tatars far less than in earlier centuries. The rivalries, which had led to the break-up of the Golden Horde, now prevented the three Khanates of Kazan, the Crimea, and Astrakhan acting together. Moreover, the Russians had learned to fight and defeat the Tatars who, while terrible in attack, were often weak and even cowardly in defence. But their mobility and their tactics of sudden invasion at any point along the hundreds of miles of Muscovy's frontiers made them a permanent and dangerous enemy.

Of the three Khanates, Kazan was the nearest and most menacing. The Muscovites, whose memories of sufferings at Tatar hands extended through generations, considered the destruction of the Kazan Khanate imperative to their safety. It was, moreover, a sacred duty. The Tatars were fanatical Mohammedans and enemies of the Cross; their presence as close neighbours was an affront to all Christians. In the heightened religious mood of the Muscovites at this time, a campaign against the Tatars was a crusade. Furthermore, a decisive conflict between Muscovy and the Khanate had become inevitable, because the Muscovite colonizing drive eastwards was growing in momentum, and Kazan barred the way.

To Ivan, possessed by intense enthusiasms and high ideals, no venture could be more glorious than the conquest of Kazan. He would at a stroke free his Tsardom from a destructive enemy and establish himself as the Tsar-Liberator. Throughout Christendom he would win renown for defeating Mohammedanism and planting the Cross in Asia. With such incentives it was not to be expected that someone of Ivan's temperament would delay. He was only fifteen years old when, in April 1545, he impetuously launched a campaign against Kazan, but it proved indecisive.

At the end of 1547 Ivan had again proclaimed war on Kazan. His armies had set out in the following January and he had joined them on the Volga. But this campaign, too, was doomed to failure. Instead of the snow and hard frosts, normal at this time of the year, heavy rains fell. The ice on the Volga, usually thick enough to bear the crossing of a whole army, was soft on the surface and cracking. Guns, ammunition, and hundreds of men were lost through the ice. Ivan waited on the island of Robotka in the Volga for new frosts, but he waited in vain. In March 1548 he returned to Moscow and he wept with disappointment and anger as he entered the city.[2]

In March 1549, Safa Girei, Khan of Kazan, died and his two-year-old son, Utemish, succeeded him. In this age the rule of a minor, depriving the people of leadership and allowing free reign to rivalries among the warrior-lords, meant disaster. The Tatars were now alarmed; just as they had taken advantage of Ivan's minority to assail Muscovy, so now they feared that the Muscovites would attack them. They sent messages urgently to the Crimean Khan, imploring him to send his son to act as their regent and to defend them against the Muscovites. In July 1549 they also made proposals for peace. Ivan responded by inviting them to send their envoys to negotiate. When no envoys came, he set out with his army for Kazan.

The winter of 1549–50 was exceptionally severe. People dropped dead in the streets from the cold. Ivan and his troops endured great hardships, but they continued their advance, arriving before Kazan on 14 February. After elaborate preparations the Muscovite troops, 60,000 strong, launched an attack and the fighting raged all day without gain to either side. On the next day, however, an unusual thaw came. Heavy rains reduced the ground to mud and the rivers flooded. Conditions deteriorated rapidly and Ivan was again compelled to order the retreat.

The chastening experience of having to withdraw from Kazan three times within five years made Ivan all the more determined to take this formidable stronghold. He hated failure and he was sensitive to the murmurings of criticism among his people over these abortive campaigns. Popular criticism was, in fact, directed against the boyars in command. Ivan was excused on the grounds of his youth and inexperience and because he was Tsar, but he knew that the criticism could quickly turn to him. He had now learnt to curb his impetuosity and to prepare more carefully. He gave urgent attention to military reforms, including the formation of a nucleus of permanent troops, as Peresvetov had proposed. But first it was necessary to curtail the rule of precedence.

This pernicious system of *mestnichestvo*, fixing immutably the seniority within the boyar-aristocracy and restricting the appointment of the most able men to positions of authority, was destructive in every field of government. But its most serious effect was to cripple military operations. Opportunities to attack the Tatars were lost, while commanders quarrelled over their appointments and whether they were in accord with their precedence. Even when such disputes did not go to the extreme of immobilizing the army, they caused uneasy relations between commanders in the field and undermined the morale among the troops. The Muscovites themselves recognized the evils of the system, but it was entrenched by tradition and the rivalries of the boyars.[3]

In November 1549 before marching against Kazan, Ivan had decreed that as between commanders in the field the rules of precedence would not apply. He repeated this decree in Vladimir in December and again in Nizhni Novgorod in January (1550), as the army advanced. But, although the Tsar himself was in command, disputes over seniority broke out between commanders even as they stood before Kazan, preparing to attack. This was a factor contributing to Ivan's reluctant decision to retreat. At the same time it impressed him so strongly with the need for military reforms and especially the restriction of the rules of precedence, that in February (1550), while still at Kazan, he sent orders to Moscow for the drafting of new regulations.[4]

The new decree on precedence, issued in the following July, confirmed Ivan's previous decrees and, without abolishing the system, it strengthened the authority of the commander-in-chief, known as the *voevoda* of the great army, and established a chain of command, giving junior officers greater responsibility. At the same time it prohibited the application of precedence during a campaign. With this strengthening of the leadership and discipline, the Muscovite army was to operate with greater efficiency in the coming campaigns.[5]

In the summer of 1550 Ivan also created a new permanent force, known as the *streltsi*, the shooters or arquebusiers, who were to serve as the nucleus of a regular army. This force was not a complete innovation. With the improvements in firearms, introduced at the beginning of the century, detachments of arquebusiers had been enlisted, primarily from the towns.[6] Ivan's new force of *streltsi* was taken from among the arquebusiers, and was itself armed with arquebuses and halberds. These troops had quarters in the Vorobiovo suburb and received pay of four rubles a year. They were exempt from taxes, even on the crafts and trade which they were allowed to carry on in peacetime. At first 3,000 *streltsi* were recruited. At Kazan and in other campaigns they proved their worth and their number increased. Towards the end of the century some 20,000 *streltsi* were serving in the garrisons of towns all over the country.[7]

On his return to Moscow in March 1550, Ivan had plunged into a fury of activity. Reforms, especially the new legal code, the *Sudebnik*, claimed his attention. Reports that the Crimean Khan, Saip Girei, was advancing into Muscovy meant moving troops to defend the frontiers. Ivan himself travelled south to Kolomna and Ryazan to inspect defences and encourage his men. For a time he remained with them, but the Tatars did not appear and he returned to Moscow.

At this time the Kazan Tatars made new proposals for peace. Yusuf, Khan of the Nogai Tatars, who wandered over a vast region north of the Caspian Sea and divided by the Yaik or Ural river, was a man widely respected by Tatars and Turks, and he offered to mediate. Ivan expressed his readiness to negotiate, but also made haste with preparations for a decisive campaign.

Returning from Kazan in the previous year, Ivan had climbed a hill, called Kruglaya, at the mouth of the Sviyaga river. From the top he had found that he had a magnificent vista over the flat plain to Kazan, Vyatka, Nizhny Novgorod, and the deserts of the Simbirsk region. Impressed by the strategic advantages of this position, he had said before descending, "Here will be a Christian town. We will cut off Kazan. God will give her into our hands."[8]

At the onset of spring in 1551, Ivan sent Shig Alei, the displaced Khan who had sought Moscow's protection, with 500 of his leading

Tatar troops and a strong detachment of Muscovites to the mouth of the Sviyaga river. Their orders were to establish a town on the hill. For this purpose trees were felled in Uglich and floated down the Volga. From Nizhni Novgorod, Prince Peter Serebryanny-Obolensky also set out with troops and on 11 May (1551) he planted the Muscovite banner on the hill. The main Muscovite army arrived by river on 14 May and within four weeks the town of Sviyazhsk was built.

The sudden appearance of this Muscovite stronghold, menacing the Kazan Khanate, made a strong impression on the peoples to the north and east of the Volga and the Kama. The Chuvash, Mordva, Votyak, and Cheremis were Finnish tribes which had been conquered by the Tatars, but had never been united with them in religion or language. They now sent their leading men to Moscow to swear allegiance to the powerful Tsar.

Among the Tatars the new proximity of the Muscovites in Sviyazhsk intensified the existing uneasiness. The leading warrior-lords of Kazan were united in wanting to seek peace with Moscow, but the Crimean Tatars in Kazan, led by the Ulan Korshchak, were unyielding in their hostility to the Tsar. They constantly urged the Kazantsi to wait for the troops promised from the Crimea, from Astrakhan, and from the Nogai Tatars, arguing that with such reinforcements they could defeat the Tsar, as they had defeated him in the past. No troops came, however, and the Kazantsi finally expelled the Crimeans from their city. Muscovite troops overtook them at the Vyatka river, killing all except Korshchak and his suite who were later executed in Moscow.

The Kazantsi at once sent their envoys to Ivan, proposing peace and asking that Shig Alei should rule over them once again. Ivan agreed and sent Adashev to confirm the peace terms and to instal Shig Alei as Khan, but only of the southern regions of the Khanate. The northern region was now claimed as part of the Tsardom, attached to Sviyazhsk. This unexpected loss of territory shocked the Tatars. Shig Alei was especially aggrieved. "What will become of my realm?" he complained. "Can I make claims on the love of my subjects when I give up to Russia an important part of their country?" [9] But Ivan would not consider the return of this territory which with his new stronghold at Sviyazhsk gave him greater control over the troublesome Khanate. Meanwhile the Muscovites were overjoyed by the release of many prisoners who had been languishing in Tatar hands. Sixty thousand men were sent by river to Moscow and others returned to their homes in the Vyatka and Ryazan regions.

The country rang with the praises of Ivan for thus liberating his subjects.

To the Kazan Tatars Ivan showed every courtesy, but they did not respond. Shig Alei constantly pressed for the return of the northern region of the Khanate, but was firmly rebuffed. Then he learnt that leading Tatars were plotting rebellion and he devised a brutal deception to dispose of these enemies. He invited them to a banquet in his palace and, when all had assembled, his guards drew their swords and slaughtered them to a man. The floors of the palace ran with blood. Even the Tatars were horrified by this savagery. Fearing for their lives many fled and throughout the Khanate there was such an upsurge of anger against the Khan, that Ivan again ordered Adashev to Kazan, this time to protect Shig Alei from his people. But the outcry had grown too strong to be ignored. The Tatars begged Ivan to remove the Khan and to appoint a Muscovite governor in his place. Adashev travelled to Kazan yet again, this time with the task of informing Shig Alei that he had been dethroned in response to popular demand.

Ivan appointed Prince Semeon Mikulinsky as his governor in Kazan, and arrangements were made to escort him with ceremony into the city. The Tatars to whom news of this appointment had been proclaimed seemed content, but then, suddenly, their mood changed. The Tatar nobles whom Mikulinsky had allowed to ride ahead to rejoin their families spread the story that the Muscovites planned to put to death all the inhabitants of Kazan. The story was quite false, but it aroused every fear and suspicion which the Tatars felt towards their age-old enemy.

Learning of this alarm in Kazan, Mikulinsky, Obolensky, and Adashev rode ahead to reassure the people. They found the gates of the city closed and the Kazantsi armed, manning the walls and towers. All their attempts to persuade the Tatars to admit them failed. The gates of Kazan remained closed to the Muscovites.

This Tatar defiance, coming so suddenly after their humble submission, infuriated Ivan and finally convinced him that Kazan could be subdued only by force. He summoned the Boyar Council and declared his determination to free Muscovy "from the ferocity of these eternal enemies with whom there can be neither peace nor rest."[10]

Losing no time, Ivan ordered troops to move with supplies by river to Kazan. He intended to follow by land, but at this juncture disturbing reports came from Mikulinsky in Sviyazhsk. The Finnish tribes had rebelled and were joining forces with the Kazantsi. The more serious news, however, was that the plague was raging in Sviyazhsk. Ivan at once sent Prince Gorbaty and Peter Shuisky with troops to reinforce the stronghold and to put down the rebellion among the Chuvash and Cheremis tribesmen. Several days later he was distressed to learn that the virulence of the plague had increased. Many had died and morale among the remaining troops and commanders was so low that they had given themselves up to drinking and pleasures, and showed little resistance to Tatar raids; tribesmen had even driven away their horses.

This last report angered Ivan. He sent Archpriest Timofei of the Arkhangelsky Cathedral with holy water to arouse the fallen spirits of Sviyazhsk. Timofei, renowned for his learning and fiery eloquence, arraigned the troops for forgetting their honour, their duty to God and to the Tsar. He scourged them unmercifully and closed with the words: "God, Ivan, and the Church call you to repentance. Mend your ways or you will see the anger of the Tsar and hear the curse of the Church!" This was language which the men understood and no more was heard of indiscipline among them.[11]

In Kazan the spirits of the Tatars were high. They now had a resolute leader. Ediger Mohammed, son of the Khan of Astrakhan, evading Muscovite attempts to capture him, had reached Kazan with a band of 500 Nogai Tatars. He had been enthroned as Khan and had impressed the Tatars by his warlike demeanour and his oaths to fight to the end. He had inspired them with a new confidence that they would yet again defeat their traditional enemy.

On 16 June Ivan set out for Kolomna. His Tsaritsa, Anastasia, was in tears at their parting, for she was pregnant and fearful for his safety. She sank to her knees before him to pray for his success and speedy return. Ivan, too, prayed long and devoutly for the protection and safe delivery of his wife, and for victory.

On the road a courier overtook him with news that the Crimean Tatars had crossed the Northern Donets and were sweeping northwards. A further courier reported that the Tatars were advancing towards Ryazan and Kolomna. But two days later came word that they were attacking Tula. Ivan at once sent troops and when, soon afterwards, he learnt that the Crimean Khan with his main army was laying siege to Tula, he prepared to go there himself. The Russians in Tula were fighting strongly and on receiving news that the Tsar himself was coming to their aid, their spirits rose so high that even women sallied out to attack the Tatars. The Khan, on learning of the

Tsar's approach, ordered a retreat. Muscovite troops then followed and defeated him on the Shivoron river, taking many prisoners, camels, and supplies.

Free now to concentrate his forces against Kazan, Ivan set out on 3 July for Sviyazhsk by way of Vladimir and Murom with further detachments of troops. Encouraging reports reached him on the road. The plague had almost died away in Sviyazhsk, thanks no doubt to Timofei's harangues and holy water. Further, Prince Mikulinsky had so soundly defeated the northern tribesmen that they had sworn allegiance afresh to the Tsar. They had also brought abundant supplies of grain, wild honey, and meat which, with the supplies gathered by Ivan's troops as they advanced, ensured adequate provisions for the campaign ahead.

The troops hoped now to relax and enjoy the plenty which surrounded them in Sviyazhsk, but Ivan was determined to lose no time. On 15 August he sent to Kazan in the name of himself and of Shig Alei notes calling on the Tatars to submit once more and promising his forgiveness. The Muscovites then began their crossing of the Volga and on 20 August they stood before Kazan. Here they received the Tatar reply to the Tsar's notes. Ediger expressed abusive contempt for Ivan and especially for Shig Alei, and poured blasphemous scorn on the Christian faith; he ended his reply with a challenge to the Muscovites to fight.

By 23 August Ivan had moved his troops into their siege positions. He then summoned all commanders and officers to a field opposite the town. As he rode out to face them, accompanied by his suite, his banner was unfurled with impressive ceremony. It bore a holy image of the Virgin which was believed to have been miraculously created and not made by human hands. Also embodied in the banner was the cross which Dmitri Donskoi had had with him when he had defeated the Khan of the Golden Horde on the famed field of Kulikovo 172 years earlier. To Ivan and to every Muscovite they were not only sacred objects, but were capable of working new miracles and bringing new victories.

After prayers Ivan addressed his commanders. It was the speech of a young Tsar, dedicated and zealous, and heard in the excitement and tension of the eve of a momentous battle, by men who believed with all the fervour of a living faith in the power of prayer and sacrifice and in their anointed leader.

"The time of our great enterprise approaches [Ivan declared]. Strive together to suffer for piety, for the holy Church, for the

Orthodox Christian faith, for our brothers in race, those Orthodox Christians who endure long captivity and suffer at the hands of these godless Tatars. . . . Let us be ready to lay down our lives; if we die, that is not death, but life; if we do not die now, we will die later, and how will we rid ourselves of these infidels in time to come? I have myself marched with you. Better that I die here, than live to see Christ blasphemed and the Christians, entrusted to me by God, suffering at the hands of the godless Kazantsi! If merciful God shows us his grace and grants us his aid then I will rejoice in bestowing great rewards on you, and he who suffers unto death, I will gladly reward his wife and children. . . ."[12]

On behalf of the princes and boyars, Prince Vladimir Andreevich replied with the words, "Be brave, Tsar. In one spirit we all fight for God and for you!" Ivan then turned to the holy image of Jesus and declared in a loud voice, which carried across the plain: "Lord, in thy name we march!"[13]

Within Kazan a similar religious and national fervour united the Tatars in determination to fight to the end. They had put away the rivalries and dissensions which had divided them in the past. Like the Muscovites, too, they saw the approaching struggle as the decisive stage in their long and embittered relationship. Calling on Mohammed and on Allah himself to grant them victory, the Tatars stood to their arms confidently. Khan Ediger had a force of 30,000 seasoned troops and 2,700 Nogai Tatars, as well as the inhabitants of Kazan and ample supplies for a long siege. Kazan itself was strongly built and fortified. High walls of oak beams, reinforced from inside by hardened river mud and gravel, surrounded the city, and within the walls were mosques, towers, and palaces built of stone.

Ivan disposed his army of 150,000 men so that they completely invested Kazan. They had no sooner taken up their positions when a force of 15,000 Tatars made a sortie. The *streltsi* suffered the full impact of this sudden attack and took to flight. Reinforcements were hastily brought up. The *streltsi* re-formed. Savage fighting followed and the Tatars were slowly beaten back to the gates of Kazan. Losses were heavy on both sides, but the Muscovites felt the first glow of victory.

Soon afterwards, however, a violent storm reduced them to despair. Rains deluged their camps and sank supply barges, which were secured to the bank of the Kazanka river. High winds tore from their pegs the Tsar's pavilion, the marquees of the three field churches, and many tents of the troops. Recalling the disasters which had compelled their withdrawal in the two previous campaigns the Muscovites became despondent. The serious loss of provisions made yet another retreat seem inevitable. But Ivan did not share the general alarm. He sent immediately to Sviyazhsk and to Moscow for fresh supplies. He also ordered warm clothing for his men, for, staking all on the success of this campaign, he was prepared to keep the enemy under siege, if necessary, throughout the winter.

The Muscovites, spurred on by their Tsar and their commanders, worked at their emplacements with feverish haste. They raised fences and palisades, and dug deep trenches. Ivan himself was tireless. He rode constantly inspecting the siege works and encouraging his troops. The work was not only arduous but dangerous, because day and night the Tatars made sudden sorties. They were, however, unable to dislodge their enemies or to prevent the siege closing more tightly on their city. But the Muscovites, deprived of sleep and even rest, and on short rations, began to feel the stress of the campaign.

Tatar pressure increased greatly when from the woods near the large village of Arsk, several miles from Kazan, mounted Tatars, led by a Tatar Prince, named Yapancha, launched savage attacks. By means of signals from the walls of Kazan, their attacks were co-ordinated with sorties from the fortress. On 30 August, however, Princes Gorbaty and Serebryanny with a strong force defeated Yapancha, taking 340 prisoners, and clearing his forces completely from the woods.

Brought to the Muscovite lines, these prisoners were tied to stakes in front of the siege works. One of their number was released and sent to the walls of Kazan, where he shouted to the Tatars the Tsar's message: "Ivan promises these prisoners life and liberty and to you his forgiveness and favour, if you will surrender to him!" The Kazantsi, standing on the walls, heard the message in silence. Then they coldly drew their bows and, shouting to their unfortunate fellow-Tatars, "Better that you should die by our clean hands than by the dirty hands of the Christians!", they loosed a stream of arrows. Each one of the prisoners was transfixed to his stake and pierced by many arrows, and none survived.[14] Ivan witnessed this incident, and the fury and hatred of the Tatars amazed him. He realized now what a merciless struggle lay ahead.

On the next day Ivan decided on major action. He ordered the Dane in his service, who was skilled in the use of explosives, to blow up Kazan's water supply.[15] From prisoners and refugees he had learnt that the Tatars drew their water from a spring and an underground stream, flowing into Kazan from the Kazanka river. Ivan sent Alexei Adashev with the Dane to direct the operation of digging under this stream and placing the explosives. The work proceeded rapidly. Eleven barrels of powder were set in position and on 4 September the stream was blown up, killing many Tatars and making a gap in the city wall. The Muscovites immediately attacked, but were driven back.

The siege continued. The Tatars had found a small spring to replace their normal water supply and they now fought with the courage of despair. Many among the Muscovites were, however, near to exhaustion, and their morale faltered at the onset of another bout of bad weather. Torrential rains turned their trenches and earthworks to mud. Prince Kurbsky considered that this was the work of Tatar sorcerers. At dawn each morning, so he reported, they appeared on the walls of Kazan, where they cried out in frightening tones and waved vestments towards the Muscovite positions, invoking evil powers to create clouds and rain. This belief in the power of Tatar sorcery and the continued bad weather seriously troubled the Muscovite camp. Ivan, too, was worried by it, and he ordered a special miracle-working cross to be brought from Moscow. With this cross, water was blessed and then sprinkled around the Muscovite positions. All believed devoutly in this method of exorcism and, indeed, the rains ceased and clear weather returned almost immediately.[16]

In the meantime the Muscovites had built high towers on which they had mounted guns and, when the towers were moved closer to the walls, they fired down on to the Tatar defences. Ivan saw, however, that his cannon-fire caused only minor damage and he ordered new mines to be laid. His Danish expert again directed the operation and on 30 September a great section of the defence works was blown up. The Tatars, confused by the noise and by falling beams and debris, gave way to panic, but then rallied and rushing from the gates of Kazan launched a furious attack. Savage hand-to-hand fighting continued for several hours, but gradually the Tatars were forced back into their fortress. Some Muscovites fought their way through the gates, but had to withdraw. Ivan was cautious and not prepared at this stage to throw in reinforcements which might be trapped within the Tatar defences.

On 1 October Ivan ordered preparations for the general assault to be made on the following day. His troops were to take communion and then await the explosion of new mines. At the same time, anxious to avoid further bloodshed, he once again called on the

Tatars to surrender, but of one voice they swore to stand firm to the end.[17]

Ivan confirmed the disposition of his troops and his orders that all were to be in readiness to attack after the explosion of mines. He then withdrew to his chapel to pray. Prince Vorotynsky interrupted him with word that the engineers had completed their task. Forty-eight barrels of powder had been placed, but the Kazantsi had discovered their tunnelling and there was no time to lose. Ivan sent messages to all troops, alerting them for the attack. He moved his own personal detachment to positions before the town where he would join them. He then returned to his prayers.

Towards dawn a tremendous explosion shook the ground. Ivan went to the entrance of the church pavilion to see debris flying through the air. He returned to hear the completion of the liturgy, but this was broken by a second, more terrible, explosion. From the Muscovite positions sounded a great roar of "God is with us!" and the troops surged forward.[18]

The Tatars stood firm in the midst of the destruction caused by the two explosions and they held their fire. As the Muscovites drew nearer the Tatars fired a salvo from cannon, arquebuses, and bows. The Muscovite ranks were suddenly thinned by this murderous fire, but the gaps were quickly filled as they rushed forward. Some hurled themselves through the breaches in the walls, others clambered by means of ladders and from towers up the walls. The Tatars fought with fury, throwing boiling pitch, heavy beams, and stones on those who tried to scale the walls. But the Muscovites, feeling victory within their grasp, fought their way into Kazan. For several hours they were held fighting in the streets. Bodies, severed legs, arms, and heads littered the ground, and blood flowed in rivulets, but, although hopelessly outnumbered, the Tatars would not submit.

At this decisive stage the Muscovite advance faltered. Many of the troops turned aside to pillage the houses and rob the dead. The Tatars at once took advantage of this pause and in a revived attack began to drive them from the streets. Learning of this dangerous situation Ivan sent trusted officers with orders to cut down any men found pillaging or running away. He himself took up a position at the main gate, holding the holy banner, to turn back troops who were in flight. He also ordered reinforcements into the city.

With the support of the fresh troops, the Muscovites again resumed the offensive. Khan Ediger, still fighting bravely, fell back

with his remaining men to the palace which had been strongly fortified. Then, realizing that further resistance was bound to fail, he
attempted to fight his way to the gates in the lower part of the city,
but found the way barred. With his Tatars he climbed upon the
mound of bodies, both Tatar and Muscovite, and reached the top of
the wall. A small party then escorted him into a tower that was still
standing.

At this point the Tatar troops apparently took authority into their
own hands. From the tower they shouted to the Muscovite commanders: "Listen! While we had the Khanate, we died for our Khan
and our land. Now Kazan is yours. We also give up to you our
Khan, alive and unhurt. Take him to Ivan. But we are going to the
open field to drink the last cup to the dregs with you!"[19]

This Tatar band then made its way down the other side of the wall
to the banks of the Kazanka river. Princes Andrei and Roman
Kurbsky with a small mounted detachment managed to overtake
them. But they were only a few hundred strong and, although
they fought bravely, they were quickly overwhelmed. Their attack
nevertheless held the Tatars long enough for a strong force, led by
Princes Mikulinsky, Glinsky, and Sheremetev to gallop into the field
in time to prevent them escaping into the woods beyond the river.
A fierce engagement followed. The Tatars, outnumbered and weary,
refused to surrender. They were cut down to a man and of the
5,000 only a few, seriously wounded and unable to struggle any
longer, were taken prisoner.

In Kazan the fighting had now ceased. Smoke arose from many
fires and the cries of the wounded and of women and children
mingled with the shouts of the victors. The leading Muscovite
commander, Prince Mikhail Vorotynsky, reported to Ivan, "Rejoice,
devout autocrat! By thy courage and thy fate, victory has been
won. Kazan is ours; her Khan is in your hands; his people have
been destroyed or taken prisoner, countless riches have been gathered.
What are your orders?"[20] Ivan replied, "Give praise to the Almighty!" and at once took part in a service of thanksgiving. Then
Khan Ediger was brought before him and was received with respect
and every kindness. "Unfortunate man," Ivan said to him, "did you
not realize the power of Russia and the deceit of the Kazantsi?"[21]
Ediger bowed low before him and received the Tsar's pardon.

Ivan then made a ceremonial entry into Kazan where he was
hailed by his troops and by the remaining Muscovites who had at
last been freed from Tatar captivity. It is said that the sight of the

corpses of the fallen, piled in heaps at various points in the fortress, moved him to tears of pity. Before leaving the city he gave orders for the fires which were still burning to be extinguished, and for all booty and prisoners, including women and children, to be handed over to his troops except only for Ediger, the jewels and regalia of the Khan, and the Tatar cannon, which he kept for himself. Finally in the centre of the city he raised with his own hands a cross and laid the foundation of a church in the name of the Annunciation of our Lady; two days later the church was complete and consecrated.

Returning to his camp, Ivan addressed his senior commanders and the troops who were drawn up before his pavilion, and his words expressed not only his own exultation but that of his people.

"Boyars, commanders, officers! [he said]. You have on this momentous day suffered in the name of God for your faith, your fatherland, and your Tsar. You have won such fame as has never been known in our time. No one has ever shown such bravery. No one has won such a victory. You are the new Macedonians, the worthy descendants of the heroes who with Grand Prince Dmitri crushed Mamai . . ."[22]

On 11 October Ivan began his return journey to Moscow. He had made provision for the government of the Khanate, appointing Princes Alexander Gorbaty and Vasily Serebryanny as joint administrators. He had sent couriers to all parts of the Khanate, calling on the people to have no fear, but to swear allegiance and pay him the same tribute as they had paid the Khan. Many of his boyars counselled him to remain with his army at Kazan until the spring. They feared revolts among the Tatars and the tribesmen, and considered that the Tsar should hold his army ready to subdue these wild peoples. But Ivan, guided, it was said, by the Zakharini, his brothers-in-law, rejected this advice. He was impatient to return to Moscow to see his wife and to receive the acclaim of his people. The *streltsi* and other troops whom he stationed in Kazan and Sviyazhsk would maintain the peace. Moreover, to keep the whole of his army at Kazan during the long winter would have raised problems. His troops were not regular soldiers, but special levies called up to serve in a campaign. They had fought long and hard, and were eager now to return to their homes. He therefore distributed liberal rewards and disbanded them.

Ivan's homeward journey was a triumphal progress. At Nizhni Novgorod he was greeted by the inhabitants with cheers and prayers of gratitude. At Vladimir he received a message which completed his happiness. There Boyar Trakhaniot galloped to him with the news that the Tsaritsa had borne him a son, named Dmitri. She had already had two daughters, one of whom had since died, but a son and heir to the throne was his greatest desire. Beside himself with joy, Ivan wept and threw his arms around Trakhaniot. Then, seeking some way in which to show his pleasure and gratitude to this bearer of good tidings, he suddenly gave him the cloak from his shoulders and his own horse. He also sent his brother-in-law, Boyar Nikita Romanovich, to Moscow, bearing his tender greetings to Anastasia. Ivan then made his way to the Troitsa monastery where he was greeted by the former Metropolitan, Josef, and he spent some time in prayer, giving thanks for victory at Kazan and for the birth of a son.

Early on the morning of 29 October, accompanied now by his brother, certain of his boyars as well as his suite and his personal guard, Ivan approached Moscow. A welcome unprecedented in its fervour and scale awaited him. The people had come out from the city and waited to meet him. For a distance of four miles along the banks of the Yauza river from the outer suburbs they massed, leaving only a narrow route. Ivan rode slowly through the crowd, acknowledging their acclamations of him as "Conqueror of the barbarians— Defender of the Christians".[23] All who were near enough pressed forward to kiss his feet, his hands, his garments. Their jubilation was so mingled with religious fervour that they showed towards him something of the adoration that they might have shown the Saviour Himself.

At the Sretensky monastery, standing at the place where the Muscovites had received the Vladimir ikon of the Mother of God which had miraculously saved Vladimir during Tamerlane's invasion, Ivan dismounted. Here, bearing the revered ikon, the Metropolitan, accompanied by bishops and senior boyars, greeted him. He knelt in prayer before the ikon and then addressed those present. Again, while exulting in his victory he showed himself to be humble and devout, without trace of arrogance. He paid tribute to the bravery of his military leaders and fighting men, and to the power of the prayers of the church and the people. The Metropolitan then spoke extolling the Tsar's virtues and his victory for Christ over Mohamet. Finally, in a moving scene, the aged Metropolitan and Bishops, boyars and others present knelt humbly before the young Tsar in gratitude.

Reaching Moscow Ivan was reunited with his Tsaritsa, embraced his baby son and spent several days with his family. He then opened the celebrations with a great banquet in the Granovitaya Palace. His people rejoiced, drinking, singing, and dancing throughout the city, and hailing as heroes their fighting men as they returned to Moscow. But in the midst of their celebrations they turned constantly in veneration towards their Tsar. More than Dmitri Donskoi and Alexander Nevsky who were to them, as King Arthur to the English, paragons of courage and Christian virtue, Ivan was exalted in the popular imagination.

The significance of the conquest of Kazan in the history of Russia was tremendous. The Muscovites had begun to take the offensive against the Asiatic hordes and, after two and a half centuries of subjugation they had, they felt, at last cast off the Tatar yoke. In 1480 during the reign of Ivan's grandfather Moscow had, in fact, become independent of the Tatar Khans, but this had happened as a muted event, devoid of real meaning for the people. The conquest of Kazan with its savage fighting and heavy losses of life inspired them. It had, furthermore, given birth to the popular sense of nationhood which economic, political, racial, or religious unity alone, or even together, could not give. It had indeed brought the nation to birth.

Finally this victory established the Tsar's power in the Volga lands. The annexation of the Khanate of Astrakhan at the mouth of the Volga was soon to follow, and Moscow then ruled over the whole of the vast river. The colonization of the rich lands in the south and southeast, watered by the tributaries of the Volga and the Don, and to the east, beyond the Volga, into the expanses of Siberia, could now begin.

Notes to Chapter XI

[1] A. A. Zimin, *The Reforms of Ivan the Terrible* (Moscow, 1960), p. 381.

[2] Solovyev, Bk. III, Vol. VI, p. 449.

[3] A. A. Zimin, "Towards the History of the Military Reforms of the Fifties of the 16th Century", in *Istoricheskie Zapiski*, Vol. 55 (1956), p. 345.

[4] A. A. Zimin, *The Reforms of Ivan the Terrible* (Moscow, 1960), pp. 337–8, but see also *Voprosy Istorii*, No. 6 (1962), p. 137.

[5] A. A. Zimin, in *Istoricheskie Zapiski*, Vol. 55 (1956), p. 348.

[6] Novgorod, for instance, had in 1545 provided 1,845 arquebusiers on the basis of one for every four households. *Ibid.*, p. 357.

[7] *Ibid.*, pp. 354–8.

[8] Karamzin, Bk. II, Vol. VIII, col. 75.

[9] *Ibid.*, cols. 78–9.

[10] *Ibid.*, col. 85.

[11] *Ibid.*, cols. 88–9.

[12] Solovyev, Bk. III, Vol. VI, pp. 466–7.

[13] Karamzin, Bk. II, Vol. VIII, col. 98.

[14] *Ibid.*, col. 102.

[15] Karamzin took the word *Razmysl* in the chronicle to mean "engineer". S. F. Platonov has pointed out that the many meanings given to this word in Dahl and other dictionaries do not include "engineer". He suggests as more probable that *Razmysl* is a corrupted form of the surname Rasmussen, and also recalls that the Danish courier, Peter Rasmussen, who was in Moscow in 1602, was called "Peter Razmysl" by the Russians. S. F. Platonov, *Ivan the Terrible* (Berlin, 1924), p. 72.

[16] This was surely the Muezzins' call to prayer with which the Russians must have been familiar. It is not clear to me why it was taken to be sorcery. Karamzin, Bk. II, Vol. VIII, cols. 104–5.

[17] *Ibid.*, col. 108.

[18] Certain accounts of this battle suggest that Ivan lost his nerve when the time came to attack and, although repeatedly summoned, he refused to leave his prayers. The troops were led into the attack without his orders. Solovyev, Bk. III, Vol. VIII, pp. 470–1; Karamzin, *loc. cit.*

[19] Karamzin, Bk. II, Vol. VIII, cols. 111–12.

[20] *Ibid.*

[21] *Ibid.*

[22] *Ibid.*, col. 114.

[23] *Ibid.*, col. 118.

CHAPTER XII

THE BETRAYAL 1553

IVAN returned from Kazan determined to rule as autocrat. The experience of leading his army and achieving a signal victory and then the unprecedented acclaim of his people had brought him to maturity and made him self-reliant. The boyars as a class had ceased to intimidate him; indeed, soon after the capture of Kazan, he apparently said to them, "Now I no longer fear you!"[1] He still revered Sylvester as his moral and spiritual adviser. His confidence in Adashev and other members of the Chosen Council was undiminished. But he was ready now to decide his own policy independently and without leaning on others, as he had done in the past. His victory at Kazan had, moreover, given new impetus and strength to his ambition to destroy Moscow's enemies and to establish the Tsardom among the great nations.

Sylvester, Adashev, and several members of the Chosen Council observed this new independence in their young Tsar with misgiving. They had tasted power and, more than the strongest and most insidious drugs, power claims its addicts. Called upon to yield to the Tsar's sole rule, they struggled to keep power in their hands. Sylvester was the most obdurate. This simple, but fanatic and forceful, priest had become arrogant and possessed by ideas of his own infallibility. If the Tsar rejected his advice, as he had begun to do, then, Sylvester claimed, he would surely incur the wrath of God. But, undeterred by threats and by the conflict of wills developing between them, Ivan persisted in his determination to free himself from the priest's domination. At this point, however, his relationship with Sylvester and his other advisers underwent a drastic change.

At the beginning of March 1553 Ivan was seized by a raging fever. His condition deteriorated so rapidly that his life was soon in danger and the last rites were administered. It was a development completely unexpected; a long reign had appeared to stretch before him, and now suddenly he was near to death. News of his illness spread quickly through the city and into the country. People crowded in the Kremlin and waited anxiously, saying among themselves,

"Our sins must be great beyond measure, when God takes from Russia such a sovereign."[2] Within the palace the leading boyars gathered, deeply disturbed about the succession to the throne.

In the bedchamber Ivan lay, still conscious, when his secretary, Ivan Mikhailov, approached and advised him that the time had come to make his last will and testament. Ivan in a weak voice gave orders for the deed to be drawn up, making his son, the infant Tsarevich Dmitri, his sole heir and successor. The deed was completed in haste and Ivan then called on his closest boyars and counsellors to kiss the cross in allegiance to his son. Towards evening on this day Princes Ivan Mstislavsky, Vladimir Vorotynsky, and Dmitri Paletsky, Boyars Ivan Sheremetev and M. Morozov, and Counsellors Ivan Viskovaty, Alexei Adashev, and Vishnyakov swore the oath. The Tsaritsa's kinsmen, Boyars Daniel Romanovich and Vasily Yuriev also swore allegiance. But Prince Kurlyatev and Treasurer Funikov excused themselves on grounds of illness.

On the following day in answer to the Tsar's summons all the boyars went to the palace to swear allegiance. Ivan received them, but was too weak to administer the oath himself. Princes Mstislavsky and Vorotynsky prepared to carry out this function on his behalf in the adjoining chamber. The quiet which had surrounded Ivan, disturbed only by whispered messages and the soft intoning of prayers, was now suddenly shattered by furious quarrelling among the boyars. Ivan heard the uproar and was stunned to learn of the opposition which many boyars were expressing to the oath. Some said boldly that Dmitri was in swaddling clothes and unfit to rule and that, if he succeeded, the country would suffer another time of anarchy such as it had endured in Ivan's childhood. But the boyars' quarrels and angry refusals to swear allegiance to Dmitri were rooted less in fears of anarchy than in the struggle for power.

The Grand Princes of Moscow had followed the practice of making their eldest sons the heirs to the throne, and to Ivan there was no question but that his only son, even though a few months old, must succeed him. But this custom had not yet acquired the force of law and the succession gave rise to savage rivalries. In addition to Dmitri, two princes of Ivan's family were living, Prince Yuri, his brother, and Prince Vladimir Staritsky, his cousin. Yuri was mentally defective and there could be no question of his contending for the throne, but Prince Vladimir was able, energetic, and ambitious, and supported by his equally determined mother, Efrosinia.

The noisy quarrelling continued among the boyars in the bed-chamber and the adjoining room without consideration for the dying Tsar. Summoning his strength to make himself heard, he spoke to his boyars.

"If you will not kiss the cross in allegiance to my son, Dmitri [he said], it means that you already have another sovereign. But you kissed the cross more than once in allegiance to me, swearing that you will seek no other sovereign. I will hold the cross for you to kiss—I command you to serve my son, Dmitri. . . ."[3]

Outcry and argument again broke out among the boyars. Then Feodor Adashev, father of Alexei, Ivan's closest favourite, said bluntly to him, "In allegiance to you and your son, Tsarevich Dmitri, we will kiss the cross, but we will not serve the Zakharini, Daniel and his brother. We have already witnessed many disasters, caused by the boyars during your minority!"[4] Three influential princes— Peter Shchenyatev-Patrikeev, Semeon Rostovsky, and Ivan Turuntai-Pronsky—continued to object to the oath. "Over us the Zakharini will wield power," they said. "Why should we submit to the Zakharini and serve the young sovereign? We would do better to serve the grown Prince Vladimir Andreevich."[5]

The antagonism towards the Zakharini had now become intense. On the succession of the infant Dmitri to the throne his mother, Anastasia, would become regent in accordance with Muscovite practice. But she was a pious young woman without experience of government, and power would, in fact, pass into the hands of her two brothers. It may be that the Zakharini had behaved arrogantly and stupidly since the Tsar's marriage with their sister had elevated their family so suddenly and placed them near the throne. Apart from personal behaviour, however, the Zakharini were scorned for their comparatively humble origin. But the further and equally important reason for the hostility was that the Zakharini were not members of the Chosen Council, that inner ring, surrounding the Tsar, which had monopolized power in the Kremlin.

During the years since 1547 Sylvester and Adashev had taken advantage of Ivan's boundless confidence in them to appoint their own supporters to all important offices. Ivan himself even sent those whom he wished to promote to these two men for prior interview and approval. Moreover many princes and boyars, seeing in Ivan's mistrust of their class a barrier to their appointment to high office, had drawn close to Sylvester and Adashev and had sought their favour. Thus Prince Dmitri Kurlyatev, who had been an active friend of the Shuisky and had taken part in the disorderly scene in the Council when Vorontsov had been dragged away, had been appointed boyar and made a member of the Chosen Council through the influence of Sylvester. Prince Dmitri Paletsky, another close ally of the Shuisky and one who had suffered disgrace on their downfall, was close to Sylvester, and his daughter had in November 1547 been married to Ivan's brother, Yuri.[6]

The power of Sylvester, Adashev, and their chosen allies seemed beyond challenge. But the family of the Zakharin-Yuriev stood outside their influence and through the Tsaritsa they were close to Ivan. For this reason the party of the favourites constantly denounced them. Kurbsky, a member of the Chosen Council, called them traitors and despoilers of the Tsardom. Sylvester even attacked the gentle Anastasia, likening her to Eudoxia, the wife of the Emperor Arcadius, who had persecuted St John Chrysostom, taken to represent Sylvester. By insinuation and other methods the favourites sought to undermine the position of Anastasia and her family and to whip up the hatred of the boyars and other classes against them. The preservation of the position and power of Sylvester, Adashev, and the Chosen Council depended on Prince Vladimir Staritsky, who was on very friendly terms with Sylvester, succeeding to the throne.

Prince Vladimir and his mother were already active. On receiving the first news of Ivan's illness, they had rallied their retainers, paid out sums of money to others, and canvassed the boyars for support. Their behaviour was so blatant at the time when the Tsar seemed on the point of death that some boyars remonstrated with them. Prince Vladimir Vorotynsky and Counsellor Ivan Viskovaty called on Prince Vladimir to swear allegiance to the Tsarevich without further delay. "Don't you dare quarrel with me and tell me what to do!" Prince Vladimir expostulated.[7] But Vorotynsky stood his ground, reminding him of his sworn allegiance to Ivan. Then a special deed binding him to serve the Tsarevich was drawn up, but Prince Vladimir at first refused to execute it. Certain boyars, loyal to Ivan and his son, tried to bring pressure to bear on him, refusing to allow him to leave the palace or to approach the ailing Tsar. But now Sylvester, who had been silent, openly came out in support of Prince Vladimir and thundered against these boyars.

By this time most of the boyars had sworn allegiance to Tsarevich Dmitri, and many were loudly persuading the recalcitrant boyars to be loyal to the Tsar. The arguments grew more heated. Ivan made desperate appeals to them to swear, and more did so. But some, like

Prince Dmitri Paletsky, Prince Kurlyatev, who was one of the last to take the oath, and Treasurer Funikov, made haste secretly to contact Prince Vladimir and his mother and to promise them support. Finally, protesting loudly, Prince Vladimir swore allegiance, but his oath carried no conviction.

Ivan, weak from fever and believing himself to be near to death, lay in an agony of anxiety and distress. He had thought that he had the support of his closest boyars, and he had never doubted the entire loyalty of his chosen advisers. Suddenly in this illness he had seen that some at least of them were ready to throw over his family and dynasty on his death. Sylvester, his spiritual guide, openly espoused the cause of Prince Vladimir. Adashev, whom he had raised from insignificance to an eminence in which he was courted by the greatest in the land, had sworn allegiance but his father's protest had clouded the son's oath. To Ivan this was not simply ingratitude, but betrayal of him as a friend and as their divinely appointed Tsar.

What distressed him most at this time, however, was the threat to the lives of his wife and children. He was a devoted husband and father, and he was tortured by the fear that, when he was no longer alive, Prince Vladimir or rival boyar factions would kill Anastasia as well as their son and daughter.

Turning to the boyars who had sworn allegiance, Ivan implored them to protect his young family.

"You have given me and my son your oath that you will serve us, but other boyars do not wish to see my son as sovereign. If it is God's will, then I will die, and then I beg you not to forget the oath you have sworn; do not deliver up my son to be killed by the boyars, but flee with him to a foreign land, wherever God directs!" [8]

Anastasia's brothers, the Zakharini, had not raised their voices throughout the disputes. They were craven and concerned only about their own fates on the Tsar's death. Their faint-hearted conduct did not escape Ivan's notice. "You, Zakharini!" he said angrily. "Why are you so afraid? Do you think that the boyars may take pity on you? You will be their first sacrifice, and so you must be ready to die for my son and his mother. You must not give up my wife to be abused by the boyars!" [9] But he knew that he could not count on them and among all those surrounding him and protesting their loyalty, there was now not one man to whom he could give his unqualified trust. His burning fear in these hours of illness and impotence was that all would desert them on his death.

For several weeks Ivan lay ill and exhausted. Over Moscow and throughout the country uncertainty brooded. Then, contrary to all expectations, the crisis passed and he began to recover. He had taken a vow during this illness that, if he survived, he would make a special pilgrimage of thanksgiving to the Kirillo-Belozersky monastery. It involved a long and arduous journey, and Adashev, Kurbsky, and others counselled him against it. He was, they said, still weak from his illness; his baby son would suffer during such a journey; his presence was required in Moscow, because the Tatars of Kazan were in revolt and had to be suppressed. But Ivan stubbornly refused to be dissuaded. Probably he wanted to get away from the oppressive atmosphere of the Kremlin, which seemed to breed deceit and treason, and he wanted to think about his own position and future conduct, surrounded, as he now felt himself to be, by treachery.

In May, Ivan set out on the pilgrimage with his wife and son. Halting at the Troitsa monastery he visited the cell of Maxim Grek, the renowned scholar whom Vasily III had summoned to Russia to translate the church books. Maxim had been disgraced for his political views and exiled to distant monasteries, but Ivan had freed him, and he now lived a life of prayer at the Troitsa. His influence had been great and he was close to Sylvester in outlook. Indeed, to Ivan in his cell, Maxim spoke like Sylvester, urging him to give up his arduous journey and, when Ivan refused, threatening him with the wrath of God; finally he prophesied that the Tsarevich would die on the road.

Ivan continued his journey with Anastasia and his son. At the Josef Volokolamsk monastery he had long conversations with Vassian Toporkov, the former Archbishop of Kolomenskoe, who had enjoyed the special favour of Vasily III, and had been deposed during the boyars' rule. Ivan turned to the old man as a friend of his father and an opponent of Sylvester and asked, "How must I rule in order to keep my nobles obedient to me?" Vassian, himself hating the boyars and believing fervently in the absolute power of the autocrat, counselled him earnestly and at length. The essence of his advice was that the Tsar should disregard all advisers and, keeping all power in his own hands, rule alone. Ivan is said to have exclaimed, "If my father were alive, even he would not have given me such sound advice!"[10]

Kurbsky and others among Ivan's strongest critics were to maintain that this conversation with Vassian corrupted him. But it was not the advice of the old monk that inspired Ivan's mistrust and hatred of the boyars. This hostility was the bitter fruit of the terror in childhood and then of what he had felt to be his betrayal by those whom he had trusted implicitly.

Encouraged by the affection and advice of the old priest Ivan resumed his return journey. But now a further tragedy overwhelmed him, for suddenly his little son died. It seemed almost as though Dmitri had been born only as an instrument revealing to Ivan the perfidy of his friends and counsellors. From this wearisome pilgrimage he returned with Anastasia to the gloom and loneliness of the Kremlin.

Notes to Chapter XII

[1] Karamzin, Bk. II, Vol. VIII, col. 124.
[2] Solovyev, Bk. III, Vol. VI, p. 526.
[3] *Ibid.*, p. 526.
[4] *Ibid.*, pp. 526–7.
[5] Karamzin, *op. cit.*, note 189.
[6] Solovyev, *op. cit.*, p. 526.
[7] *Ibid.*, pp. 527–8.
[8] *Ibid.*
[9] *Ibid.*, p. 532.
[10] *Ibid.*, p. 533; Karamzin, *op. cit.*, cols. 131–2.

CHAPTER XIII

REFORMS, ASTRAKHAN, AND THE TATARS
1554–60

THE events of this spring of 1553 undoubtedly made a deep and lasting impression on Ivan, but this was not at once apparent in the man or his behaviour. Indeed, during the next six years he was an enigma. It is impossible to know whether he was pursuing Christian principles of charity and forgiveness of his enemies, or whether he was behaving with astute calculation. He was capable of humility and charity, but he was equally capable of vengeful cruelty, of biding his time and then striking suddenly and savagely.

On his return to Moscow from his pilgrimage, Ivan showed no anger towards those who had sought to betray him and his family; he did not punish or dismiss them. As before he received Sylvester with every courtesy and listened to his counsel. He treated Alexei Adashev in the same friendly manner, and in 1555 even promoted him to *okolnichy*, the rank immediately below that of boyar. Possibly Ivan was moved by enduring respect and affection for both men, and it may be that he did not regard Alexei Adashev, who had sworn allegiance to the Tsarevich, as a betrayer. At the same time he certainly realized that he could not do without them and their fellows in the Chosen Council at this stage.

Towards Prince Vladimir Andreevich of Staritsa he behaved with apparent generosity which masked an abiding mistrust. It happened that on 28 March 1554, some nine months after their return to Moscow, Anastasia gave birth to another son, named Ioann or Ivan. Without delay Ivan had a new testament prepared by which, in the event of his death, Prince Vladimir would become guardian of the young Tsar and also of the regent. It provided further that, if the Tsarevich died before coming of age, Prince Vladimir would succeed to the throne. For his part Prince Vladimir had to swear a solemn oath to fulfil his duties as guardian and regent honourably, not sparing even his own ambitious headstrong mother, if she plotted against Anastasia and the Tsarevich. He swore also to carry out his functions as regent in accordance with the advice of the Tsaritsa, the

Metropolitan, and the Tsar's counsellors, and he undertook never to hold more than 100 of his private troops in Moscow at any time. Short of having him executed, a step he was probably unprepared to take at this stage in view of the support the Prince had among the boyar-princely aristocracy, this was the practical and, indeed, the only arrangement that Ivan could make to ensure the succession of his son and the protection of his beloved wife.

Among those at court who had refused, or shown reluctance, to swear the oath to Tsarevich Dmitri, Ivan's mild forgiving mood was, however, a source of uneasiness. A sign of this apprehension and also of the continuing discontent among the boyars was the conspiracy of the Rostovsky, an eminent princely family, to flee to Lithuania. In July 1554 Prince Nikita Rostovsky was seized, as he attempted to escape over the frontier. Under interrogation he revealed that Boyar Prince Semeon Rostovsky, his father, had sent him to the Lithuanian Grand Duke with the message that the Rostovsky family wished to swear allegiance to him. Prince Semeon also revealed that he had had two meetings with Lithuanian ambassadors, when he had spoken slanderously of the Tsar and had divulged state secrets. The Boyar Council sentenced him to death, but on the intercession of the Metropolitan and other churchmen Ivan commuted the sentence to one of imprisonment at Beloozero.

Apart from the troubles caused by the boyars who were unwilling to accept the facts of the national state and the supreme authority of the Tsar, Ivan found this a difficult and testing time for other reasons. He was isolated and under constant pressure from Sylvester, Adashev, and their powerful group. He wrote later:

> "Who indeed can recount in detail both the persecutions and oppressions I suffered in my ways of life, in my movements and in repose, and likewise in my attendance at church and in all my manner of life? . . . They imposed these things upon us in God's name, deeming that they were inflicting such persecutions upon us for the good of our soul and not through cunning."[1]

He had to watch that they did not "hold counsel in secret and without our knowledge" and take independent action "deeming us to be incapable of judgment".[2] "And if I did not acquiesce then they said that this would lead to the downfall of my soul and the destruction of the Tsardom."[3]

In domestic policy, however, Ivan was more in agreement with them, and he was impatient to implement the reforms of this period. But this, too, involved him in conflict at times, especially with

Sylvester who was quick to show anger whenever his advice was passed over or rejected. Aggrieved by the Tsar's new independence, he began attributing every ailment and every misfortune, no matter how insignificant, suffered by the Tsar, the Tsaritsa, or their children to the wrath of God, incurred by Ivan's wilfulness.

A further aggravation for Ivan was the fact that Sylvester and his party went out of their way to comfort those who were in disgrace or opposed him. They were guilty, in Ivan's words, of "indulging every whim of Prince Vladimir". Semeon Rostovsky received special consideration in exile through Sylvester's intercession. Finally, "they stirred up great hatred against our Tsaritsa Anastasia and likened her to all the impious Tsaritsas . . .".[4]

The seven years, following the conquest of Kazan and then his illness, were not, however, merely a period of strife at court: it was a time also of intensive military and reforming activities. Ivan now took the offensive against the Tatars. He subdued the rebels of Kazan, captured Astrakhan, and in a series of daring exploits his troops intimidated the Khan of the Crimea. In the midst of these military campaigns he promulgated a series of reforms.

The first period of reform, lasting from 1549 until 1552, had brought a new discipline and efficiency to the army which had shown its mettle in the Kazan campaign. It had also seen the promulgation of the new legal code (*sudebnik*) and of local government measures which had gone some way towards establishing a new system of administration.

In this second period of reform, lasting from 1553 until 1560, the changes already introduced were rapidly developed. In local government the functions of the sheriff (*starosta*), who was replacing the governor (*namestnik*), were defined. He had special duties to suppress robbery and murder, which were rife throughout the country, to prevent the flight of peasants from the land, and to protect them from the powerful magnates. The sheriffs who now had wide jurisdiction were listed by name and required to swear to perform their duties faithfully, and corruption or negligence could be punished by death.

The displacement of the governors by the sheriffs was accompanied by the gradual abolition of "feeding" by the Tsar's officers, especially in the north. This led to a significant increase in the national revenues, now collected by the sheriffs and local officials. The Great Office (*Bolshoi Prikhod*) was established and quickly became the most important treasury department in the land. Both the increase in the national revenues and the greater efficiency in administration were particularly valuable at this time, when military commitments were heavier than ever, and when so many army commanders had to be compensated for loss of their "feedings" by payments from the treasury.

The creation of a strong centralized state depended to a great extent on the encouragement and security of the growing class of serving gentry. It was notable that, while the boyar-aristocracy retained so many of their privileges, the gentry were called upon to bear more extensive duties. But the problem remained of finding estates to give this class a sound economic basis. Attempts to obtain land from the vast holdings of the church had failed, and Ivan judged it unwise to press his attack on the landowning and other privileges of the church which was such a powerful supporter of the centralized state and of his authority as autocrat. But a number of measures were introduced which furthered the welfare of the gentry as a class. Two new central departments, set up in Moscow, one to allocate lands to the serving gentry, and the other to regulate their military service, bore witness to the special attention being given to them.

In the 1550s, and mainly in the years 1555-6, a system of central departments was, in fact, instituted, making Moscow even more indisputably the capital and the administrative centre of the nation. Most of these departments, or *Prikazi*, had as their head a *dyak* or secretary with clearly defined functions. The secretaries began keeping records of laws and regulations, and developed the practice of meeting to discuss and co-ordinate their functions. Increasingly the central administration was bearing responsibility for the whole country.

At this time Ivan was particularly concerned with army reforms. First, it was essential to define the duties of all landowners to serve and provide troops. Many boyars and others, holding patrimonial estates, had in the past served their princes in accordance with specific agreements which had since lapsed and had not been replaced. For such boyars military service had been voluntary and some neither served nor provided troops. In 1555-6 Ivan issued statutes, defining their obligations. Every owner of lands, whether hereditary or held on service tenure, was in future required to serve personally and also to provide in respect of each defined measure of land an armed man with mount and adequate supplies. A landowner who did not serve personally or who failed to supply the troops required of him had to make a payment into the treasury, calculated on the basis of his liability. Strictly enforced, these statutes produced a marked increase in the strength of the Tsar's army which had by 1560 probably come to number 150,000 troops, and by 1580 as many as 309,000.[5]

Such extensive administrative and military developments bore heavily on the peasantry, however, and created conditions in which the growth of serfdom became inevitable. The payment of taxes, the calls of military service, the demands of their landowners, and the struggle to wrest a living from the soil, from hunting, fishing, and handcrafts, burdened the peasants increasingly. Many were in debt to their landlords, and the fate of the defaulting debtor was that he became the *kholop* or virtually the slave of his creditor. In growing numbers peasants escaped by flight from this bondage and the impossible hardships of their lives. During the 1550s villages became deserted as a result of mass flights.

This movement to the freedom of the virgin lands to the east and south disturbed Ivan. The young and growing nation could ill afford to lose men on such a scale. He introduced several measures with the purpose of halting this migration and made it one of the urgent duties of the sheriffs to prevent flights and recover runaways. But, concerned as he was with the needs of the state and especially of the army, he gave little thought to the possibility of lightening the peasants' burdens.

These reforms were introduced to the accompaniment of frequent disturbances caused by the Tatars. Within two months of the conquest of Kazan, Tatar bands were plundering Russian merchants and supply caravans. A punitive expedition from Sviyazhsk hanged 112 of the raiders, and order was restored. But it lasted for only a few weeks. In March 1553 Prince Gorbaty, the governor of Kazan, reported serious revolts among the Tatars, and from Sviyazhsk came news of rebellion by Cheremis and Votyak tribesmen. Detachments sent to restore order had been boldly attacked and defeated.

The Muscovite government acted promptly. Daniel Adashev, brother of Alexei, led troops to Vyatka and from there patrolled vast regions of the Kama, Vyatka, and Volga rivers during the summer. In September 1553 four of the leading Muscovite commanders— Prince Simeon Mikulinsky, Peter Morozov, Ivan Sheremetev, and Prince Andrei Kurbsky—set out from Moscow with strong forces and began laying waste the regions which had rebelled. Between them they took captive 6,000 Tatars and 15,000 Tatar women and children. But major revolts continued to break out, involving heavy casualties to both Muscovites and Tatars, and terrible devastation of the land. Finally in 1557 the last of the rebels among the Tatars and Finnish tribesmen capitulated and swore allegiance afresh to the Tsar.

Five years of punitive warfare had thus proved necessary to subdue the Kazan Khanate and one reason for the persistent rebellion was that the Nogai Tatars were actively helping the rebels. The Nogai had previously maintained friendly relations with Moscow. Their traders were famed among the Russians for the herds of magnificent horses which they drove hundreds of miles across the steppes to sell in Moscow. But then the Nogai had turned to raiding along the trade routes, destroying villages and plundering merchants.

Ivan sent complaints to the Nogai princes, but couched in friendly language, promising them presents, and inviting them to send envoys to Moscow to discuss future relations. He knew that his capture of Kazan had shaken the Tatars, and indeed the whole Mohammedan world, and he was anxious to avoid pushing the Nogai into active alliance with the Crimean Tatars against Muscovy. Even before the capture of Kazan, the Sultan of the powerful Ottoman Empire, aroused by the Muscovite threat to the Khanate, had called on the Nogai to rally to the defence of their brothers and in response to his appeal a band of Nogai, led by Ediger, had fought bravely at Kazan.

The danger of the Muslims in the south and east uniting against him was constantly on Ivan's mind. The great weakness of the Tatars, however, was their constant fighting among themselves. Bitter feuds made even the bonds of family and religion ineffective. No matter what dangers threatened the Tatars, Moscow could always find allies among them to further her policies. It was this factor of Tatar rivalries which made the conquest of Astrakhan a simple, almost bloodless campaign.

The Khan of Astrakhan, known as the Tsar, was Yamgurchei. He had offered his allegiance to Ivan, but had declared his hostility on learning of the conquest of Kazan. Among the Nogai, Prince Yusuf was the enemy of Moscow, but Izmail, his brother, was her ally. Even before Kazan's capture, Izmail had sent messages to Ivan, urging him to take Astrakhan, depose Yamgurchei, and elevate the former Tsar, Derbysh, in his place. He renewed these proposals after the fall of Kazan. In October 1553 Izmail sent ambassadors to Moscow, asking for protection against the Tsar of Astrakhan, and promising active support of the Nogai.

Ivan took keen interest in this proposal. Astrakhan was of great importance to Muscovite trade and with the city in his hands he would control the great Volga waterway from source to mouth. Further, Ivan considered Astrakhan to be part of his tsardom, believing mistakenly that it was the town known as Tmutarakan, which in the time of Kievan Rus, before the Mongol invasion, had been under the rule of Grand Prince Vladimir, who had bestowed it upon his son Mstislav. It was, therefore, he believed, part of the patrimony of the Tsar of Muscovy.

Ivan sent Alexei Adashev to talk with the Nogai ambassadors, and they drew up a plan of campaign. On the melting of the ice in the spring of 1554, Prince Yuri Pronsky-Shemyakin led 30,000 troops by river to Astrakhan, where he was joined by a further force from the Vyatka region, commanded by Prince Vyazemsky. Supported by the Nogai, the Muscovite forces routed Yamgurchei's army, captured Astrakhan, and made Derbysh Tsar again.

Among the Nogai themselves, however, fighting broke out. In February 1555 Ivan received news that Izmail had killed his brother, Yusuf, and defeated his army. It had been a savage battle with heavy losses on both sides, which had seriously weakened the Nogai Horde. But now Izmail, far from enjoying the fruits of victory, was fearful of being attacked by Yusuf's sons, and he begged Ivan for protection. Meanwhile, Derbysh was wavering in his loyalty. He had agreed to pay Ivan a tribute of money together with 3,000 sturgeon annually, and as one paying tribute to Moscow he feared the hostility of the Crimean Khan and of the Sultan. Indeed, in April 1555, he sent word to Moscow that Yamgurchei, supported by the sons of Yusuf, by Crimean Tatars, and by a force of Turkish janissaries, was advancing on Astrakhan. In the confused fighting which followed Yamgurchei was killed and Izmail was defeated by his nephews. But then in a sudden and unpredictable change-over, typical of the Tatars, the nephews joined forces with Izmail, who regained command of the Nogai Horde. Izmail then sent word to Moscow that Derbysh was in league with the Crimean Khan. Ivan promptly despatched troops down the Volga, but Derbysh fled to Azov, and Astrakhan, her people readily swearing allegiance to the Muscovite Tsar, was finally annexed without bloodshed.

This time Astrakhan and the mouth of the Volga remained in Russian hands. The nomadic Nogai were allowed to fish the rivers, to camp in the vicinity of Astrakhan, and to trade, but they were under the watchful eye of the garrison. Ivan ordered the Cossack Ataman, Lyapin Filimov, to make a permanent settlement at the Volga portage and to post troops on the banks of the Irgyz river to ensure peace in this region. From time to time the Tatars became restless and they fought among themselves, but Moscow's domination of Astrakhan and the Volga lands was not seriously challenged.

The morale of the Muscovites was now high. They had seen that the Tatars, so brave and terrible in attack, could be cowardly in defence, and this applied especially to the Crimean Tatars whom they had once feared most of all. Ivan displayed this new Muscovite confidence when in the summer of 1555 he decided to mount an attack on the Crimea. He was, in fact, the first Muscovite sovereign to carry the war into the Crimean Khanate: it was a clear demonstration that, after years of being on the defensive, Muscovy had taken the offensive.

In summer, 1555, the Crimean Khan, Devlet Girei, invaded Muscovy with an army of 60,000 men. Ivan at once sent Prince Ivan Mstislavsky with troops to Kolomna and, accompanied by Prince Vladimir Andreevich, he himself followed to take command. Learning that the Tsar was waiting at the head of his army, the Khan withdrew his horde. Boyar Ivan Sheremetev with 13,000 troops followed the retreating Tatars and, although vastly outnumbered, he engaged them and was defeated, but only after prolonged and heavy fighting. This minor victory raised Tatar morale and the Khan turned to advance again on Tula. Certain among Ivan's commanders expressed misgivings about meeting the Khan himself at the head of such a strong force, and counselled him to fall back to defend Moscow. But Ivan was determined to defeat the Khan in pitched battle and led his army on to Tula. He was on the march when he learnt that the Tatars were hurriedly retreating towards the Crimea.

In March of the following year Ivan sent out two reconnaissance parties to obtain confirmation of reports that the Khan was yet again preparing to invade. He himself proceeded with his armies to Tula to wait in readiness. The Khan advanced towards the frontier, but retreated immediately on learning that Ivan was prepared. The summer did not pass, however, without action. Secretary Rzhevsky, commanding one of the reconnaissance parties, boldly made his way some 700 miles down the Dnieper to the Tatar port of Ochakov on the Black Sea. He caused major damage to enemy settlements and then safely withdrew.

This exploit dismayed the Khan as much as it delighted Ivan. Devlet Girei believed that it surely portended a full-scale Muscovite invasion. His fears increased when Prince Dmitri Vishnevetsky, the Ukrainian Cossack leader who had recently transferred his allegiance from Lithuania to Muscovy, established a stronghold on Khortitsa island in the Dnieper. From this stronghold Vishnevetsky threatened the Tatar camping grounds and, when the Khan tried to dislodge this Cossack party, he failed ignominiously. The Cossacks withdrew only in the autumn when their supplies were exhausted.

The Khan was now desperate. His appeals to the Sultan had brought no help, for the Turks were preoccupied elsewhere. At the end of 1558, however, the Khan received reports that the Tsar had marched with his armies into Livonia. He quickly assembled a force of 100,000 men and advanced into Muscovy. But Ivan was in Moscow, and his troops were in readiness along the frontier. Once again the Khan retreated, not daring to risk battle.

Intent on holding the initiative, Ivan sent two strong raiding parties southwards at the beginning of 1559. Vishnevetsky led 5,000 men down the Don and Daniel Adashev with a force 8,000 strong made his way down the Dnieper. Both expeditions had resounding success. Vishnevetsky inflicted serious damage on Tatar positions around Azov. But Adashev embarked his men in boats at Ochakov, sailed into the Black Sea, captured two Turkish ships, and landed on the Crimean peninsula. There he laid waste Tatar camps and freed Muscovite and Lithuanian prisoners before withdrawing his troops without serious loss. This was an amazing and unprecedented exploit and, indeed, a singeing of the Sultan's beard.

During the summer (1559) Ivan waited in readiness to meet the Tatar invasion which seemed inevitable after these daring raids. But the Khan did not appear. The Cossacks of the Don and the Ukraine, the Nogai and the Astrakhantsi were all independently raiding the Crimean Khanate, where the Tatars were further weakened by severe famine. To Moscow the Khan sent proposals for peace and complaints about being attacked from all sides. But his complaints drew from Ivan only a stern reproof for his past predatory raiding, an admonition to pursue a peaceful policy towards his neighbours in future, and the threat that the Russians now knew the way to the Crimea by sea as well as by land.[6]

The Russian triumphs over the Tatars now received a worthy commemoration. Ivan had made a vow after the conquest of Kazan and Astrakhan to raise a monumental cathedral to mark these great events in his reign. The site chosen was the southern end of the Red Square in Moscow, and during the years 1555 to 1560 two Russian architects, Postnik and Barma, built the Cathedral of St Vasily the Blessed, which is one of the glories of Russian architecture.

The tall octagonal tower of the central church, mounted on a high platform, was surrounded by four large and four smaller octagonal chapel towers, each of which was of a different height and surface texture, and of a different colour, and the whole structure sloped away towards the river. The result was a building rich in design, confusing, but compelling and profoundly moving. It followed national Russian tradition, but within this tradition it showed tremendous individuality.

The cathedral was, in fact, a triumphant expression of the personality of the newly emergent Muscovite nation. It was at the same time peculiarly an expression of Ivan himself with all his simplicity and violent extremes. Like him, too, the Cathedral of St Vasily was essentially Russian and, still dominating the Red Square, it stands as an enduring monument to one of the most truly Russian and one of the most outstanding of the Tsars and as a monument to the birth of the nation.[7]

Notes to Chapter XIII

[1] J. L. I. Fennell (ed. and trans.), *The Correspondence between Prince A. M. Kurbsky and Tsar Ivan IV of Russia* (Cambridge, 1955), p. 93.

[2] *Ibid.*, p. 87.

[3] *Ibid.*, p. 93.

[4] *Ibid.*, p. 95.

[5] A. A. Zimin, *The Reforms of Ivan the Terrible* (Moscow, 1960), pp. 444–8.

[6] Solovyev, Bk. III, Vol. VI, p. 495.

[7] The legend that Ivan engaged an Italian architect to build the Cathedral and that on its completion he had the architect's eyes put out so that he could never build another like it is entirely without foundation. Postnik and Barma, two Russians from Pskov, were responsible for the building, which bears no signs of Western influence, and they were not blinded.

The Cathedral, as seen in the Red Square today, has lost something of its original simplicity and harmony of design, because in the 17th century a chapel and a belfry were added and then at a later date an enclosed gallery was built around it. G. H. Hamilton, *The Art and Architecture of Russia* (London, 1954), pp. 131–3.

Between Ivan and his contemporary, Philip II of Spain, there is a strong, but superficial resemblance. But both men left to posterity monumental buildings which were very real reflections of their respective personalities. The monastery of San Lorenzo de Escorial was a massive forbidding retreat. The Cathedral of St Vasily was a lively, joyous but savage expression of national triumph.

CHAPTER XIV

THE DRIVE WESTWARD 1553-64

WITH a strong instinctive movement the Russian people were now stretching outwards towards their natural frontiers. They had conquered their Tatar enemies on the Volga and no barrier stood to their trade and colonization eastwards. They had taken the offensive against the Tatars of the Crimea and in 1560 it seemed that they could extend their frontiers to the shores of the Black Sea without difficulty.

The westward striving of the Russians was, however, especially strong and persistent. Novgorod, Kiev, and the Dnieper river had been an intrinsic part of their earliest history and represented for them the trade and kinship with Western Europe which the Mongol invasion had destroyed. They were impatient, too, to recover the lands, still inhabited by Orthodox Russians, which their western enemies had seized while Russia lay powerless under the Tatar yoke. Ivan III and other Muscovite princes had claimed them as part of their patrimony. But Sweden, the Teutonic Knights, Lithuania, and Poland had always stood firm against the Russians, and their hostility was all the greater because they feared the massive new nation now stirring in the east.

During his campaigns against the Tatars, Ivan's thoughts had been turning increasingly towards the west. To him the greatest glory that he could achieve, after the conquest of Kazan, was the recovery of the Russian lands, held by his western enemies, and the revival of Muscovite trade with the west through the Baltic Sea. But it was also a matter of practical necessity. The Tsardom was, he knew, backward, compared with Western Europe. This applied especially to the manufacture of arms and to the science of war, which his people had to master so that Muscovy would be strong, able to defend herself and to reclaim the territories belonging rightfully to her. He was determined that in every field Muscovy should take her place with the nations of Europe sharing in the free intercourse of ideas and trade.

In these objectives Ivan was reflecting the aspirations of his people.

But Sylvester and many among his boyars opposed his western policy at this stage. They urged him to take advantage of the craven weakness of the Crimean Tatars, revealed by the exploits of Adashev and Vishnevetsky, and to conquer the Crimea as he had conquered Kazan and Astrakhan. Afire with crusading zeal, Sylvester could think only of winning a further great victory for the Cross over the Crescent. This, he held, was the mission of the Orthodox Tsar, not war against Livonians and Lithuanians who were Christians of a kind and to be won to Orthodoxy by great deeds of faith and by friendly counsel, rather than by the sword. In spite of the pressure upon him, however, Ivan obstinately pursued his own policy and Sylvester, to his fury, found his counsel rejected.

Ivan was not yet ready to attempt the conquest of the Crimea. He saw clearly the tremendous obstacles and he was not carried away, as were Sylvester and his supporters, by the victories over Kazan and Astrakhan, or by crusading fervour. He recognized that the daring expeditions of Adashev and Vishnevetsky could not be repeated in moving an army of 100,000 or more men across 700 miles of steppelands, as would be necessary in a major campaign against the Crimean Tatars. But the most serious danger was that such a campaign would certainly involve him in war with the great Turkish Empire, then at the zenith of its power. The Crimean Khan was vassal of the Sultan and, indeed, in his campaigns against Muscovy, his horde had often been supported by Turkish janissaries. Any attempt to invade the Crimea in force would, Ivan knew, inevitably bring him into conflict with the Sultan. He had always avoided this danger. When Adashev brought back Turkish prisoners, Ivan made haste to return them to the Pasha at Ochakov with the message that the Tsar was at war with his enemy, Khan Devlet Girei, but with the Sultan he wanted only eternal peace.

The time was not ripe for the conquest of the Crimea and history has endorsed the wisdom of Ivan's decision. More than two centuries were to pass before Russia was able to conquer the peninsula and to suppress the troublesome Crimean Tatars.

An unexpected event in 1553 had intensified Ivan's eagerness to turn westward. An English seaman, named Richard Chancellor, had brought his ship into the White Sea and had thus shown that the Baltic was not the only route for trade with the rest of Europe. Chancellor was master of the *Edward Bonaventure* and pilot-general of an expedition of three ships, entrusted to the command of Sir Hugh Willoughby, with the object of finding the north-east passage to the fabled riches of Cathay. The ships had sailed from Gravesend on 18 May 1553. Off North Cape a storm had separated them. Willoughby's *Bona Speranza* with the *Bona Confidentia* put into a deserted fjord and there during the Arctic winter he and the crews of both vessels were frozen to death.

Richard Chancellor a more able seaman than Willoughby, sailed further eastwards into the White Sea, and anchored at the mouth of the Dvina river. There he learnt from fishermen that he was in the realm of the Tsar of Muscovy and after some delay he was summoned to Moscow. He was shown great courtesy in the Kremlin and the magnificence of his audience impressed him. In the outer chamber, where he waited,

> "sat one hundred or more gentlemen, all in cloth of gold very sumptuous and from there I came into the Council Chamber, where sat the Duke himself with his nobles which were a fair company: they sat around the chamber on high, yet so that he himself sat much higher than any of his nobles in a chair of gilt, and in a long garment of beaten gold, with an imperial crown upon his head, and a staff of crystal and gold in his right hand and his other hand leaning on the chair."[1]

Chancellor presented the letter which he carried from Edward VI, addressed to "the Kings, Princes and other Potentates, inhabiting the northeast parts of the world towards the mighty Empire of Cathay",[2] requesting free passage, help, and trade "for these our servants".[3] After an exchange of formal courtesies the audience was concluded. Chancellor withdrew, but two hours later he was summoned to dine, which in itself was a gesture of high favour. Again Chancellor was impressed by the richness of the court, although the banqueting hall was "not great as is the King's Majesty's of England". The Tsar sat in a gown of silver, wearing his crown, and "there sat none near him by a great way".[4] But the display of gold, kept for this purpose, bore witness to the wealth and power of the Tsar. Two hundred people sat down to dinner and all were served in golden vessels, "the cups also were of gold and very massive".[5]

At his farewell audience Chancellor received the Tsar's formal reply to Edward VI, news of whose death had not yet reached Muscovy. Ivan expressed his willingness to receive English ships and after negotiations with "one of your Majesty's counsel" to allow "free mart with all free liberties" to English merchants throughout his dominions.[6]

Chancellor set out on his return voyage from the White Sea in

February 1554, bearing the Tsar's letter. In the following year the Russia or Muscovy Company was incorporated by Royal Charter and Chancellor sailed again, accompanied this time by the Company's agents, bearing a letter from Philip and Mary, requesting trading privileges. Again Ivan received the Englishmen with great courtesy and he was much taken with George Killingworth, one of the agents, who sported a beard "which was not only thick, broad and yellow coloured, but in length five foot and two inches of assize".[7] Apparently without question Ivan granted the Company extensive trading rights, but, since the agents were not empowered to meet Ivan's demands for materials of war and skilled men, he appointed an embassy to negotiate in London.

In July 1556 Chancellor sailed from the White Sea in the *Edward Bonaventure* with Osip Nepea, the first Russian ambassador to England, but the voyage had a tragic end. The ship was wrecked on the Aberdeenshire coast, and Chancellor himself lost his life, while saving the Russian ambassador from drowning. Not until February 1557 did Nepea and the nine surviving members of his suite reach London. He was received in audience and richly entertained, but the royal letter which he took back to Moscow conferred trading privileges far less than those granted to the Company. What was agreed concerning the sale of arms to the Tsar is not known, but permission was granted for skilled Englishmen to be enlisted for service in Muscovy.

The Company, having gained a foothold, was now eager to expand its privileges and to obtain monopolies as well as the right to trade with Asiatic countries by land across Muscovy. Anthony Jenkinson, like Chancellor a gallant seaman, was appointed to carry out these negotiations, and when Nepea sailed from England in May 1557 he took passage in Jenkinson's ship. In Moscow Jenkinson quickly won the affectionate respect of Ivan, and he was to play an important part in the troubled relations which developed between Ivan and Queen Elizabeth.

Anthony Jenkinson was granted all that he asked of Ivan. He himself led the first venture to establish trade with Asia by land and, receiving every facility, he travelled as far as Bokhara. His reports on the potential markets there led the Company to send a series of expeditions into Persia, and Ivan gave these ventures extensive privileges, while at the same time extending the rights of the Company, until it enjoyed virtually a monopoly of European trade with Muscovy.

Indeed, during the thirteen years after Chancellor's discovery of the North Sea route, Ivan consistently received all Englishmen with favour and acted with great generosity towards the Company. But he obtained very little in return. He had engaged a number of skilled workmen, and he had probably been able to import small quantities of arms, but no firm evidence survives on this subject which was enveloped in secrecy. The few Russian merchants who made the voyage to England in the Company's ships, usually to trade on the Tsar's behalf, were exempted from paying aliens' dues, but enjoyed no other privileges. In fact, Elizabeth, who had come to the throne in 1558, actively supported her merchants in extracting every advantage and yielding as little as possible in return.

Ivan's demands, however, caused Elizabeth embarrassment and he did not appreciate that she had to act with caution. Protests against English trade with Muscovy, especially the engaging of English craftsmen and the alleged sale of arms, had already been made in London by the Kings of Poland, Sweden, and Denmark, and by the Emperor. In 1561 the Senates of Cologne and Hamburg even stopped shipments of arms to England, until the Queen gave assurances that such arms were for her own use and not for reshipment. Elizabeth gave her royal word that all munitions were intended solely for the defence of her realm. At this time she placed a ban on the export of arms, but protests continued to come from Denmark, Sweden, and Poland, and it is difficult to accept that they were entirely groundless.

This storm of opposition to England's trade with Muscovy showed how deep was the fear of the Tsar in the Baltic and East European countries. It also demonstrated the strength of the obstruction which Ivan experienced in his attempts to re-establish trade and contact with the rest of Europe. His western neighbours were especially concerned to withhold from Muscovy the new techniques and military equipment which the West had developed, while the Russians were still divided among themselves and beset by Tatars. Having no Baltic seaboard, Ivan had welcomed the English discovery of the White Sea route, for by this route he hoped to beat the blockade.

It was in a very real sense a blockade. The Baltic countries allowed trade with Muscovy only in goods which were of no military or industrial value, and they made strenuous efforts to prevent any skilled men taking service with the Tsar. When in 1539 Peter Friazin had fled to Livonia, he was asked whether he knew a German, named Alexander, in the Tsar's service. Friazin replied that he knew the man and added that Alexander had informed the boyars that he had a friend in Dorpat who was skilled in gunnery and was ready to serve the Tsar. The Livonians at once sought out this gunner and he disappeared.

In 1547 Ivan sent a Saxon, named Schlitte, to Germany to enlist as many learned and skilled men as possible for service in Muscovy. After obtaining the approval of the Emperor, Charles V, Schlitte managed to engage 123 men, whom he assembled in Lubbeck. The Livonians were alarmed. They immediately made strong representations to the Emperor, concerning the grave dangers which would come from allowing the Muscovites to learn modern skills and arts of war. Their protestations impressed Charles who promptly gave them authority to prevent the enlisted men taking passage to Muscovy. The party was dispersed and Schlitte himself was imprisoned. One of these men, a certain Master Hans, was more determined than the others. He tried to make his way to Moscow alone, and was seized and imprisoned. As soon as he was freed, he made a further attempt, but was captured near the frontier and this time executed.[8]

Ivan himself bitterly resented these efforts to keep his country weak and backward, and to deny her trade. To him it was intolerable that Muscovy should be deprived of direct access to the Baltic Sea, which he considered her right historically. He was all the more determined to recover a foothold on the shores of the Baltic, because it was essential to his ambitious policy of expanding Muscovite power. After the capture of Kazan he, therefore, concentrated his attention on Livonia, the weakest and most hostile of his western enemies.

Livonia formed part of the dominions of the feudal Order of Teutonic Knights, which had come into existence after the Third Crusade. These wealthy and warlike knights, who elected their own Grand Master, had been highly successful in their campaigns of conquest and crusading, and in 1237 they had absorbed the kindred Order of Knights of the Sword. Their drive eastwards against the Russians had, however, been halted in 1242 when Alexander Nevsky, Grand Prince of Novgorod, had routed them on the ice of Lake Peipus. Nevertheless by the mid-14th century the Teutonic Order ruled the Baltic coastlands from Esthonia and Livonia to East Pomerania. But the Order had begun to decline rapidly after its defeat by Jagiello, the great Lithuanian King, at Tannenberg in 1410. It lost its warlike crusading zeal, and the knights became corrupted by wealth and power.

Muscovy had been at peace with the Order for many years, mainly because she had been engaged elsewhere. Ivan's father, Vasily III, was too preoccupied with Lithuania and with the Tatars of Kazan and the Crimea to disturb his alliance with the Grand Master, although he had matters in dispute with the Order. During Ivan's minority the boyars had neglected the country's interests. But now Ivan was ready to settle outstanding issues, and to wrest from the Order direct access to the Baltic Sea.

In 1554 Livonian ambassadors had come to Moscow with proposals for the renewal of the peace which had expired. Alexei Adashev, appointed to negotiate with them, pointed out bluntly that Livonians had offended and obstructed Russian merchants and had perverted Russian churches to their own uses. But the main Muscovite complaint concerned the failure of Dorpat to pay tribute to the Tsar and this was to be the pretext for war. Dorpat, independently ruled by its bishop, had long paid tribute to the Grand Princes of Muscovy. An agreement, concluded in 1503 with the bishop, had confirmed the tribute but for fifty years there had been no payments. For these reasons, Adashev said, the Tsar had "laid his anger upon" the Grand Master, the bishop, and the whole country, and he therefore refused to renew the treaty of peace.[9]

The Livonian ambassadors at first denied knowledge of tribute. This drew from Adashev a stern rebuke, which reflected the Muscovite attitude.

> "How remarkable it is that you do not wish to know that your forefathers came to Livonia from beyond the sea, intruding into the hereditary lands of the Russian Grand Princes, as a result of which much blood flowed. Not wishing to see the further pouring of Christian blood, the forebears of the sovereign permitted the Germans to dwell in the lands they had taken on the conditions that they paid tribute to the Grand Princes, but the Germans have broken their promise; they have not paid tribute, and now must pay all arrears."[10]

The uncompromising Muscovite attitude cut short the prevarication of the Livonian ambassadors, who undertook that tribute would be paid in future and that all arrears would be settled within three years. They agreed, too, that all Orthodox Churches in Livonia, damaged by Protestant fanatics, should be returned to their Russian inhabitants who would in future worship in freedom. Russian merchants would enjoy free trade with Livonian and other merchants in all goods except coats of mail. Foreigners, engaged to serve the Tsar, would have free passage through Livonia, and all help would be denied the Grand Prince of Lithuania and King of Poland against Muscovy.

When the Tsar's representative arrived in Dorpat to ratify the agreement, however, he met with further prevarication. The Livonians now maintained that, before ratifying, they would have to secure the approval of their overlord, the Roman Emperor. But after hearing the angry expostulations of Ivan's ambassador they ratified the agreement. Three years later Livonian ambassadors again arrived in Moscow. No tribute had been paid and they had the effrontery now to request that the payment of tribute should be cancelled.

Ivan's patience was at an end. In November 1557 he appointed the Tatar, Shig Alei, to command an army of 40,000 men which, supported by detachments of tribesmen from the east, advanced to positions near the Livonian border. In December a new embassy from Livonia arrived in Moscow with proposals for the payment of the outstanding tribute, but as soon as Ivan learnt that they had come again empty handed, he angrily ordered them to depart.

In January 1558 Russian troops, moving from Pskov, invaded Livonia and laid waste the lands for a distance some 150 miles from the frontier. Shig Alei then withdrew and sent a courier to the Grand Master, calling on him to submit to the Tsar. The Master requested safe-conduct for his ambassadors and Ivan at once halted hostilities. But then came news that Livonians in Narva were continuing to attack the Russian stronghold of Ivangorod, despite the cease-fire. Angered by this deceit, Ivan ordered his army to capture the town, which fell on 11 May (1558).

Ivan was delighted with this conquest. The Muscovite Grand Princes had long coveted Narva. Standing on the left bank of the Narova river, some ten miles from its entry into the Gulf of Finland, it had been one of the most flourishing ports on the Baltic in the times of the Hanseatic League. It was still of great importance as a stronghold and port, and its capture marked a successful beginning to Ivan's campaign to secure access to the Baltic.

A Livonian mission was already in Moscow to negotiate an armistice when news of the capture of Narva reached the city. This made Ivan even more insistent that his terms should be accepted in full. The Grand Master and the bishop had to come personally to Moscow, bringing tribute from the whole country, swearing humble obedience and formally surrendering Narva and other towns to the

Tsar. The Livonian mission, then in Moscow, at once departed to report these demands to the Master and the war continued.

Ivan's army now swept across Livonia. Many towns surrendered without a shot fired. The Master, Furstenberg, an old man, escaped to Valk, where he laid down his office and in his place the knights elected Gottgard Kettler as the Grand Master of the Order. In July 1558 Prince Peter Shuisky, commanding a strong force, captured Dorpat. Twenty Livonian towns, large and small, were in Muscovite hands by the autumn. Ivan was confident now of his hold on Livonia, and he even granted estates to members of the Muscovite gentry in the newly conquered lands.

The Livonian campaign had been so successful that in September, after posting garrisons in all towns, the main army withdrew to Muscovy. Kettler, able and energetic, took advantage of this withdrawal to attack the Russian garrisons. But his bold action brought swift retribution. In January 1559 a Muscovite army, 130,000 strong, invaded Livonia and methodically laid waste the country, killing all who were captured, and not even little children were spared.

Kettler was now desperate for money and troops. He turned first to Erik, son of the Swedish King, Gustavus Vasa, offering regions of Livonia in return for active help against the Muscovites. Erik was eager to accept the offer, but the old King restrained him. He himself had in 1554 gone to war with Ivan over a frontier dispute, and had been compelled to sue for peace. He had counted then on the support of Poland and Livonia, but they had been too preoccupied with their own affairs, and reluctant to become involved in war with the Russians. Gustavus Vasa had signed a peace with Ivan and he had no intention of breaking it in the Livonian cause.

Reval appealed independently to the Danish King, Christian III, for help. Recalling that this region of Esthonia had once been a province of Denmark, the people of Reval asked him to accept them again as his subjects. But Christian III was, like Gustavus Vasa, an old man, unwilling to antagonize the Tsar. He offered, however, to intercede for Reval in Moscow, but he died after appointing his embassy which set out in the name of his successor, Frederick II.

In Moscow the Danes diffidently asked that the Tsar should restrain his troops from invading Livonia, which was Danish territory. Ivan did not angrily reject the Danish approach. He was anxious to move his troops to his southern frontiers to stand ready against an expected Crimean Tatar invasion. He replied, therefore, that out of respect for the Danish King he would concede an armistice to the Order from May to November, 1559. But he made this gesture, he stated, in the expectation that during this period the Grand Master himself or his envoys would come to Moscow to declare allegiance and sign a treaty of eternal peace.

Kettler had then approached Sigismund II Augustus, Grand Prince of Lithuania and King of Poland, and on 16 September 1559 an alliance was concluded between them. Sigismund Augustus as Lithuanian Grand Prince undertook the defence of the Order against the Tsar and in return the Master agreed to cede the southeastern region of Livonia with Dunaburg to Lithuania.

Sigismund Augustus was not a strong ruler or a dominating personality and at times he appeared to be wholly overawed by the Tsar. Pleasure-loving and lazy he earned the name "King-To-morrow" from his habit of hesitating and procrastinating, and it was a habit of which Ivan took advantage. But he was to show increasing vision and determination during the second half of his reign in pursuing the task of uniting Lithuania and Poland, and welding them into a single nation.

At this time Poland and Lithuania, although linked by a dynastic union since 1386, were still independent of each other. Lithuania was a vast country which under the rule of the Jagellon dynasty had come to embrace the whole of White Russia and much of the Ukraine, including Kiev and extensive regions to the east of the Dnieper. These eastern possessions of Lithuania, populated by Orthodox Russians and formerly under Russian rule, were regarded by Ivan and his predecessors as part of their patrimony. Poland, less than half the size of Lithuania, was separated from Russia by the great mass of her dynastic partner. But the mounting westward drive of the Russians since the mid-15th century made the Poles eager to consolidate the union between the two states. The Lithuanians were still holding back, fearing Polish domination.

Sigismund Augustus had observed with increasing uneasiness the growth of Muscovite power during the reign of Ivan and he realized that conflict was inevitable. But he was anxious to avoid war, at least until he had persuaded the Poles to fight side by side with the Lithuanians against the Muscovite enemy. Between 1549 and 1556 Sigismund Augustus, as Grand Prince of Lithuania, had made three approaches to Ivan to conclude a permanent peace. The most that Ivan would concede on each occasion was an armistice for a limited period. His chief reason for refusing a permanent peace was his determination to secure a foothold on the Baltic coast, and also to recover Kiev and other Russian towns in Lithuanian hands. His hostility was aggravated by the refusal of Sigismund Augustus to acknowledge his title of Tsar. Ivan nevertheless agreed to the first armistice, because at that time he was preoccupied with his campaigns against Kazan, the second armistice because he was at war with Sweden, and the third armistice because he was concentrating on bringing the Livonian war to an early conclusion.

Displaying the flexibility and patience which had marked the reign of Ivan III, his grandfather, Ivan now gave priority to the need for a Baltic seaboard and postponed the recovery of the Kiev region. At the same time he was considering the possibility of a temporary alliance with Lithuania against the Crimean Khan. The Dnieper lands, forming part of Lithuania, had a common frontier with the Crimean Khanate and suffered as much as Muscovy from the predatory raids of the Tatars. Ivan reasoned that such an alliance would ease his burden of defence against the Tatars and enable him to conclude the Livonian war more speedily.

In 1558 Ivan actually sent proposals for this alliance to Sigismund Augustus. Discussions between their ambassadors at once reached deadlock, because the Lithuanians insisted that the towns, especially Smolensk, captured by Ivan's predecessors should first be returned. But the real obstacle to the alliance, as the Lithuanian ambassadors openly admitted, was their fear of Muscovy, which had become a greater danger to them than the Crimean Khanate.

The Livonian war which was Ivan's chief motive for seeking peace with Lithuania was, in fact, to give rise to war between Muscovy and Lithuania–Poland. Sigismund Augustus recognized that he could no longer delay meeting the Muscovite threat. In his alliance with the Master, he had undertaken to defend the Order, and in January 1560 his ambassador arrived in Moscow to present a formal note, demanding that the Tsar cease all military operations against Livonia. Ivan's reply was blunt and held no hope of compromise. "By the all-powerful will of God, since the times of the great Russian ruler, Rurik," he stated, "the Livonian lands had rightfully formed part of his tsardom".[11] War with Lithuania had thus become inevitable.

Notes to Chapter XIV

[1] Hakluyt, I, p. 256.
[2] *Ibid.*, p. 241.
[3] *Ibid.*
[4] *Ibid.*, pp. 256–7.

[5] Hakluyt, I, pp. 256–7.

[6] G. Tolstoy, *The First Forty Years of Intercourse between England and Russia 1553–93* (St Petersburg, 1875), pp. 7–8.

[7] Hakluyt, II, p. 267.

[8] T. S. Willan, *The Early History of the Muscovy Company 1553–1603* (Manchester, 1956), pp. 11–14.

[9] Solovyev, Bk. III, Vol. VI, p. 499.

[10] *Ibid.*, p. 500.

[11] *Ibid.*, p. 519.

CHAPTER XV

THE TERROR BEGINS 1560-4

THE year 1560 was notable in Ivan's reign, for it marked the beginning of his unfettered personal rule. Historians have often described it as the year of his dramatic transformation in character, when the devout and dedicated Tsar suddenly became the cruel self-willed tyrant. But the transformation was apparent rather than real. He had always been given to extremes of conduct; it was something deep-rooted in his character and, indeed, in the character of his people. But in this year two events—his liberation from the tutelage of Sylvester and Adashev and, following soon afterwards, the death of his beloved Tsaritsa[1]—combined to give him freedom to rule without restraints of any kind. The two events also faced him with a terrible loneliness from which he suffered acutely and which aggravated his fears.

By this time Ivan's position and authority were already beyond challenge. In large measure this was due to his force of personality and intellect. He was tall and powerfully built, with an imperious Roman nose and small lively penetrating grey eyes. He could be benign and gracious or fearful to confront, and at all times he was Tsar, a natural leader and head of the nation.

Foreign visitors to the Kremlin were always strongly impressed. Anthony Jenkinson, reporting on his visit to Muscovy in 1557, wrote that Ivan

"doth exceed his predecessors in name . . . even so much by report he doth exceed them in stoutness of courage and valiantness, and a great deal more. . . . He is not only beloved of his nobles and commoners, but also had in great dread and fear throughout all his dominions, so that I think no prince in Christendom is more feared of his own than he is, nor better beloved."[2]

For seven years after taking power into his own hands, Ivan retained Sylvester, Adashev, and their supporters at court and in positions of authority. He found that they clung to power, resenting his independence. The conflict of wills must have come near to explosion on many occasions. Ivan exercised restraint because he needed their services, but he was now always guarded in his dealings with them and insisted on his own policies being pursued. Gradually, however, their presence became intolerable, and it was their hostility towards Tsaritsa Anastasia which apparently exhausted his patience.

In October 1559 Ivan and Anastasia were in Mozhaisk, some sixty-five miles southwest of Moscow, when a report reached him that the Livonians had broken the six-month armistice, agreed earlier in the year. The winter had set in earlier than usual and the cold was intense. Great drifts of snow blocked the roads and made travel almost impossible by horse or by sledge. But Ivan was so anxious about events in Livonia that with his wife he set out at once for Moscow. As a result of the hardships and cold, suffered as they forced their way through the snow, Anastasia fell ill.

Ivan himself wrote later, "How shall I recall the hard journey to the ruling city from Mozhaisk with our ailing Tsaritsa Anastasia?"[3] It remained with him as a bitter memory. He accused Sylvester and his associates of neglecting to provide medical help for Anastasia at this time. Further, he charged that by their "cunning scheming" they destroyed all the benefit that Ivan and his family might have derived from their pilgrimages and prayers for the salvation of their souls and for their bodily health.[4] All this they did out of hostility to the Tsar, but especially to the Tsaritsa.

The reasons for this hatred towards Anastasia are not known. Ivan wrote cryptically that "for the sake of one sole little word from her, she ranked as worthless in their eyes and they cast their anger upon her".[5] They had, of course, been opposed to her at the time of Ivan's illness, because she represented the family which would assume power, if the Tsarevich while still a minor succeeded to the throne. Since that time, however, their hatred seems to have become directed at Anastasia personally "for one sole little word". It was an extraordinary development. From all available sources Anastasia appears as a gentle, devout woman, not an intriguer or even a strong personality with marked likes and dislikes. Sylvester, like so many fanatic churchmen, was certainly capable of intense hatreds. But Adashev, who fed the poor and cared for ten lepers in his home, even washing them with his own hands, was widely loved as a good man and an ardent Christian; it is difficult to believe that he could have hated this simple woman or have deliberately harmed her by withholding medical care or in other ways.

From the time of this journey from Mozhaisk, Ivan turned his face from Sylvester and Adashev. But still he was restrained, neither dismissing nor venting his anger upon them. In the spring of 1560 Adashev was appointed to an army command in Livonia and later in the summer he was made governor of the newly captured town of Fellin.

At about the same time as Adashev's departure from Moscow, Sylvester withdrew to the Kirillov-Belozersky monastery, where he was shorn as a monk. [6] Towards Sylvester, even at this stage, Ivan remained respectful. But he was to explain his attitude later, when he wrote:

> " . . . the priest Sylvester, seeing his advisers set at nought, for this reason left of his own free will; but we, having given him our blessing, did not dismiss him, not because we were ashamed, but because we did not wish to judge him here on earth, but in the world to come, before the Lamb of God, for the evil he has done to me, while serving me and yet in his cunning manner overlooking me. There will I accept judgment for as much as I have suffered spiritually and bodily at his hands. For this reason I have allowed his son to remain unmolested even to the present day—only from our presence is he debarred." [7]

During these months Anastasia had been declining. She had never recovered from the winter journey to Moscow and in July (1560) she became gravely ill. Fear aggravated her condition, for in this month a terrible fire, breaking out again in the Arbat, threatened Moscow. Strong winds blew great clouds of smoke over the Kremlin and the flames reached towards the Tsar's palace. Anastasia was afraid that the fire would trap them, and Ivan had her carried to safety in the village of Kolomenskoe. He himself stayed behind to fight the fire, exposing himself to danger and by his example inspiring others to carry water and pull down buildings to prevent the flames spreading. Many lost their lives and many were maimed before the fire was finally extinguished.

Ivan hastened then to Kolomenskoe, but Anastasia was failing and the doctors could do nothing further for her. On 7 August she died. She had been a devoted, but anxious, wife and mother, who had borne six children during her thirteen years of marriage and had watched four of them, tightly swaddled as was Muscovite practice, die in infancy. [8] She had loved Ivan dearly, depending on him not only as a husband, but as a protector. She had always known that, if he died, she would be parted from her children who would be killed either by quick violence or by the lingering death of neglect and cold in some distant snow-swept monastery. Her tearful partings from Ivan were always especially distressing for this reason and such desperate fears must have pressed heavily upon her during Ivan's illness, when the overt hostility of Sylvester and others left her in no doubt about her fate, if he died. Indeed, fear must have been her constant companion as she lived her daily life in the *terem*, the women's quarters, or visited the dark Kremlin churches, where ancient ikons, blackened by the fumes of oil lamps, looked down from the walls like figures of doom.

Anastasia had also been loved by the simple people as the gentle devout Tsaritsa, and on her death the people of Moscow grieved. A great crowd escorted her coffin, as it was carried, the Tsar in tears walking behind it, to the Novodevichy monastery.

Ivan and his court went into deep mourning, but it was of short duration. Only eight days after her death, the Metropolitan, church hierarchy, and the boyars waited upon him and formally proposed that he should take another wife. The succession was always of concern to the whole nation in these decades when life was brutish and short and death was impatient. Ivan, too, was anxious to ensure the succession, for none could know if his two sons, Tsarevichi Ivan, aged six, and Feodor, born three years later, in 1557, would survive him. On 18 August (1560), therefore, he announced that he would marry the sister of Sigismund Augustus. At the same time he threw aside mourning. The Kremlin began to ring with the noise of banquets and entertainments, and no one was sober. Some of the older boyars, aghast at this drunken revelry, kept apart, only to find themselves laughed at by the young courtiers and humiliated by such pranks as having wine poured over their heads.

In every age men have tended to regard long grief as proof of love, while brevity of sorrow could only mean heartlessness or indifference. But Ivan's sudden abandon to merriment and drinking did not indicate indifference or heartlessness. He had not forgotten Anastasia. Seventeen years later in a letter he was bewailing his separation "from my young one"; [9] it was the cry of a man recalling a time when he had enjoyed the quiet companionship of a wife whom he loved and when he had been at peace with himself. He sent rich donations to the monasteries of Mount Athos so that the monks would pray for the repose of her soul. He was never to forget this one person who he knew had loved him and been incapable of betraying him.

In his revels after the death of his Tsaritsa, Ivan drew about him a new group of favourites. Foremost among them were Boyar Alexei

Basmanov and his son, Feodor, as well as Prince Afanasy Vyazemsky, Vasily Gryaznoi, and Malyuta Skuratov-Belsky. They were not men of the calibre of Sylvester and Adashev, and were rather drinking companions. According to Prince Andrei Kurbsky, they poisoned the mind of Ivan against the supporters of Sylvester and Adashev, and were responsible for prompting the first executions of the terror. But it is more probable that these victims brought the fury of Ivan upon their own heads.[10]

After the departure of Sylvester and Adashev, Ivan had shown clemency to their supporters. He merely ordered them to refrain from seeing or communicating with their former leaders and required them to swear a fresh oath of loyalty to him as Tsar. His leniency was promptly shown to have been misguided. In Ivan's words:

> "they transgressed the oath on the Cross; they not only did not keep away from those traitors, but they began to help them still more and to scheme in all manner of ways in order to return them to their former dignity and to plot all the more fiercely against us; and since their malice showed itself to be unquenchable and their will inflexible—for this reason the guilty ones received punishments according to their guilt".[11]

Ivan struck without mercy. The widow, Maria Magdalina, accused of communicating with Adashev and practising witchcraft, was executed with her five sons. Daniel Adashev and his twelve-year-old son, also his father-in-law Turov, the three brothers Satiny, and Ivan Shishkin with his wife and children were all found guilty of liaison with Adashev and executed.[12]

Others, like Prince Andrei Kurbsky, were involved less deeply and punished mildly. It was probably the result of these efforts of friends and followers to maintain contact that Adashev was moved further away to Dorpat, where he died of fever.[13] Sylvester was exiled to the Solovetsky monastery on the barren islands in the White Sea, where he died.

From the time of these executions Ivan became more ruthless in dealing with his boyars and any who affronted or opposed him. Criticism infuriated him and, always quick to anger, he was now often inflamed with heavy drinking, and there was no one to calm or restrain him. One evening, when he was making merry with his companions who were wearing masks, stamping and dancing in Russian fashion, Prince Mikhail Repnin reproached him angrily with behaviour unbecoming to a Christian Tsar. The Orthodox Church condemned all forms of dancing, merriment, and especially the wearing of masks, as Ivan well knew. In reply, however, Ivan put a mask over Repnin's head, saying, "Come, make merry and join with us". Repnin tore off the mask, stamped on it in a fury, and shouted, "It's not for me, a boyar, to play the fool and demean myself!" Ivan, too, lost his temper and sent him from the palace. Several days later, as he stood by the ikonostasis in the cathedral during the intoning of the gospel, Repnin was savagely murdered on the Tsar's orders.[14] On the same day Prince Yuri Kashin was also cut down as he entered church, but the reason is not known.

The young Prince Dmitri Obolensky-Ovchinin, a nephew of the favourite of Elena, Ivan's mother, lost his life, because in the course of a quarrel with young Feodor Basmanov, he shouted, "I and my forebears have always served the sovereign usefully, but you serve by vile sodomy!"[15] Prince Dmitri Kurlyatev, who had been close to both Sylvester and Adashev, was exiled with his wife and daughters to a distant monastery where all were forced to take vows and, according to Kurbsky, they were later strangled. But Ivan was not always so merciless in his punishments. Prince Mikhail Vorotynsky, exiled with his family to Beloozero, certainly fared better. His guards were writing at the end of 1564 that during the previous year the prince had not received the fresh sturgeon, raisins, plums, and figs, to which he was entitled. Vorotynsky himself petitioned because he had not had his allowance and a long list of articles, including 200 lemons, all of which were part of his regular rations in exile.

Moreover, Ivan could be unexpectedly mild and forgiving, even towards individual boyars whose crime was treason. Suspecting Prince Ivan Belsky of planning flight to Lithuania, Ivan ordered him to swear on the Cross that he would not depart from the realm or from his principality. Further, twenty-nine men were required to act as sureties for him and 120 men to be sureties for them. Notwithstanding these extraordinary precautions, Belsky later in the same year pleaded guilty to treason in that he had sent messages to Sigismund Augustus, asking for a safe conduct to Lithuania. Ivan nevertheless pardoned him. Others enjoyed similar clemency from their unpredictable Tsar.

Meanwhile the war in Livonia continued. Ivan had rejected the formal demand, made by Sigismund Augustus in January 1560, to cease all military operations against the Order. Still deterred by Muscovite power, and prevented by a desperate financial crisis in Lithuania from enlisting the mercenary troops on whom he largely depended, Sigismund Augustus hesitated to take the offensive. The Grand Master, Kettler, offered some resistance, but it was of no avail against the Muscovite army, which now occupied new areas of Livonia, and in August (1560) Prince Kurbsky captured the important stronghold of Fellin.

Under this pressure the Order was now disintegrating. The large island of Oesel offered allegiance to Frederick II and became a Danish possession. In June 1561 the people of Reval swore allegiance to the King of Sweden, Erik, the son and successor of Gustavus Vasa.

The Livonian knights and the merchants pressed for union with Lithuania–Poland. Kettler entered into negotiations with Nikolai Radziwill the Black, Voevoda of Vilno, and in November 1561 the agreement was concluded. Livonia, the rights of her citizens guaranteed, became formally part of Lithuania–Poland. Kettler himself received with the hereditary title of duke the Duchy of Courland which was created from the southwestern portion of Livonia. The Order of Teutonic Knights had ceased to exist, and three powers—Muscovy, Sweden, and Lithuania–Poland—prepared for war to decide on the possession of the Livonian lands and, above all else, of the Baltic ports.

Erik XVI, King of Sweden, having occupied Reval, at once proposed peace with the Tsar, for he knew that Lithuania–Poland would seek to expel the Swedes from Livonia. For his part Ivan was unwilling to have two active enemies opposing him at the same time. Without raising the issue of Reval, which he coveted, he received the Swedish ambassadors and in due course a peace for seven years was signed between Muscovy and Sweden.[16]

Ivan had resolved at this time to settle his dispute with Lithuania by marrying one of the King's sisters. Such dynastic marriages were normal instruments of policy in the 16th century, and Ivan made the proposal with two purposes in mind. He hoped, first, that it would gain him a distinct advantage when he came to negotiate a final peace concerning his conquests in Livonia. His second purpose was more far-reaching. Sigismund Augustus, the last of the famed Jagellon dynasty, was childless, and Ivan saw marriage with his sister as giving him title to the throne of Lithuania–Poland on the King's death, which would facilitate his claims not only to Livonia but also to White Russia and the Ukraine.

So confident was Ivan that Sigismund in his anxiety for peace with Muscovy would welcome such a marriage that he carefully briefed his ambassador, Feodor Sukin, on the choice to be made between

Anna and Catherine, the King's two sisters. Sukin was to make full enquiries and, if possible, see them both with his own eyes, choosing the sister who was more beautiful, healthy, and good-natured. In Moscow Ivan discussed the bride's conversion to Orthodoxy and made provision for her reception and accommodation, pending her Orthodox baptism and then her marriage.

Ivan's expectations were, however, to be disappointed. Sigismund Augustus was prepared to consider such a marriage only after the conclusion of a peace treaty on his terms. Moreover, when the Lithuanian ambassador, Shimkovich, arrived in Moscow, he insisted that the representatives of both sides should meet at the frontier to negotiate and that in the meantime all military operations should be suspended. The proposal that negotiations should take place anywhere but in Moscow raised one of those breaks with tradition which to the Muscovites were insuperable obstacles, involving the prestige and honour of the dynasty. The ambassador was informed that such meetings had always and could only take place in the Tsar's capital. He withdrew and the proposals for marriage and for peace lapsed.

Hetman Radziwill now marched against the Russians in Livonia. In September 1561, after a five-week siege, he took the small town of Tarvast. But the Russians defeated the Lithuanian army near Pernau and then razed Tarvast to the ground. Skirmishing took place during 1562, but Sigismund Augustus without raising the marriage proposal tried desperately to revive negotiations for peace. He lacked an army capable of holding the Russians and he had so far been unable to win the active support of the Poles and even of many of his Lithuanian subjects against the Tsar. He was playing for time. But Ivan was not deceived. He roundly accused Sigismund Augustus of not wanting peace and of seeking secretly to persuade the Crimean Khan to invade Muscovy.

At the beginning of 1563 Ivan himself led a strong army to the Lithuanian border. His objective was Polotsk, the town on the western Dvina which was important not only as a frontier stronghold, but also for trade directed through Riga. After a siege of two weeks Polotsk surrendered. Ivan was jubilant. Nothing was closer to his heart than this struggle for access to the Baltic, and Polotsk, completing his control over the Dvina waterway, gave it to him. Before returning to Moscow he appointed three commanders—Peter I. Shuisky, Vasily, and Peter S. Serebryanny-Obolensky—in command of the town with detailed instructions to reinforce its defences.

The fall of Polotsk alarmed Sigismund Augustus, for he had thought it impregnable. Moreover, the Muscovites were now advancing towards Vilno. The Lithuanians at once showed greater eagerness to renew negotiations, but Ivan was in no haste. He was filled with overweening confidence that, when he chose, he could continue his victorious advance into Lithuania. At this stage, however, because he wanted to return to Moscow and to attend to Crimean affairs, he granted Sigismund Augustus a six-month armistice.

On 26 February (1563) Ivan departed from Polotsk. He settled his army in quarters around Velikie Luki and then hastened to Moscow. His journey became a triumphal progress, like the journey he had made from Kazan over ten years ago. People gathered along the roads to set eyes on their little father, who continued to lay low their enemies. It seemed all the more like a repetition of the Kazan journey when, on 31 March, a boyar rode furiously to meet him with the news that the Tsaritsa had given birth to a son, named Vasily.

In 1561, realizing that Sigismund Augustus did not welcome the proposal of marriage and that he would only agree on unacceptable terms, Ivan had given up the idea of marriage with his sister. He had done so reluctantly and with a feeling of humiliation which had added an element of venom to his campaign for Polotsk. Promptly, however, he had started a new search for a bride, this time among the Asiatic rulers. He heard that Temgruk, a Circassian leader, had a daughter of remarkable beauty. He had her brought to Moscow and became infatuated on sight. The Metropolitan himself prepared her for baptism and under the name of Maria she was married to Ivan on 31 August 1561. Now she had gladdened his heart with the birth of Vasily. But he survived for only five weeks, and the marriage itself did not endure. Maria was an Asiatic beauty, wild and cruel in spirit and remote from the devout and dutiful Anastasia, whose memory Ivan cherished. Contemporaries wrote that she encouraged him in his cruel and dissolute tastes. But apparently she appealed only to the sensualist in him and, once he had reached satiety, he lost interest in her.[17]

At the time of his second marriage Ivan was eager to reach some understanding with the Crimean Khan. While at war with Lithuania he needed to guard his southern frontier against Tatar attacks. The letter which he wrote to Devlet Girei was a clever blend of threat and flattery. In it he recalled the profitable alliance between Ivan III and Mengli Girei, and proclaimed the might of Muscovy which he had demonstrated in his conquests of Kazan, Astrakhan, and much of Livonia. Privately his ambassador, Afanasy Nagoi, informed the Khan that Adashev and others had been disposed of, because they were opposed to the Tsar's friendship with the Khan.[18]

This approach was timely. The Khan was weary of the pressure of Sultan Suleiman upon him, when all he wanted was independence and the freedom to raid and plunder. The Khan therefore revealed to Nagoi the Sultan's great design. This was nothing less than the joining of the Don and Volga rivers by a canal, the establishing of fortresses on the Volga at Tsaritsyn and Perevolok, and a third near the Caspian Sea. From these bases the Turks, supported by all the Muslims of the steppelands, would recapture Kazan and Astrakhan, and overrun Muscovy. But the plan made small appeal to the Khan. He saw his horde bearing the brunt of this great campaign and coming under even closer Turkish control. For the present, however, the Sultan's project was merely under discussion and the Khan assured the Tsar that he could count on his friendship. From the Nogai Tatars, too, Ivan received assurances of their continued alliance.

Towards the end of 1563 two deaths moved Ivan deeply. The first was his brother, Yuri, the companion of his childhood miseries. Yuri was simple, either congenitally or, more probably, as a result of the terrors experienced during his tender years. Always in Ivan's absence he held office as Governor of Moscow, but it was merely a nominal appointment, for Yuri was too backward to exercise any authority. Ivan had always shown a certain protective affection towards him and now, on his death, he sent donations to Mount Athos for prayers to be said for the repose of his soul.

Towards Yuri's widow, Juliana, Ivan behaved with strange perversity. She was, like Anastasia, devout and humble, much loved by the people and held as an ideal of Muscovite womanhood. She had declared on the death of her husband that she would depart from the world and be shorn as a nun. Fulfilling her vow she made the journey from the Kremlin to the Novodevichy nunnery on foot, and was followed by the Tsar, Tsaritsa, Prince Vladimir Andreevich, and a great crowd of people. But on arriving at the nunnery Ivan in a sudden outburst of anger ordered that the bare cell, where she hoped to end her days in prayer, should be crowded with furniture and every luxury of the court, and he appointed a suite to attend on her. It was as though he was determined to deny her the peace of prayer and meditation for which a part of him yearned and could never achieve.

On the last day of 1563 Metropolitan Makary, venerable with age, died. He had held the high office of Metropolitan for twenty-one years. As Archbishop of Novgorod before his elevation to supreme office he had been a dominating figure, but in Moscow he had effaced himself. For a time he appeared to have been over-shadowed by the simple priest, Sylvester. But he emerged from his studious and devotional way of life when the interests of the church were challenged. At the *Stoglavny* assembly he had resisted the efforts of the Trans-Volga Hermit group, supported by the Tsar himself, to deprive the church of its property. He had then boldly defended the church and had also carried out important reforms, most of which were embodied in the *Stoglav* or Hundred Chapters.

At other times of crisis, however, he apparently absented himself. When Ivan was ill and disputes raged over the succession to the throne, the Metropolitan's voice might have been expected to decide the issue, but Makary was not present or, if he was, he took no part in the dissension. At the same time he did not incur Ivan's anger or mistrust. Indeed, it seems that Makary, a practical churchman and reformer, and a scholar, devoted his energies to the affairs of the church and was content to leave affairs of state and direct dealings with the Tsar so far as possible to Sylvester. Many considered him indecisive and cowardly, especially because he failed to censure the Tsar's sinful activities or to wield the great influence of his office on many occasions. But, although he stood aloof from all that happened at court, some events undoubtedly distressed him. In his testament, written a few days before his death, he wrote that, overwhelmed by sorrows, he decided several times to lay down his office and retire to a distant monastery. But each time the Tsar and the church hierarchy prevailed on him to remain.[19]

Makary's most memorable work was the compiling of the lives of the Russian saints in the *Mineya Chetya* and the continued recording of the Russian rulers in the *Stepennaya Kniga* which had begun in the 9th century with Rurik. This was the work of a scholar and historian, aware of the birth of the new nation and anxious to record it for coming generations, and it was the work which Makary loved, rather than the stresses and conflicts of office.

Makary was closely associated with the introduction of printing into Russia. The invention of printing had been known to the Russians for many years and the Grand Princes had been keenly aware of its importance. Ivan III had paid an allowance to the renowned Lubeck printer, Bartolomeo, with what return is not known. In 1547 Tsar Ivan gave orders for printers to be engaged in Germany to train his own subjects in Moscow. In 1561 he erected a printing house under the direction of two Russian masters, Ivan Feodorov, a church deacon, and Peter Mstislavets, who published two books from the Bible and also a Book of the Hours.

Ivan's intention was to print the Gospels in full, using the earliest sources to correct corruptions which had come in the course of decades of copying by hand. In this project he had the eager support of Makary, who indeed, may have originated it. But among the people and the simple priests it raised furious objections. The Gospels, as they knew them, were sacred and any change in the text, whether a corruption or not, was sacrilege. The two printers suffered popular persecution and were apparently dependent on the protection of Makary. After his death they were forced to flee to Lithuania. The printing press was then transferred to Alexandrovsk suburb, where under the Tsar's protection certain religious books were produced.[20]

Early in 1564 all the bishops came to Moscow and elected as Metropolitan a monk of the Chudov monastery, named Afansy, who had formerly been an archpriest of the Blagoveshchensky Cathedral and the Tsar's confessor. This was undoubtedly Ivan's choice for the office and the assembly of churchmen obediently observed his wishes in electing him to be the new Metropolitan.

Notes to Chapter XV

[1] Kurbsky distorts these events, alleging that it was after the death of Anastasia that Sylvester and Adashev were expelled because of accusations that they had poisoned her. It is clear, however, that both men departed from court, and were not expelled, and that their departure preceded her death. Moreover, Ivan in listing in his letter to Kurbsky the crimes of Sylvester and Adashev makes no mention of the poisoning of his Tsaritsa. Had there been any suspicion of this at the time, Ivan would have thundered his condemnation and would hardly have allowed either man to live undisturbed in exile from Moscow. See pages 139–40 concerning the death of Anastasia and the hostility of Sylvester, Adashev and their party towards her. Kurbsky in his *History* alleged that the Tsar's new favourites made him believe that Sylvester and Adashev had bewitched the Tsaritsa. Kurbsky not only distorted facts, but was incapable of being consistent. In 1572 Ivan told the Lithuanian ambassador that the boyars were responsible for the death of Anastasia. J. L. I. Fennell, *Correspondence*, pp. 85–93. N. Ustryalov ed., *Statements of Prince Kurbsky* (St Petersburg, 1833), pp. 78–9, 391.

[2] Hakluyt, II, pp. 429–30.

[3] Fennell, *op. cit.*, p. 97.

[4] *Ibid.*, p. 98.

[5] Solovyev, Bk. III, Vol. VI, p. 539; Fennell, *op. cit.*, pp. 98–9.

[6] Sylvester as a simple priest belonged to the White Clergy who married before being ordained and usually cared for the people of their parish. Only members of the Black Clergy, who were celibate, could take monastic vows.

[7] Fennell, *op. cit.*, p. 99.

[8] Tsaritsa Anastasia's children were Anna (1549–50), Maria (1551–4), Dmitri (1552–3), Ivan (1554–81), Evdokia (1556–8), Feodor (1557–98).

[9] Fennell, *op. cit.*, pp. 190–1.

[10] Solovyev, *op. cit.*, pp. 539–42.

[11] Fennell, *op. cit.*, p. 101.

[12] Solovyev points out that these executions are mentioned only by Kurbsky and must therefore be accepted with some reservation. Solovyev, *op. cit.*, p. 540.

[13] Kurbsky states that Adashev was held in prison and died of privations. This, too, must be treated with reservation. Fennell, *op. cit.*, p. 98.

[14] In his letter to Kurbsky Ivan wrote, "And in the churches these things did not take place as you lyingly assert." Solovyev, *op. cit.*, p. 546; Fennell, *op. cit.*, pp. 101–3.

[15] The words which Obolensky-Ovchinin is alleged to have spoken in this quarrel may, of course, be an invention by Kurbsky. References to Ivan's drinking and debauchery are numerous, but details are lacking. He was notorious for his love of women. Elizabeth I of England in conversation with Ivan's ambassador referred euphemistically to the Tsar as a "well-known admirer and appreciator of beauty". Solovyev, *op. cit.*, p. 541; N. Casimir, "Historical Notes Relating to Czar John the Terrible of Russia and Queen Elizabeth of England" in *Reliquary*, XVI, 1876–7.

[16] Solovyev, *op. cit.*, pp. 575–6.

[17] Karamzin, Bk. II, Vol. IX, col. 26.

[18] *Ibid.*, col. 24.

[19] *Ibid.*, col. 27.

[20] The work of printing a corrected version of the Old and New Testaments was carried out in Ostrog by the Volhynian Prince, Konstantine, who had managed to secure the services of Ivan Feodorov. This Russian Bible, corrected from a Greek Bible sent by the Patriarch of Constantinople, was published in 1581. Ivan had a considerable private library, but information about its contents is lacking. He also made use of the Josef Volokolamsk monastery library, which contained 1,150 volumes, a large collection for these times. S. V. Bakhrushin and others, *History of Moscow* (Moscow, 1952), I, pp. 246–7; Karamzin, *op. cit.*, cols. 28–9.

CHAPTER XVI

THE DEFECTION OF KURBSKY 1564

PRINCE ANDREI KURBSKY belonged to an old princely family, descended directly from Vladimir Monomakh, and thus boasting a lineage as illustrious as that of the Tsar. In the 14th century one of Kurbsky's forebears had made himself grand prince of Yaroslavl. His descendants were numerous, however, and, since they observed no rule of primogeniture, the principality had been split into some forty petty estates. In the following century the Grand Princes of Muscovy had absorbed the whole principality, but apparently the Kurbsky family accepted this change without question and served faithfully. Not even during Ivan's minority, when most princely families were involved in disreputable and treacherous activities, did the Kurbskys besmirch their name. They were a family of unimpeachable loyalty.

Prince Andrei, the eldest of three sons, was outstanding in intelligence and ability. He was energetic and brave and, although still only in his early thirties, some two or three years older than Ivan, he had already had a brilliant career. He had distinguished himself in command of troops at the capture of Kazan, in the Livonian war, and elsewhere. When six months after the Kazan campaign, the Tatars rebelled and the Votyak and Cheremis tribesmen attacked Russian garrisons, Ivan entrusted to Kurbsky and two others the task of restoring order. During the winter of 1553-4 Kurbsky fought twenty major engagements and finally enforced obedience among these new subjects of the Tsar. Ivan was impressed and grateful, and in 1556 elevated him to the rank of boyar.

Kurbsky was, however, more than a brave and spirited military commander. By the standards of the time he was highly educated and advanced far beyond his fellow princes and boyars in the breadth of his outlook. He took a keen interest in books and learning, and delighted in studying the latest ideas and developments in the west. His high intelligence and vitality, and his dashing, at times tempestuous, nature made him seem on first impression one of the most attractive men at court.

Towards the end of 1559 Ivan summoned Kurbsky and said to him, "I am compelled either to take the field myself against the Livonians, or to send you, my favourite: go and serve me truly!"[1] Kurbsky was then in high favour, but his position was soon to be overcast by the departure of Sylvester and Adashev and the execution of many of their supporters. Kurbsky himself had been one of their closest colleagues and indeed at this time he suffered some punishment, presumably for continuing in contact with Adashev in Fellin. But he was not in disgrace. He was still one of the Tsar's most trusted and favoured officers, and he continued to hold an important command near the Livonian frontier.

For all his intelligence, learning, and ability, however, Kurbsky was a man incapable of loyalties, or even concern, for anyone or anything apart from himself. He was uneasy after the execution of so many of those who had been close to Adashev and himself, and he feared that he might meet the same fate. Towards Ivan he felt a deep resentment which may have been sown much earlier and been nurtured secretly, or which may have come to birth as Ivan began to rule alone. This resentment was soon to turn into a black vindictive hatred.

Early in 1564 Kurbsky, commanding an army 15,000 strong, was defeated by a force of 4,000 Poles near the town of Nevel, some sixty-five miles north of Vitebsk. Kurbsky himself was wounded in the fighting, but more than his wounds he was troubled by fears of Ivan's anger on learning of such an ignominious defeat. It was apparently at this point that he decided to flee to Lithuania.

King Sigismund Augustus and his counsellors were well aware of Kurbsky's weak loyalties and made every effort to win him over. His renown as a general had spread beyond Muscovy, and his defection would be a moral and political victory over the Tsar as well as a distinct military gain. The King himself wrote a letter to him and another letter, signed by Nikolai Radziwill the Black, the Lithuanian Hetman, by Volovich, the vice-chancellor, and a group of senators, was delivered at the same time to him in Dorpat before his flight. Both letters invited him to transfer his allegiance to Lithuania, where he would be warmly welcomed. Further messages from the King and from Radziwill promised him the royal favour as well as riches and estates appropriate to his dignity.

Kurbsky, his decision made, had a moving farewell meeting with his wife and nine-year-old son in Dorpat. He asked his wife whether she would rather have him dead before her, or part with him alive forever. Dutifully she replied that his life was more important than her happiness. In tears they took leave of each other and Kurbsky blessed his son.[2] Whether this account of his parting with his family is true or not, the fact is that he did not hesitate to abandon his wife and son to execution or, at very least, distant exile, while he himself fled to safety and riches in Lithuania. He evidently made no attempt to provide for their flight or their safety, although from Dorpat this could not have been impossible to arrange.[3]

By night on the last day of April 1564, Kurbsky crept from Dorpat and found the two horses, saddled and hidden by a trusted servant beyond the walls of the town. Riding towards the Lithuanian frontier he met couriers who handed him a safe-conduct from the King and a further letter from Lithuanian senators, assuring him that he could count on the promises of honourable treatment. He rode on to the town of Wolmar, occupied by the Lithuanians in Livonia, where he received a royal welcome.

Once safely installed in the Lithuanian camp, Kurbsky threw his energies into a remorseless campaign against his former master. His hatred of Ivan had now become a furious obsession. He harassed the Lithuanians with plans for attacking Muscovy and, when they showed caution, he castigated them with failing to wage war boldly. He was tireless in urging Sigismund Augustus to spur the Crimean Khan by means of rich gifts to invade Muscovy. His efforts were successful, for Devlet Girei led 60,000 of his Tatars in a massive raid on the Ryazan region at a time when Ivan still believed the Khan to be his ally.

Ivan was, in fact, in Suzdal, expecting daily to receive the treaty of alliance, signed by Devlet Girei, when news of the Tatar raid reached him. He had no troops in Ryazan, but two of his new favourites, Boyar Alexei Basmanov and his son, were at the time on their estates in the region. They rallied the local inhabitants, who fought off the invaders. Ivan had, on learning of the invasion, left his Tsaritsa and his son in Alexandrovsk and had set out from Moscow with troops. But he had travelled only a short distance when a message reached him from Basmanov that the Tatars were in full flight. Kurbsky himself commanded a motley army of some 70,000 troops against the Russian garrison in Polotsk at this time, but his campaign proved an utter failure.

In his desperate efforts to attack, damage, and revile the Tsar, Kurbsky had no thought for Muscovy or his former countrymen. Tatar hordes and Western enemies could devastate the land, burn

Moscow and other cities, and carry off the people: nothing mattered to him so long as it contributed to the denigration and defeat of the Tsar.

Far more than all his plotting and military ventures, however, Kurbsky's writings were effective in furthering his purposes. He applied his considerable literary ability and his great skill as a propagandist with such effect that, long after all the protagonists were dead, Ivan's reputation remained blackened by his calumnies.

Karamzin, whose history has influenced generations of historians in their interpretation of Ivan and Kurbsky, has related the story of the delivery of Kurbsky's first letter. His servant, Vaska Shibanov, handed it to the Tsar himself, as he stood on the Red Staircase, the grand entrance to the palace, saying that it was "from my master, your exiled subject, Prince Andrei Mikhailovich". Angrily the Tsar stabbed at his foot, transfixing it to the ground with the iron-tipped staff which he always carried. He then leant on the staff and ordered Shibanov to read the letter aloud to him. Without flinching and with the blood pouring from his foot, Shibanov read the letter.[4] This story, typical of so many grimly colourful stories about Ivan, was almost certainly untrue.[5] The letter was probably made public rather than delivered personally, for its main purpose was to revile Ivan.

Kurbsky wrote this first letter from Wolmar soon after his flight. He was to write several other letters as well as his damaging *History of the Great Muscovite Prince*.[6] But the main importance of his letters and *History* now, four centuries after they were written, is that they prompted two lengthy replies from Ivan, which make this correspondence one of the most illuminating documents in Russian history.

Both men were ardent controversialists. Ivan was more learned and expressed himself more powerfully than his adversary. He had the further advantage of writing from sincere conviction, not from malevolence which led Kurbsky to lie and distort facts. Nevertheless, Kurbsky provided some insight into the discontent and opposition of the boyars, while Ivan's long letters, conveying vividly the gale-force of his anger, also revealed him as a monarch with a deep sense of responsibility and mission.

Kurbsky, in fact, had two purposes in writing his letters; he wanted to defame Ivan and at the same time to justify himself, for his defection had made a stir in Muscovy and in Eastern Europe. He referred to the "brilliant victories" that he had won for the

Tsar's glory, to his labours and his wounds "inflicted by barbarian hands in various battles", but "to you, O Tsar, was all this as naught. . . ." [7] And he exclaimed:

> "What evil and persecutions have I not suffered from you! . . . But I cannot now recount the various misfortunes at your hands which have beset me owing to their multitude . . . of everything have I been deprived; I have been driven from the land of God without guilt, hounded by you!" [8]

His charges and complaints seemed to ring with truth, and all in Lithuania were ready to believe them. But they were in fact exaggerated and almost groundless. Ivan in one of the quieter passages of his reply wrote:

> "Unjust evils and persecution you have not received from me; and ills and misfortunes we have not brought upon you; it was for your crime, for you were in agreement with our traitors. Falsehood and treacheries which you have not committed we have not imputed to you." [9]

The letters indeed reveal that Kurbsky was ready to go to any lengths in distorting facts to serve his ends. Ivan, although eager to explain and justify himself, did not disclaim what he had done, but admitted and defended or excused his actions.

Kurbsky's malevolence sprang from personal hatred and from his opposition to Ivan's determination to rule absolutely and alone. The Grand Princes of Muscovy had always, he maintained, ruled with the advice and help of their boyars, and this had been the strength of Muscovy. The departure from this tradition had, he alleged, begun with the baleful influence of the Greek Princess, Sofia, wife of Ivan III and grandmother of Ivan, and had been continued by Ivan's mother, the foreigner, Elena Glinskaya. In his *History* he dwelt on the beneficent influence of the Boyar Council in the days when it had important advisory powers and shared in the rule of the country. But Kurbsky did not limit this function of advising and assisting to his own boyar class. He also extended it to include the people, and he evidently had in mind the Assembly of the Land (Zemsky Sobor), which had first been summoned in 1550.

Kurbsky thus declared himself in favour of the new state of Muscovy, united under the Tsar, and did not seek to revive the old independent principalities. His sole political objective was to restore the procedure whereby the Tsar would rule not alone but with the advice and help of his boyars and people.[10]

In spite of his political ideas, as stated in his letters and his *History*,

however, Kurbsky belonged emotionally to the time when Muscovy
was split into independent principalities. He was at heart the ruler
of a principality, his loyalty and interests concentrated in his petty
domain. The union of Muscovy under the strong rule of the Grand
Prince and the birth of the nation meant to him only the loss of his
independence; it had not led him to acknowledge new loyalties. He
had served only for personal honour and gain and, when these were
threatened, he fled.

Such was the mentality of many of the boyars and princes whom
Ivan mistrusted and feared. Neither as individuals nor as a class did
they seek to overturn the existing regime. They had demonstrated
this during the ten years of Ivan's minority when, ruling unchecked,
they might have effected extensive changes. But they had changed
nothing, and had merely by their incessant quarrelling reduced the
government of the country to chaos. To Ivan, however, it was
evident that the boyars were plotting to assassinate him and destroy
the nation. Kurbsky's treason and his frantic efforts to attack him
and reduce Muscovy to ruins seemed to provide dramatic proof of his
gravest suspicions.

Ivan's immediate fury was, however, due more to Kurbsky's gross
temerity in writing publicly and charging the Tsar with all manner of
crimes and cruelties, and with failing in his responsibilities.

This was more than Ivan could endure. Normally he would have
dismissed with contempt such a letter, written by a traitor. But this
letter read like a summons to other boyars to follow his example, and
its attempt to denigrate the Tsar and to show disaffection could not
be ignored.

In a fury Ivan replied and his letter, in one edition taking up
eighty-six pages, compared with just over four pages of Kurbsky's
first letter, is a magnificent document.[11] Composed in the white heat
of anger, Ivan often breaks from one argument to pursue another.
His letter is not easy to read, but it abounds in illuminating phrases
and sentences. It reveals his intimate knowledge not only of the
history of his own people, but of ancient Greece and Rome, of
Byzantium and Persia, and to him history was not the chronicle of
long-dead events, but the vital living record of rulers and peoples
who had faced trials such as he himself was facing. But the dominant
influence in his letters was the Bible. He had read and studied it so
intensively that it had dyed his mind and become a part of his
thinking. Indeed the stark minatory style of many passages in his
letters makes them resound like a book from the old testament.

Ivan opened his letter with a statement of his ancestry from which the autocracy "has come down even to us, the humble sceptre-bearer of the Russian Tsardom". He then asserted the nature and source of his power and condemned Kurbsky for committing not merely treason, but apostasy.

"By the grace of God and with the blessing of our forefathers and fathers [he wrote], as we were born to rule, so have we grown up and ascended the throne by the bidding of God. . . . This is our Christian and humble answer to him who was formerly boyar and counsellor and voevoda of our autocratic state and of the true Christian faith, but who is now the perjurer of the holy and life-giving Cross of the Lord and destroyer of Christianity, the servant of those enemies of Christianity who have apostasized from the worship of the divine ikons and have trampled on all the sacred commandments and destroyed the holy temples and befouled and trampled on the sacred vessels and images, like Isaurian and the one who is called Putrefaction, and the Armenian . . . to him who has cast in his lot with all these, to Prince Andrei Mikhailovich Kurbsky, who with his treacherous ways wished to become master of Yaroslavl, let this be known!"[12]

Ivan then addressed Kurbsky direct. "Why have you set yourself up as a teacher of my body and soul? Who placed you as a judge or as one in authority over me?"[13] he demanded. "What is it, you cur, that you write and for what do you grieve, having committed such evil? What will your counsel, stinking worse than dung, resemble?"[14] The reason for Ivan's great anger on this score was less on the ground that he himself was the subject of accusations than that Kurbsky should dare to criticize anyone, for he had himself committed the greatest sin of all, apostasy. He had betrayed the Tsar, appointed by God, and so he had betrayed God.[15]

Ivan's unwavering vision of the divine source of his power emerges strongly from his letters. The other factors which are shown to be dominant in his mind are the need of the young nation for a strong central rule and his duty to provide that rule. Kurbsky's references to the Tsar's "well-wishers", meaning Sylvester and Adashev, draws from Ivan furious disavowals that they were anything but evil counsellors, seeking to usurp his power and thereby to destroy the nation.[16] He refers to the "devilish scheming" behind Kurbsky's deeds,

"since you took counsel with the priest [Sylvester] that I should be sovereign only in word, but that in deed you and the priest should rule. . . . Bethink yourself: did God, having led Israel out of captivity, appoint a priest to command over men or numerous governors? No, he made Moses alone lord over them, like a Tsar."[17]

Ivan was convinced that it was his holy duty to wield this tsarish power as, so he was persuaded, his forebears wielded it, for "from the beginning they have ruled all their dominions, not the boyars, not the magnates".[18] He cited Greek and Roman history to show how quickly nations and empires fell from greatness, if not "under one authority".[19]

In his reply Kurbsky attempted to dismiss the Tsar's letter as a "grandiloquent and big-sounding screed . . . belched forth in untamable wrath with poisonous words, such as is unbecoming not only to a Tsar, so great and glorified throughout the universe, but even to a simple lowly soldier".[20]

Kurbsky's contemptuous strictures were, however, not unmixed with bravado. Like a man who opens a furnace door and is hurled backwards by the blast of heat, he was at first overwhelmed by the intensity of the Tsar's anger and the fury of his anathemas. But his strictures were not without some justification. Ivan had demeaned himself in answering, especially in such detail, Kurbsky's letter, and thereby bringing himself to the level of the traitor. Nevertheless he had written not only from anger, but also with a passionate sincerity, as though driven to explain himself and also to assert and explain his absolute power and his duty to wield it for Muscovy.

Ivan's second letter to Kurbsky was far shorter and quieter in tone. Written in 1577, after he had suffered betrayals and tasted despair, it expressed in its first pages the bewilderment of a man who cannot understand why he had been so deceived and beaten down by misfortunes. It was the mood of a man who saw himself as Job. The arrogant conviction of the divinely appointed Tsar had been mellowed by a greater consciousness of human frailty and in particular of his own frailty. In the war between arrogance and humility, constantly waged within himself, humility was more often gaining the upper hand, but it was always liable to be dissipated by his sudden unpredictable rages.

In his second letter strong recrimination gave way to complaint and even remorse. "And why did you separate me from my wife?" he asked, recalling the harmony of his first marriage and Anastasia's death seventeen years ago, which he had come to blame on Sylvester and Adashev.

"If only you had not taken from me my young one, then there would have been no 'sacrifices to Cronus'. You will say that I was unable to endure this loss and that I did not preserve my purity—well, we are all human. . . . If only you had not stood up against me with the priest! Then none of this would have happened; all this took place because of your self-willedness".[21]

Ivan then renewed his imprecations, but he closed his letter with the injunction to Kurbsky, "Think on these things to yourself and unfold all these things for yourself. And we have written all this to you neither boasting nor puffing ourselves up—God knows—but to remind you to mend your ways, that you might think of the salvation of your soul."[22] In this chastened mood, many years after the event, it was almost as though he might have received Kurbsky as a prodigal, had he dared to return to Muscovy.

In these two letters to Kurbsky, Ivan revealed something of the complexity of his character and of the conflicts within him. He strove after moderation and restraint, but they usually eluded him. He had a lofty sense of mission to Muscovy and of responsibility to his people, but at times it overwhelmed him and then, because he was merely human, he gave way to debauchery. His conviction of his divinely bestowed power made him arrogant, but then the enormity of this power made him humble. Storms of vindictive anger seized him and he regretted them and his furious anathemas. The more he suffered misfortunes, the more he was conscious of his burden of sin, for misfortunes were, he believed, punishments from God.

Ivan was a tragic man, because he was unable to subdue his own egocentric nature. The essence of his tragedy was that he was incapable of the complete dedication to his office which he knew it required of him, and that he was incapable of submitting before God with the humility which Job had demonstrated.

Notes to Chapter XVI

[1] Solovyev, Bk. III, Vol. VI, p. 542.
[2] Karamzin, Bk. II, Vol. IX, col. 34.
[3] The fate of Kurbsky's wife and son is not known.
[4] Karamzin, *op. cit.*, col. 34.
[5] A more reliable source—the synodal copy of the Nikon Chronicle in the *Full Collection of Russian Chronicles*, Vol. XIII, p. 383—states that Shibanov did not bring the letter. He was captured subsequently by Ivan's officers and sent to Moscow where he was interrogated under torture and then executed. Fennell, *Correspondence*, pp. 21–3.

[6] N. Ustryalov (ed.), *Statements of Prince Kurbsky* (St Petersburg, 1833).

[7] Fennell, *op. cit.*, pp. 5, 7.

[8] *Ibid.*, p. 5.

[9] *Ibid.*, p. 133.

[10] Klyuchevsky, II, p. 165.

[11] Fennell, *op. cit.*, pp. 2–179.

[12] *Ibid.*, p. 14.

[13] *Ibid.*, pp. 40–1.

[14] *Ibid.*, pp. 30–1.

[15] *Ibid.*, p. 19.

[16] *Ibid.*, pp. 2–3.

[17] *Ibid.*, pp. 46–7.

[18] *Ibid.*, pp. 26–7.

[19] *Ibid.*, p. 61.

[20] *Ibid.*, pp. 180–1.

[21] *Ibid.*, pp. 190–3.

[22] *Ibid.*, p. 197.

CHAPTER XVII

THE OPRICHNINA 1565

KURBSKY'S treason made a devastating impact on Ivan at the time. It was not the first occasion that he had been betrayed by a man whom he had trusted, and betrayal always distressed and hurt him deeply. But Kurbsky had exceeded all others in perfidy. One of the Tsar's ablest commanders and his closest favourite, he had not only gone over to the enemy, but now publicly arraigned his former sovereign, while at the same time driving the enemies of Muscovy to invade her lands and massacre her people.

It was, however, the intensity of Kurbsky's hatred that most disturbed Ivan. This was because he saw in Kurbsky not an individual who had fled from just punishment but the representative of the whole boyar-princely class, voicing their implacable malevolence towards him. His suspicions intensified, Ivan readily believed that the boyars and princes hated him and his dynasty. All were meditating treason against him. All were waiting to follow in the steps of Kurbsky, who in the security of the enemy camp expressed the vitriolic thoughts which they were thinking.

As in childhood, Ivan felt himself isolated and surrounded by enemies. What added to his fury was that he had to depend on these very boyars and princes to govern and lead his troops. He had no others, experienced in bearing such responsibilities. But Ivan could never accept impotence or nurse fears and suspicions without acting. He devised now a cunning and desperate plan of escape from this dependence and insecurity.

At the beginning of winter 1564 a rumour spread in Moscow that the Tsar was going away. His personal attendants had instructions to make themselves ready. Military serving men, summoned by name from distant towns, were told to bring their wives and families with them. No one knew where the Tsar was going. Mystery shrouded the preparations. The rumours took on an ominous note.

Early on the morning of 3 December the Kremlin square filled with sledges. The Tsar's personal servants at once began loading them with holy ikons, clothing, the whole of the Tsar's treasury, and the magnificent gold plate which reflected the wealth and prestige of the court. The people watched uneasily, for these were preparations such as had never been made when the Tsar went on pilgrimages or to hunt and relax in the country.

In the Uspensky Cathedral the church hierarchy and the boyars were waiting when Ivan arrived. The Metropolitan celebrated mass and Ivan prayed fervently. After receiving the Metropolitan's blessing, he took leave of the assembly, graciously giving his hand to the boyars and merchants to kiss. He sat in his sledge with the Tsaritsa and his two sons, and attendants wrapped them in furs against the savage cold. Then, accompanied by Alexei Basmanov, Mikhail Saltykov, Prince Afanasy Vyazemsky, and others of his new favourites, and escorted by mounted guards, he set out from Moscow.

At the village of Kolomenskoe he was delayed for two weeks. Heavy rains had brought an unseasonal thaw, reducing the roads to mud and making the ice on the rivers dangerous to cross. When able at last to leave Kolomenskoe, he travelled to the Troitsa monastery and thence to Alexandrovsk where he arrived on Christmas day.

In Moscow churchmen, boyars, and people were uneasy. The Tsar's secret journey, and his care in taking all his personal goods and wealth boded ill of some kind. A month passed without news. Then on 3 January (1565) couriers arrived from Alexandrovsk, bringing two documents, one addressed to the Metropolitan, and the other to the merchants and the people.

Ivan's message to the Metropolitan referred in detail again to the disorders and misdeeds of the boyars during his minority. He charged that they had not changed their ways. Commanders betrayed his trust and were ready to aid the Khan and other enemies to prey upon Muscovy. But when the Tsar in his righteous anger against these unworthy subjects punished them, the Metropolitan and other churchmen interceded on their behalf and thwarted his will and his justice.

"Consequently," wrote Ivan, "not wishing to endure your treachery, we with great pity in our heart have quitted the Tsardom and have gone wherever God may lead us!"[1]

The second message was read out to the assembled merchants, traders, and people of the city. In it Ivan affirmed to his faithful subjects that his anger was not directed against them and he assured them of his goodwill.

Panic broke out among the Muscovites after the reading of these two messages. The Tsar had abdicated, leaving them without leader or defender. He was the pivot and crux of the whole society and no disaster could appal them so much as the abdication of their Tsar, and especially Ivan, the Tsar-Conqueror and Liberator.

The life of the city came to a standstill. The markets and government offices stood empty, as the people huddled in groups bewailing their fate. "The sovereign has deserted us! We will perish! Who will be our defender against the foreigners? What will happen to the sheep without the shepherd?"[2]

Boyars, princes, and churchmen shared in the popular panic. They joined with others in urging the Metropolitan to go to Alexandrovsk to implore the Tsar to return. Of one voice, all declared:

"Let the Tsar execute the malefactors; in life and death his will is supreme, but the Tsardom cannot remain without its Head! He is our Sovereign, given to us by God; we know no other. We will all to a man go with you to petition the Sovereign and weep before him."

In more threatening tones, the merchants and people added, "Let the Tsar point out his traitors to us. We will destroy them ourselves!"[3]

Hasty preparations were made for the journey to Alexandrovsk. The Metropolitan, it was generally agreed, should remain in the capital, which was in a ferment. In his place Pimen, Archbishop of Novgorod, and Levky, Archimandrite of the Chudov monastery, were chosen to petition the Tsar. They set out without delay, followed by an anxious multitude, comprising representatives from all sections of the community.

On 5 January (1565) the two churchmen with the crowd, straggling at their heels through the snow, reached Alexandrovsk, hidden away in the dense forests to the north of Moscow. They had made in a day and a half the journey of seventy-five miles which had taken Ivan three weeks.

Admitted to Ivan's presence, the churchmen implored him to take away his wrath from his people, not to forsake the Tsardom, but to rule as he saw fit. Then they begged him to admit his boyars. Ivan received the boyars and representatives of the gentry, merchants and people. He heard their tearful pleas, and then spoke sternly about the treachery which he had endured. Finally he agreed to return to his capital, but on conditions. The first was that he should be free to rule as he considered necessary and, more specifically, that he should be free to punish traitors without restraints, intercessions, or reproaches.

Overjoyed by his decision to return, all were ready to agree to any conditions that he cared to make. The churchmen conducted prayers in which Ivan and those present joined. They then hastened back to Moscow on Ivan's direction that the business of the city must not remain in suspense.

The people of Moscow waited impatiently for the return of their Tsar. But it was not until 3 February (1565) that he made a ceremonial entry into the city. On the following day he summoned the church hierarchy, senior boyars, and officials before him, and all who now set eyes on him were deeply shocked.

On his departure two months earlier and even in Alexandrovsk a month ago, Ivan had been a powerfully built handsome man. His small grey eyes were alert and full of fire, and his fine head of hair, thick beard, and heavy moustache added to his distinguished appearance. But now they could hardly recognize him as the same man. He had become stooped and his features had so shrunken that he seemed an old man. He was suddenly bald. His lively expressive eyes were dulled. It was apparent that, while at Alexandrovsk, he had lived through some terrible mental and spiritual crisis which had ravaged him physically and had left him prematurely aged.

At this assembly Ivan announced the second condition of his return to Moscow, and it was a condition which bewildered everyone. For the safety of himself and of the Tsardom, he said, he would create a special guard and provide a private establishment for himself. This establishment was to be known as the Oprichnina,[4] which would be an independent state within the Tsardom, belonging to the Tsar and ruled by him alone, not as Tsar but as proprietor. He was, in fact, creating an independent principality of his own or, as Klyuchevsky called it, a parody of the old independent principalities.[5] Into this personal realm he would withdraw, isolating himself from the boyars and princes whom he mistrusted, and even from the people. It was a grotesque conception which was to spread confusion and suffering throughout the country.

The first steps in establishing the Oprichnina were the requisitioning of lands and the selection of special life-guards, the Oprichniki. The land confiscated or set aside for this purpose was at first mainly in the central regions, but it soon spread more widely, especially in the north, until it embraced nearly half of the area of the vast Tsardom.

The basis on which land was taken is uncertain. Many boyars were dispossessed because Ivan particularly mistrusted them. His first concern, however, was apparently to make this Oprichnina self-sufficient and wholly independent of the rest of the state. Broadly the lands taken, sometimes in single estates or even parts of estates and parts of towns, and forming a patch-work pattern, fell into three categories. The first was an inner region, mainly to the east and southeast of Moscow, which provided the Oprichnina with food and other supplies. The second category included the northern regions, too distant to provide estates for the military serving men, and comprising mainly black lands whose peasants, after the abolition of the "feeding" system, paid taxes direct to the treasury; this category provided the finances of the Oprichnina. The third category of lands embraced the vast area stretching from Vologda and Galich in the northeast of Moscow around to Mozhaisk in the west, where the Oprichniki were mainly settled on estates.[6]

The first and third categories included many inherited estates, belonging to members of the boyar-princely aristocracy, who were summarily dispossessed. They were entitled to equivalent estates elsewhere outside the Oprichnina. Lands were specially allocated to some, but more frequently the landholder, ejected suddenly from estates which his family had occupied for generations, had to search for free lands. In the bitter cold of the winter of 1565 some 12,000 landholders with their families, but with few of their possessions, were forced to leave their homes, many on foot, to seek new lands to the east.

This trek was to continue during the next seven years as further areas were taken for the Oprichnina. Many of the dispossessed found lands in the north, and in the Sviyazhsk, Kazan, and lower Volga regions. But, while they were settling these undeveloped districts, the state was deprived of their military service and in the central area the established traditions of service were disrupted.

Ivan, assisted by Alexei Basmanov, Malyuta Skuratov, and other new favourites, chose his new life-guards and allocated to them the estates taken into the Oprichnina. The number of these guards was fixed initially at 1,000, a figure which recalled his abortive attempt fifteen years earlier to appoint 1,000 chosen men as a special corps. He had planned then with the support of the Chosen Council to settle them on lands near Moscow. The plan had been abandoned because the lands available were insufficient. The Chosen Council would not have supported the dispossession of members of the boyar-aristocracy from their patrimonial estates, and at that time Ivan had not felt strong enough to take such ruthless action alone. But he had a long memory and he desperately wanted the security which a corps of trusted guards would give him. The failure of this attempt to establish his "Thousanders" had undoubtedly rankled with him and the Oprichniki probably had their beginnings in memory of that failure.[7]

Ivan took great care in the selection of these guards. He himself examined many of them, enquiring about their forbears and their connexions to ensure that they were not allied with the old aristocracy. But in this, too, much depended on his personal whim. The guards were chosen mainly from the lower gentry, from the "children of boyars" who were the descendants of boyars who had lost the rank of boyar, and from the military serving class who held lands distant from the central regions, where the boyar-princely aristocracy had occupied estates since the time of the independent principalities. But also Ivan selected some of his Oprichniki from that very class against which he inveighed so tirelessly. Prince Vasily Shuisky, descended from the Rurik line and member of the family which had terrorized him in childhood, was personally chosen to serve in the Oprichnina. Ivan Romanovich, Ivan's brother-in-law, and possibly also Boris Godunov, whose sister was to marry Tsarevich Feodor, were also chosen as Oprichniki.[8]

All life-guards had to swear absolute loyalty to Ivan personally. They bound themselves to report all traitors, to make no friendships outside the Oprichnina, and to honour no loyalties to parents, family, or country above their loyalty to him. In return Oprichniki received estates, often with other property confiscated from the former landholders, and also pay and considerable privileges.

Ivan's separate establishment involved more, however, than his chosen Oprichniki. It had its own boyars and officials, suites of courtiers and attendants, and its servants including carpenters, bakers, and cooks. All were carefully chosen as men uncontaminated by any of the elements which Ivan considered treacherous.

In Moscow certain streets and suburbs, including the Arbat and half of the Nikitskaya and suburbs extending towards the Novodevichy nunnery, were taken into the Oprichnina, and here some guards were settled. All living in these parts of the city, who had not been chosen for the Oprichnina, had to move elsewhere. In the area between the Arbat and the Nikitskaya streets, which was outside the Kremlin, Ivan ordered a special palace to be built, surrounded by a stone wall, which was to house the court and the headquarters of the Oprichnina.[9]

The remaining parts of the Tsardom, excluded from the Oprichnina, were known as the Zemshchina[10] which Ivan entrusted to the rule of Princes Ivan Belsky and Ivan Mstislavsky, and other senior boyars. He directed that all the state ministries should continue to function as in the past, carrying on the administration of the country. The ministries were to report to the boyars and the boyars were authorized to report to the Tsar himself on any matter of importance and especially on military affairs.

Ivan thus remained, as before, the sovereign, ruling over the whole land. At the same time, like an independent prince of earlier times, he also ruled in his principality, or Oprichnina, as proprietor. Many contemporaries, especially in Poland–Lithuania, mistakenly believed that he had divided his realm into two parts, and Ivan himself always took pains to deny such conceptions. In fact, the parallel institutions of the Oprichnina and the Zemshchina often worked together. The Foreign Office (Posolsky Prikaz) continued to conduct relations with foreign governments and the financial ministries had to co-ordinate their work at many points. It was not the existence of the Oprichnina, but the disruption caused in setting it up and the conduct of its personnel that tended to divide the Tsardom for a time.

Ivan's purpose in setting up the Oprichnina is not certain. For some years historians were agreed that his chief purpose was to uproot the descendants of the independent princes from their traditional lands and to destroy the boyar-princely aristocracy, which had terrorized him in childhood and which constantly by its seditious activities threatened destruction to the nation. But more recent researches into the circumstances of the setting up of the Oprichnina and the acquisition of lands for its personnel disprove this thesis. Indeed, it would seem that Ivan himself was unclear as to his basic purpose. In his selection of his Oprichniki and in the confiscation of estates he so often acted capriciously that no clear pattern emerges. His immediate purpose was, however, clear. This was the creation of a separate domain under his direct and personal control, where he could feel secure.[11]

Notes to Chapter XVII

[1] Karamzin, Bk. II, Vol. IX, col. 43.
[2] *Ibid.*, cols. 43–4; Solovyev, Bk. III, Vol. VI, pp. 551–2.
[3] Karamzin, *loc. cit.*

[4] Karamzin, *op. cit.*, col. 46. Oprichnina derives from the word *oprich*, meaning separate or apart. Oprichnina also meant that part of a man's estate set apart for his widow. See also Klyuchevsky, II, pp. 177–9.

[5] Klyuchevsky, *loc. cit.*

[6] S. Veselovsky, "The Institution of the Oprichnina Establishment in 1565 and its abolition in 1572" in *Voprosy Istorii*, 1946, No. 1, pp. 86–104; A. A. Zimin, "Land Policy in the Years of the Oprichnina 1565–72" in *Voprosy Istorii*, 1962, No. 12, pp. 60–79.

[7] Soviet historians have disagreed sharply concerning the connexion between the attempt to establish the "thousanders" in 1550 and the institution of the Oprichniki in 1565. S. P. Platonov considered that in 1565 Ivan was repeating what he had attempted fifteen years earlier. S. V. Veselovsky strongly denied that there was any connexion. A. A. Zimin has analysed the evidence and I have accepted his opinion, particularly as it seems to me the most probable interpretation of how Ivan's mind worked in such matters. S. F. Platonov, *Essays* (Moscow, 1937), p. 109; S. V. Veselovsky, "The First Step in the Reform of the Central Power in the Reign of Ivan the Terrible" in *Istoricheskie Zapiski*, 1946, Vol. 15, pp. 57, 61, and *passim*; A. A. Zimin, *loc. cit.*

[8] Vasily Shuisky was the only serving member of the Shuisky family at this time, the other members being not yet of an age to serve. Ivan elevated him to the rank of boyar in 1567, and it is almost certain that he was an Oprichnik. S. V. Veselovsky in *Voprosy Istorii*, 1946, I, p. 89.

[9] At first Ivan decided to have his Oprichnina court within the Kremlin to the rear of the existing palace on the site where the apartments of the Tsaritsa and the palace of Prince Vladimir Andreevich stood. On 1 February 1565, however, the palace of Prince Vladimir was burnt to the ground in one of the frequent fires which troubled Moscow. Ivan then gave orders for his new palace to be built outside the Kremlin. He spent less and less time in this palace, however, preferring the isolation of Alexandrovsk. The Moscow palace was burnt to the ground in the great fire in 1571. A. A. Zimin, *loc. cit.*

[10] Zemshchina comes from the word *zemlya* meaning land, and might here be translated as the realm or dominion.

[11] S. F. Platonov, *Essays on the History of the Troubled Time in the Muscovite State in the 16th and 17th Centuries* (Moscow, 1937), pp. 110–15; S. F. Platonov, *Ivan Grozny* (Berlin, 1924), pp. 100–16; S. V. Veselovsky in *Voprosy Istorii*, 1946, No. I, pp. 86–97; A. A. Zimin, *loc. cit.*

CHAPTER XVIII

THE TERROR CONTINUES 1565–72

Two days after his return to Moscow, Ivan enforced the condition, made at Alexandrovsk, that he should be free to punish without restraints, reproaches, or intercessions all whom he considered traitors.

The first victim was Prince Alexander Gorbaty-Shuisky, who came of ancient lineage and had distinguished himself in many campaigns. Accused of complicity with Kurbsky and plotting to kill the Tsar, the Tsaritsa, and their children, he was now condemned to death with his son, aged seventeen years. Father and son walked hand in hand, without sign of fear, to the place of execution. The son moved ahead, not wishing to see his father beheaded, and knelt to the block. The father drew him back, saying, "But I cannot see you dead." The son was forced to watch the executioner wield the heavy sword. He lifted up his father's head and kissed the lips. Calmly he bent down and his own neck was severed at a blow.[1]

Four other men of some prominence were executed on this day. Prince Dmitri Shevyrev was killed by the horrible method of being impaled upon a pointed and greased stake which with the weight of his body slowly penetrated upwards into his intestines and towards his heart, but he survived a whole day of agony before he died.[2] Princes Ivan Kurakin and Dmitri Nemoi were compelled to become monks and to retire to distant monasteries. A close relative of Tsaritsa Anastasia, Boyar Ivan Yakovlev, incurred the Tsar's disgrace, but received more merciful treatment on giving a written undertaking, endorsed by the signatures of the bishops, that he would not flee to Lithuania, to the Papal See, the Emperor, the Sultan, or, surprisingly, join forces with Prince Vladimir Andreevich.

Another unexpected ruling concerned the renowned military leader, Prince Mikhail Vorotynsky, who had been exiled to Beloozero where he had lived for some four years, receiving a regular pension and supplies of foods and luxuries. Ivan now recalled him, ordered him to serve on the Boyar Council, and made him governor of Kazan.

Like several other boyars, however, he was obliged to give a written undertaking not to flee, and to provide sureties.

At this time the selection of his special guards, the Oprichniki, was engaging Ivan's attention. He had originally proposed a force of 1,000, but finally chose 6,000 guards. For them he devised a sinister and distinctive uniform, which was soon to strike terror in the hearts of the people. Each Oprichnik wore a black uniform and rode a black horse, and to his saddle were secured the emblems of a dog's head and a broom. The emblem signified that these guards hounded traitors and swept them from the land.

The Oprichniki were privileged troops. No one had any rights or protection against them. Members of the Zemshchina quickly came to detest them, referring to them as the "Outsiders" (Kromeshchiki) because they were outside the law. But the general hatred and fear of his guards did not disturb Ivan who considered the popular feeling to be a further guarantee of their dependence on him and of their loyalty. In fact, he was so obsessed with his personal security that he ignored the many harmful activities of his guards, especially in plundering the merchants and the townspeople.

Chosen almost entirely from the lower ranks of the serving men, Oprichniki were carried away by the sudden wealth and privilege of their new positions. Many indulged in wild spending on luxuries and on debauchery, and their immunity from the law gave them ample opportunity for such indulgence. At the same time, being on constant service, they could not attend to their estates. They had no incentive to develop them and no chance to feel that they might sink roots in this newly acquired land. Consequently their sole interest was to draw what money they could from these estates, and soon they were burdening their peasants with new dues and new labours. In desperation their peasants began to flee from these impositions. Whole villages became deserted and lands everywhere suffered from the decline in the labour force and from neglect.

Ivan appeared to be detached from such problems. His concern at this time was with the expansion and security of the Tsardom and his own safety. Although his new palace, erected outside the Kremlin, was like a fortress and surrounded with stone walls, he did not feel at ease in Moscow. He had conceived a dislike of the city and increasingly spent his time with his family and with the whole establishment of the Oprichnina at Alexandrovsk. There in the midst of the dense forests, he had built himself a fortified town which was impregnable. Within it his palace was surrounded by a moat, a stone wall, and protected by ramparts. His court officials and his guards occupied special quarters, and no one dared to depart without his personal knowledge. Moreover, the approaches to Alexandrovsk were closely guarded for a distance of two miles, so that no one could enter or leave without permission.

In this refuge Ivan lived a life in which both his devotions and his diversions were extreme. At 4 a.m. he rose and went with the Tsarevichi and with Malyuta Skuratov to attend matins. He had specially chosen 300 Oprichniki who formed what was called the "Brotherhood", all of whom held mock monastic offices in a parody of monastic life over which he presided as abbot. The 300 "Brothers" attended matins and any who failed to appear were at once imprisoned for eight days. Ivan himself prayed most devoutly during this early morning service, lasting two or three hours. His prostrations were so ardent that his forehead was often bruised from striking the ground.

At 10 a.m. the "Brothers" dined in their refectory and every day was a banquet day at which wine and spirits flowed freely and great quantities of rich foods were consumed. But Ivan did not eat with them. He stood at the lectern, reading aloud from the sacred books, while the company feasted. Later, when he himself dined, he liked to discuss the laws of Orthodoxy, and he delighted in the intricacies of theological argument. Sometimes after dinner he would visit the torture chambers to witness the interrogation of some unfortunates, arrested on suspicion by the Oprichniki. At 8 p.m. he attended vespers and at 10 p.m. he retired to his bedchamber where blind men took turns to tell him stories, until he was ready to sleep. But he did not sleep long; at midnight he rose to attend another service.

While in his chapel Ivan often received reports and issued instructions. The boyars responsible for the affairs of the realm, the Zemshchina, did not dare to make independent decisions, and constantly referred to him. When any important ambassadors arrived in Moscow, Ivan with all the magnificence of his court and attended now by his Oprichniki, wearing for such occasions uniforms of gold, received them in his Kremlin palace. From time to time Ivan also left Alexandrovsk to visit particular monasteries, to examine frontier fortifications, or to hunt wild animals, especially bears, in the woods.[3]

At Alexandrovsk, Ivan adopted certain new favourites whose presence annoyed the Oprichniki and horrified the Orthodox priests. These favourites were German Lutherans. In June 1565 he had uprooted the citizens of Dorpat, because they were in secret communication with their former Master, and had settled them with their families to the east of Moscow. He had, however, shown them special consideration and had even allowed them their Lutheran pastor, Wetterman, who travelled from town to town administering to his flock.

Ivan enjoyed the company of this pastor, whom he respected as an intelligent and dedicated man, and he gave him the task of arranging his library. Of the other German Lutherans, he took four into his service. He also allowed a Lutheran church to be built and consecrated in Moscow. He even fined the Metropolitan a large sum for some offence caused to one of the Lutherans. Ivan may well have derived a perverse satisfaction from affronting the Orthodox clergy in this way, but it was also notable that in this age of bigotry he was both tolerant and enlightened, and he undoubtedly found pleasure in the company of the pastor and the other Lutherans.

In the upheavals of this time no one dared complain or petition the Tsar for fear of punishment or even more from fear that he might again forsake them. Boyars saw their estates bestowed on Oprichniki and had to set out with their families in search of new lands. Prominent men were executed. Oprichniki robbed and ill-treated the people. But the Tsar did nothing. Indeed, he took into the Oprichnina the Stroganov family, several English traders, and certain monasteries to shield them from the depredations of the Oprichniki, thus making it clear that it was not his intention to restrain his guards.

In fact, Ivan himself abetted his Oprichniki in their lawless exploits. One night in July 1568 several of his favourites, including Prince Afanasy Vyazemsky, Malyuta Skuratov, and Vasily Gryaznoi, with a detachment of guards, broke into the homes of a number of eminent officials and merchants, known to have beautiful wives. They carried the wives away by force. Later in the night Ivan, accompanied by a large escort, met them and his favourites displayed the women to him. Ivan chose certain of them for himself and left the others to their captors. With his guards he then rode through the outskirts of Moscow, setting fire to the houses of boyars and princes in disgrace, and scattering their cattle. He returned to Moscow and then ordered that the ravished wives should be returned to their homes.

The one person to whom all outside the Oprichnina looked silently in hope of action of some kind was the Metropolitan. He represented the second power in the land, and it was his accepted duty to comfort the weak and those in trouble. Metropolitan Afanasy was, however, an old man, and in 1566 ill-health forced him to retire. The election of a new Metropolitan was a matter for the archbishops and bishops meeting together, and the Tsar then endorsed their choice. But Ivan, anxious to find an able and devout man, took matters into his own hands. His choice fell first on German, Archbishop of Kazan. But in conversation before the assembly of churchmen had met for the formality of electing the Tsar's choice, Ivan found that German was speaking in the threatening tones of an old testament prophet. Later he repeated the conversation to his favourite, Alexei Basmanov, and asked his opinion. "We think, Sovereign," Basmanov replied, "that German wants to be a second Sylvester. . . ."[4]

Ivan at once began seeking a new candidate and he found the man he wanted in Philip, the Abbot of Solovetsky monastery. He was the son of Boyar Kolyshov and had become a monk when very young. By his ability, energy, and devoutness he had quickly won renown, extending far beyond the ice-bound islands of the White Sea. As abbot of the Solovetsky monastery he had transformed the lives of the monks, whose faith exposed them to all the rigours of the Arctic winter. He had developed herds of reindeer and cattle, built roads, and organized fishing so that the monks were properly fed and had useful healthful occupations.

Ivan had heard of Philip's good works many years earlier. He had presented to the monastery gold plate, pearls, rich cloths, and lands. In other ways, too, he had helped the abbot to develop the island and the monastery which was of great sanctity, because in it were preserved the relics of Savvatyi and Zosima, two of the most revered saints of the Russian Orthodox Church.

In choosing Philip for the Metropolitanate, a choice which had apparently occurred to no one else, Ivan was behaving as a devout and responsible Tsar who sought a worthy head of the church. But conflict was to prove inevitable. Ivan must have known that Sylvester, whom he had come to hate, had on finally retiring to Solovetsky been loved by Philip, who had tended him like a son in his last years. Such a background was bound to breed suspicions and hostilities in Ivan's mind.

Summoned to Moscow, Philip was astonished to learn that he was to be elevated to the Metropolitanate. Tearfully he begged to be allowed to return to his Arctic monastery, but Ivan was adamant. Philip then agreed to accept the office on condition that the Tsar abolished the Oprichnina. "Let there be but one Russia!" he pleaded. "Every divided Tsardom according to the word of the Almighty falls to ruins. I cannot sincerely give you my blessing, seeing this affliction of the fatherland!"[5] Ivan refused to consider conditions and silenced the abbot, but still insisted on his accepting office. Philip's obstinacy was then softened by the advice of the archbishops and bishops. They pointed out that his duty was not to oppose the will of the Tsar, but to calm his anger whenever possible. Philip was even persuaded to sign a paper in which it was stated that he had given his word to the archbishops and bishops that he would not interfere in the Tsar's Oprichnina and would not resign office on the grounds that the Tsar had rejected his advice or his requests or had forbidden him to meddle in civil affairs.[6]

Philip was duly consecrated Metropolitan. He delivered his inaugural sermon in the Tsar's presence and preached earnestly on the duty of rulers to be fathers of their people and upholders of justice. He warned against evil flatterers who gathered around the throne, sometimes blinding their rulers to the good of the country. Ivan heard him in silence and was apparently impressed by his words. Moreover, he continued to show Philip every favour, but it was not to last for long.

In 1567 a further bout of executions took place. King Sigismund Augustus had sent as a courier to Ivan a certain Kozlov who had been born in Moscow, but had married and settled in Lithuania. Returning from this mission Kozlov reported to the King that he had succeeded in persuading many Muscovite magnates to defect. He was sent to Moscow again, this time armed with messages from the King and Hetman Khodkevich to Princes Belsky, Mstislavsky, Vorotynsky, and to the equerry Boyar Ivan Chelyadin, inviting them to transfer their allegiance to Lithuania. These messages were intercepted, and Ivan had indignant and reproachful replies sent by hand of Kozlov to the King and Hetman.[7] Belsky, Mstislavsky, and Vorotynsky managed to escape disgrace and punishment. Chelyadin, although an old man, was executed with his wife.[8]

Among the others who were executed at this time were three princes of Rostov, who had planned to flee to Lithuania at the time of the Tsar's illness in 1553, and also Princes Peter Shchenyatev and Turuntai-Pronsky who had strongly favoured the succession of Prince Vladimir Andreevich. Ivan had not forgotten these events, and his mistrust once aroused was rarely assuaged.

Prince Vladimir Andreevich had remained unscathed during these years since he had first been proposed as Ivan's successor. In 1553 and again in the following year he had been forced to swear solemnly to serve the Tsarevichi on the accession of one or the other to the throne. He had also bound himself to observe strict conditions, designed to thwart any attempts to place him on the throne. Ivan treated him with great courtesy and even affection, and gave him a splendid palace in the Kremlin. Beneath this display of goodwill, however, he nursed a deep mistrust of his cousin. He could never forget that Prince Andrei Staritsky, father of Prince Vladimir, had sworn allegiance to him and to his mother as regent, and that four years later he had planned to seize the throne by armed force, using Novgorod as his base. The son would surely repeat his father's treachery. Ivan surrounded him with spies and kept sharp watch for any signs of sedition.

In 1563 a secretary, Savluk Ivanov, in the service of Prince Vladimir, sent a report to Moscow, stating that Princess Efrosinia and her son were causing grave harm to the Tsar. It was a vague charge of the kind often inspired only by malice, but always treated seriously. Savluk was summoned to the Kremlin and, after investigation of his allegations, Efrosinia was shorn as a nun. Towards Prince Vladimir, Ivan was more lenient. He replaced all the boyars and senior officials in his service, but took no further action. Three years later, however, Ivan removed him from his ancestral lands, taking them for himself, and gave him equivalent estates at Dmitrov and Zvenigorod. Like the changing of the senior men serving him, this was an expedient which Ivan's father and grandfather had used to destroy local loyalties to the family which had traditionally ruled in the region.

Ivan's unsleeping suspicions were stirred afresh in 1568 by rumours that Prince Vladimir was planning to defect to Lithuania. Another story was that Ivan had placed the Prince in command of troops at Nizhny-Novgorod, but was alarmed by the popular acclaim that greeted him there. Suspecting that he might lead a popular revolt, Ivan recalled him to Alexandrovsk. Many lurid reports have survived concerning the death of Prince Vladimir and his family, but it is certain that he died in January 1569.[9]

Distressed by these executions and by the mounting oppression at the hands of the Oprichniki, the boyars and merchants continued to look hopefully to Metropolitan Philip for help and comfort. He had always been a man of action and would surely come forward to protect them. By this time, however, Ivan had grown suspicious of

Philip, believing that he was in league with the boyars and plotting to destroy the Oprichnina.

The violent clash between these two men of strong and dominating temperament finally happened in the gloom of the Uspensky Cathedral. Ivan entered, accompanied by his guards, to find Philip standing before the ikonostasis, the great golden screen, glittering with bejewelled ikons, which separated the body of the cathedral from the holy sanctuary. Ivan went towards him and stood awaiting his blessing. Philip gazed fixedly at an ikon and was silent. Finally certain boyars said to him, "Holy Father, here is the Sovereign! Bless him!"[10]

Philip refused and began sternly castigating Ivan.

"In the most heathen and barbaric realms there is law and justice, there is compassion towards the people—but not in Russia! The goods and lives of our citizens go unprotected! Everywhere plundering, everywhere murder . . . and these deeds are carried out in the name of the Tsar!"

For some minutes he continued to thunder his rebukes.

Ivan listened, trembling with anger. Suddenly he struck the ground with his staff.

"Be quiet, for I will speak! Be quiet, Holy Father!" he shouted. "Be quiet and bless me!"

"Our silence," answered Philip, "will lie as a sin upon your soul and bring death!"

"Those close to me rose against me and they seek to harm me— but what business is it of yours to interfere in our tsarish counsels?"

"I am pastor of the Christian flock!"

"Philip. Do not thwart our power, for you will bring our wrath upon yourself!" replied Ivan, and he added, "Better that you leave the Metropolitanate."

"I did not ask, seek through others, or by bribery to acquire this office. Why did you take me from my desert?" Philip answered.[11]

Ivan then stormed out of the cathedral. Already he was considering how to deal with this rebellious ecclesiastic. His first step was to send two priests with Prince Vasily Temkin, whom he trusted, to Solovetsky monastery to gather what evidence they could find against Philip. The monks there spoke with reverence of their former abbot, but some damaging evidence was found, or invented, and the new abbot, Paisy, a rival of Philip, who hoped to succeed him as Metropolitan, was prepared to testify.

As soon as the witnesses had arrived from the north, the Metropolitan was summoned before a court of churchmen and boyars over which Ivan himself presided. But Philip contemptuously brushed aside the charges and evidence brought against him, and again publicly rebuked the Tsar.[12] Finally he strode from the court without waiting for its verdict.

On 8 November 1568 Philip was conducting the special service in honour of St Mikhail the Archangel in the Uspensky Cathedral, when Boyar Alexei Basmanov entered with a crowd of Oprichniki in their uniforms of black. The large congregation froze in horror, as Basmanov ordered a paper to be read aloud, declaring the sentence of an ecclesiastical court, which had sat separately, that Philip was to be degraded and dismissed from the Metropolitanate. Oprichniki tore off his rich vestments before the whole congregation, replacing them with a plain white monkish robe. They then took him away to the nearby Bogoyavlensky monastery. On the following day he was brought before the court over which Ivan presided to hear his sentence; he had been found guilty on many charges, including witchcraft, and was sentenced to life imprisonment. An archimandrite of the Troitsa monastery, named Kirill, a saintly but docile man, was at once appointed Metropolitan in his place.

For a time Philip was held in the Nikolaevsky monastery on the banks of the Moskva river, but the people gathered there in great crowds, hoping to set eyes on this saintly man. Ivan, fearing that he might become a popular martyr, had him removed to a monastery near Tver. There a year later (December 1569) Malyuta Skuratov, Ivan's most trusted favourite, strangled him in his cell.[13]

For some time Ivan had been watching Novgorod with growing mistrust. Once the city had been known as Great Novgorod and her citizens, priding themselves on their independence and on the wealth which trade with the West brought them, had looked on Moscow with a certain condescension. Moscow had grown in power, but for many years Novgorod had managed to avoid Muscovite and Lithuanian attempts to annex her. Then Ivan's grandfather, Ivan III, faced with the danger of Novgorod going over to Lithuania, had in 1471 finally conquered and annexed the city. He had, moreover, moved the leading Novgorod families to other parts of Muscovy, replacing them with trusted subjects from central Muscovy. Nevertheless the Novgorodtsi had continued to cherish the old traditions of independence and the anti-Muscovite factions, once very strong, had not completely perished.

Ivan himself had always regarded the Novgorodtsi with suspicion.

When Prince Andrei Staritsky, father of Prince Vladimir, had plotted armed rebellion in 1537, had he not looked to Novgorod for support? The city had not helped him, but thirty or forty of her leading citizens had been executed for complicity in the plot. Again in 1545, near Kolomna, had not a band of armed Novgorodtsi threatened him? They had, in fact, been peaceful petitioners, but Ivan had never believed this. To him treachery and defiance were deep-rooted in the city, and in his mood of black mistrust, when he saw conspiracy and sedition seething beneath the surface of the whole Tsardom, he was ready to believe any charge against Novgorod.

In the summer of 1569 a Volhynian, named Peter, stated in Alexandrovsk that the people of Novgorod were conspiring to defect in a body to Lithuania. A document, signed by the Archbishop of Novgorod, Pimen, and by leading citizens, had been hidden behind the ikon of the Mother of God in the St Sofia Cathedral. This paper, presumably addressed to King Sigismund Augustus, expressed their earnest desire to transfer their allegiance to him.

Ivan at once sent Peter to Novgorod, escorted by a trusted officer, to find the incriminating document. They found it, as reported, behind the ikon in the cathedral and the signatures appeared authentic. It was said at this time that Peter was no more than a vagrant who had been punished by Novgorod and was seeking revenge. He had written the paper and had most skilfully forged the signatures. Ivan, however, believed the document to be genuine. It accorded exactly with his suspicions both of the infamy of the Novgorodtsi and of Sigismund Augustus's deceitful policy of seducing the Tsar's subjects from their loyalties.

Ivan resolved now to destroy Novgorod. He would not only punish, but would virtually exterminate this centre of monstrous treachery. In December 1569 he set out from Alexandrovsk and, travelling north of Moscow, made for Klin, on the border of the Tver region. Along the road from Klin to Novgorod, a distance of 175 miles, his troops plundered and destroyed all villages and towns.

On 2 January 1570 the advance guard reached Novgorod. The city was nearly the size of Moscow, and bore many marks of her former greatness. The river Volkhov divided the merchant side to the east from the Sofiiskaya side to the west, the latter named after its great cathedral, and the two parts were joined by a wooden bridge. The western part of the city was dominated by the stone Kremlin, surrounded by a moat, and containing the cathedral. The whole city was ringed by an earthern rampart, reinforced with timbered walls and towers of stonework.

The Tsar's advance guard at once placed a cordon around the city to ensure that no one escaped. Detachments then rode to the monasteries outside the city and sealed their treasury chests. In Novgorod, abbots and monks, 500 in number, were held under guard, awaiting the Tsar's arrival. Priests and deacons, also seized in the city, were treated as debtors and beaten from morning to evening unless they paid twenty rubles apiece. All palaces, large houses, and warehouses belonging to the wealthy citizens were sealed. Merchants, officials, and traders with their wives and children were held under close guard.

On 6 January Ivan, accompanied by his son, Tsarevich Ivan, and a close escort of 1,500 guards, arrived in the merchant side of the city. The massacre began on the next day. Without trial or interrogation all abbots and monks held under guard were beaten to death with staffs, and their bodies dragged away to their monasteries for burial.

The following day was a Sunday. Ivan proceeded to St Sofia's Cathedral. On the Volkhov bridge Archbishop Pimen met him, as was the custom, and moved forward to bless him with the Cross. Ivan stood back and said angrily:

> "You, man of sacrilege, you do not hold in your hand the life-giving Cross, but a weapon and with this weapon you wish to strike into our heart. With your like-minded conspirators, the citizens of this city, you would betray our patrimony, this great Novgorod, to a foreign dynasty.... From now on you are neither pastor nor teacher, but wolf, destroyer, despoiler, traitor to our imperial purple, and mortifier of our crown!" [14]

In spite of this angry condemnation Ivan then ordered Pimen to proceed to the cathedral to conduct the service which he attended. Closely escorted all the time Ivan went next to the Archbishop's palace to dine. He had taken his seat, attended with all the ponderous ceremonial of the Muscovite court, and had even begun to eat, when suddenly he gave a terrible shout. This was the signal to the leaders of his guards to plunge into action. They seized Pimen and all the Novgorodtsi in the palace and held them under close arrest. Guards took all the rich robes and gold plate they could find from the palace and cathedral, and also from the churches and monasteries within the city walls.

Ivan and the Tsarevich then moved in procession to their headquarters in the eastern side of the city and there set up a court.

Novgorodtsi were brought to this court and interrogated. Conducted by means of terrifying inhuman tortures, the interrogations resembled those of the Spanish Inquisition at this time. Special fires and heated pans were used to scorch flesh, laid bare by cruel flogging with whips which flayed the victims to the bone. Pincers, sometimes red-hot and sometimes cold, pulled the ribs from men's chests. Nails were driven into bones and needles levered the nails from feet and hands. Some were impaled with stakes and died in agony or lingered for hours unless brutally despatched.

During these weeks the whole of the city resounded with the terrible screams and cries of men and women under interrogation. Once tortured the accused, irrespective of their evidence, were tied with legs and arms trussed to their necks. They were then dragged behind sledges to the Volkhov bridge and cast down into the water, for the river did not freeze in this area. Women and children were bound up and suffered the same fate. Little children were tied to their mother's backs and cast down into the icy water. To ensure that none survived guards in small boats patrolled the river with boathooks and pikes to kill or push under the water any who floated to the surface.

Every day for five weeks this massacre continued. The snow and ice on the bridge and along the banks of the river were deep-stained with blood. The river was choked with trussed corpses. The city was sunk in a deep silence of terror, broken only by the shouts of guards and the shrieks of men, women, and children.

The court concluded, Ivan rode around the city. He sent his men to plunder and destroy the monasteries and houses and to kill all cattle. Coming into the city he ordered the destruction to continue. Novgorodtsi who had been spared the horrors of torture and death stood dumbly, unable to hide, as their houses were reduced to ruins.

On the morning of 13 February, Ivan directed that the best men surviving in each street be brought before him. They came, some trembling at the sure prospect of a slow agonizing death; most were numbed with terror at the thought of facing their dread Tsar. But Ivan spoke graciously to them.

"You people of Great Novgorod [he said], remain alive! Pray to the Lord God, to his holy Mother, and to all the saints in our blessed tsarish realm . . . that the Lord may grant you victory over your enemies seen and unseen. God will judge Archbishop Pimen and his evil counsellors and accomplices, who have been traitors to you and to me. For all this blood, those traitors will be called to account. You must not now grieve over all that has happened. Live honourably in Novgorod. In my stead I am leaving as your governor my boyar and commander, Peter Danilovich Pronsky."[15]

The surviving Novgorodtsi were too dazed to realize that the nightmare of terror had ended. Some 60,000 men, women, and children, their kinsmen and fellow citizens, had been killed. Several months passed before the shock of this massacre began to pass. The clearing of the Volkhov river of bodies, severed limbs and heads, and unidentifiable trunks was only finished six months later. Meanwhile the spring and summer came, bringing plague and disease and, because there were no crops and no money to buy food, famine thinned even the few survivors. Only at the hands of the Mongols and the Tatars had killing and suffering been known on this scale.

From Novgorod Ivan set out immediately for Pskov. He had sent to Alexandrovsk under guard the Archbishop and those close to him to be tried and sentenced later. He was now intent on rooting out treachery in Pskov. The people of Pskov had heard of the Novgorod horrors and did not doubt that a similar fate was inexorably moving upon them. But, guided by their governor, Prince Yuri Tokmakov, and a fanatic hermit, named Nikola, they made plans. On the Saturday night, which Ivan passed in a nearby monastery, the whole population gathered in the churches at midnight. They prayed and sang fervently as though judgment day was at hand, and the ringing of bells and singing are said to have quieted the heart of the Tsar.[16]

Entering the city next morning, Ivan was astonished to find all the people standing before their houses. They bowed deeply in welcome as he approached and offered bread and salt, the traditional Russian gesture of friendship and hospitality. Impressed by this display of loyalty, Ivan's suspicions weakened. He ordered that no one should be executed and confined his guards' activities to the seizure of ikons, vestments, and monastery bells. He then cut short his stay in Pskov and returned to Moscow.

But Ivan was still not satisfied. He believed that Pimen had been involved in conspiracy with others, outside Novgorod, to transfer the city together with Pskov to Lithuania. Pimen had been brought from Alexandrovsk to Moscow and the investigations that followed produced staggering results. The charges of complicity in this conspiracy involved the men who had been closest of all to Ivan, those whom he had chosen to lead his Oprichniki and who had been mainly responsible for rooting out treachery. They were Alexei Basmanov and his son, Feodor, the Tsar's treasurer, Funikov, his chancellor, Ivan Viskovaty, and Prince Afanasy Vyazemsky, from whose hand alone in the past Ivan would accept physic when ill. All of these trusted henchmen were directly implicated. In all some 350 people were accused, and to be accused was to be judged guilty.

On 27 July (1570) ominous preparations were made in Moscow, which terrified the people. It seemed that their Tsar was planning for them the fate that the Novgorodtsi had suffered. Eighteen gallows were erected, and numerous implements of torture were set up around them. A great fire was lit and over it hung a huge cauldron of water. Realizing that soon the city would echo the agonized screams of tortured victims and that they might find themselves involved, the people hid themselves away. Ivan arrived to find the square empty, except for his attendants and the Oprichniki and the accused. He was determined that the executions should serve as an example to the Muscovites and he ordered them to be brought to witness the Tsar's justice.

Once the square was crowded with townspeople, standing silent and afraid, the proceedings began. First, Ivan freely pardoned 180 men who were the least guilty. Then the charges of conspiring with the Tsar's enemies and in particular of aiding the treason of Novgorod were read aloud and the prisoners were executed. Viskovaty was stripped naked, tied up by his feet, and slowly cut to pieces. Treasurer Funikov was dipped first in boiling water and then in cold water, and the process was continued, until he died in fearful agony. The others were hanged or hacked to pieces. In all 200 men were executed in the course of four hours.

From this public spectacle three of the most prominent of the accused were missing. Prince Vyazemsky had died under torture during his interrogation. Alexei Basmanov, it was said, was executed by his son, Feodor, on the express order of the Tsar, and then the son was killed. Archbishop Pimen was deprived of office and sent to end his life in a monastery near Tula. In the course of the next few days, moreover, other men who had been among those closest to Ivan, like Prince Peter Obolensky-Serebryanny, Ivan Vorontsov and Mikhailo Lykov, were executed to assuage the Tsar's suspicions.

Like the Novgorodtsi, too, the Muscovites suffered, as an aftermath to these executions, both famine and plague. People died in the streets of the city and on the roads leading out from it, and hundreds fled eastwards and southwards to escape disease and death. In places where the plague raged, the roads were blocked on the Tsar's orders to prevent the infection being carried to other parts of the country.

Muscovy was to suffer from frequent outbreaks of plague during the next two years and from acute shortages of food. But the people did not complain. They prayed, and with extraordinary resignation they accepted these sufferings as punishments from God. In the same spirit they accepted the furious massacres, the bloody executions, and persecution at the hands of the Oprichniki of their Tsar. Such phenomena did not weaken their respect and loyalty and, most strangely, their reverence for him. He was a strong Tsar, whom God had appointed to rule over them. He had conquered their enemies, especially in Kazan, and he had checked the infamies of boyars and princes, from which they had suffered. They loved and feared him as they loved and feared the Lord, the dread Lord of Israel.

Notes to Chapter XVIII

[1] Karamzin, Bk. III, Vol. IX, cols. 47-8.

[2] *Ibid.*

[3] *Ibid.*, p. 51, and notes, pp. 157-9.

[4] *Ibid.*, col. 54.

[5] *Ibid.*, col. 55.

[6] *Ibid.*, col. 56.

[7] It is not clear whether these messages from the King and Hetman were intercepted or whether the boyars who received them handed them to the Tsar. Karamzin, *op. cit.*, cols. 57-8; Solovyev, Bk. III, Vol. VI, p. 555.

[8] This Chelyadin had taken a prominent part in the outcry against the Glinsky after the fire of Moscow and this may well have been remembered against him. Solovyev, *op. cit.*, p. 555. According to one account of this execution, Ivan in the presence of the whole court had him dressed in the Tsar's robes and crown and seated on the throne. Ivan then bowed low before him and said mockingly, "Hail great Tsar of the Russian land! You have received from me the honour which you desired! But having power to make you Tsar, I can also cast you from the throne!" Ivan then plunged a knife into the heart of the unfortunate man, and Oprichniki hacked his body to pieces. This story is typical of many stories of the horrors of Ivan's court, but too often they are unconfirmed by other evidence and patently the testimony of hostile and unreliable chroniclers. Karamzin, Bk. III, Vol. IX, cols. 58-9 and note, p. 183.

[9] Karamzin states that Ivan charged Prince Vladimir with planning to poison him and he ordered Vladimir to drink poison. He describes a most moving scene in which after taking leave of each other, Prince Vladimir, his wife, and his children all took the poison and died in agony.

Solovyev points out that many contradictory reports have survived concerning the death of Prince Vladimir. According to them he was either poisoned, or hacked to pieces, or beheaded. Likewise the fate of his family was the subject of conflicting reports. According to Kurbsky, two of the sons died with their father. But the eldest son certainly survived and was living in 1573. Karamzin, *op. cit.*, cols. 83-4; Solovyev, *op. cit.*, p. 734.

[10] Karamzin, *op. cit.*, cols. 60–1; Solovyev, *op. cit.*, p. 556.

[11] Karamzin, *op. cit.*, col. 62.

[12] *Ibid.*, col. 63.

[13] Malyuta Skuratov told the abbot and monks of the monastery that Philip had died of fever. The monks were terrified and in Skuratov's presence they dug a grave behind the altar of the monastery chapel where they buried the body. In 1584 his remains were disinterred and taken to the Solovetsky monastery, but in 1652 they were removed to Moscow and buried in the Uspensky Cathedral. Karamzin, *op. cit.*, col. 86.

[14] Solovyev, *op. cit.*, p. 559.

[15] *Ibid.*, p. 560.

[16] *Ibid.*, p. 56; Karamzin, *op. cit.*, cols. 94–5.

CHAPTER XIX

THE LIVONIAN WAR AND THE FIRE OF MOSCOW 1565–72

IVAN'S determination to annex Livonia and to secure a permanent foothold on the Baltic had not weakened. Neither the defection of Kurbsky nor the minor defeats suffered near Nevel and at Orsha had deprived him of the initiative. Kurbsky's flight which had caused such a stir at the time had not induced other commanders to follow in his steps, and subsequent Muscovite successes had cancelled out the defeats.

Sigismund Augustus, disturbed by the growth of Muscovite power and by the exhaustion of Lithuania, was anxiously seeking to end hostilities. In May 1565 his ambassadors arrived in Moscow with proposals for an armistice on the conditions that the King would concede Polotsk and all parts of Livonia, occupied by Muscovite forces, while retaining the Livonian regions in his own hands. It was a reasonable offer, but Ivan rejected it, demanding Riga and other towns in return for which he would yield Courland and certain towns on the west side of the Dvina. The ambassadors could not accept this counter-proposal, but they suggested that the Tsar and the King might more readily reach agreement if they met personally. Ivan at first welcomed this suggestion, but then questions of protocol, to which the Muscovite always attached excessive importance, made him less eager.

The King's offer to concede all towns and lands occupied by the Muscovites nevertheless still tempted him. With Dorpat and Polotsk in his hands, it would be an impressive peace. The Livonian war made heavy demands on his troops and it threatened to drag on for many years. At this time, too, the Sultan was planning an expedition to recapture Astrakhan, which might touch off rebellion among the Tatars in Kazan and elsewhere along the Volga. If the Tsar's forces were engaged on the Volga and in Livonia, the Crimean Khan would certainly invade Muscovy. The tremendous distances separating these defence areas added seriously to Ivan's problems. Astrakhan was over 800 miles and Livonia and Kazan were both more than 400 miles distant from Moscow. In an emergency there could be no question of moving troops from one front to the other. Peace with Lithuania was thus of the greatest importance.

Ivan's understanding of the position was undoubtedly sound. But still he hesitated to accept the Lithuanian proposals. Possession of the whole of Livonia was the chief objective of his foreign policy, now that Kazan had been conquered, and he disliked compromise, except as a matter of tactics. He decided nevertheless to discuss this offer of peace more widely, to take advice and to ensure that the war had popular support, especially among the serving gentry who would bear the brunt of the campaigning. Remembering keenly the opposition of the Chosen Council and of the boyars generally to the Livonian campaign, he was not prepared to rely on the Boyar Council alone, and in any case he constantly suspected his boyars of treachery. He decided, therefore, to summon the Assembly of the Land (Zemsky Sobor) for the second time in his reign.

This Assembly which met in Moscow in the summer of 1566 was larger and more representative than the first Assembly, convened sixteen years earlier. The delegates, 374 in number, comprised members of the church and Boyar Councils, the chief military serving men of senior and junior grades, secretaries of the ministries in Moscow, leading merchants, and certain landowners from the regions near the Lithuanian frontier. They represented not the people in any democratic sense, but the various organs of the central government. They were the leading officers on whom the Tsar depended to execute his orders, command his armies, and administer the Tsardom.

The ecclesiastical council represented the church which, apart from being a powerful landowner and an important influence among the people, frequently advised the Tsar in civil matters. The boyars were traditionally the high officers of state and their council still, nominally at least, fulfilled the function of advising the Tsar. The most numerous group comprised the military serving men, the gentry on whom the Tsar relied increasingly. The merchants, who numbered 75, had not been summoned to the previous Assembly, but since they played an important part in the finances of the state and had a semi-official standing, their presence was this time considered necessary.

The only exception to the principle that all the delegates were responsible officers in the government of church and state was the group of landowners from the western regions. Presumably they were summoned because they were familiar with local conditions and because they were most directly involved.

Ivan opened the Assembly with a speech in which he put the question clearly. Should he make peace on the King's terms, or should he pursue the war until all Livonia was conquered? The delegates had studied the problem well in advance and gave reasoned replies, each group expressing its special interests. All, with one exception, spoke strongly in favour of continuing the war.[1] The Tsar, they said, had justice on his side, and they pledged themselves to give all, including their lives, in the struggle. It was an impressive display of patriotic fervour and of loyalty to the Tsar. The Assembly concluded with a resolution on which the delegates kissed the Cross, thus binding themselves by oath to carry out what they had agreed.

The Assembly's determined support for continuing the war dispersed Ivan's hesitations for the time being. Without delay he sent Boyar Umny-Kolychov to Lithuania to inform the King that, unless he conceded the whole of Livonia, no armistice was possible. Moreover, Ivan now insisted on two further conditions which previously he had been prepared to waive; the first was that the King must acknowledge Ivan's title of Tsar, and the second that he must surrender Kurbsky to the Tsar's officers. Sigismund Augustus rejected these demands and, although reluctantly, he sent a declaration of war to Moscow and again ordered his troops to march. At the beginning of 1568 Hetman Khodkevich laid siege to the fortress of Ulu but was fiercely beaten off by the Muscovite garrison.

Ivan himself, however, still had misgivings about his rejection of the Lithuanian peace terms. He alone among his people understood the overall position and was able to make a realistic appraisal of Muscovite armed strength and the demands that might be made on it. On his return to Alexandrovsk he wrote to his boyars in Moscow, directing them to reconsider the King's offer. The boyars made an equivocal reply. Ivan sent prompt instructions that they were to state clearly, if they favoured peace, what terms they would consider acceptable. The boyars then replied that peace would depend on the terms offered by the King when he renewed negotiations, a step which they confidently expected.

At this time Sigismund Augustus was more anxious than ever before to agree a permanent peace or at least an armistice with Ivan. He had even rejected an approach by the Turkish Sultan for alliance, because he would do nothing to worsen his relations with the Tsar. One reason for his anxiety for peace was that Lithuania was exhausted. But the main reason was that he needed freedom from war to consolidate the Union of Lublin, agreed on 28 June 1569, which was to have results of great significance for Eastern Europe.

During the first fourteen years of Sigismund Augustus's reign, no advance had been made towards the closer union of Lithuania and Poland. The King himself and Lithuania as a whole did not favour it, and the Poles urged it without avail. The complete change in the attitude of the King and of his Lithuanian subjects had been brought about by Ivan himself. The course of the Livonian war had made it clear that Lithuania could not stand against the might of Muscovy. Among the Poles, too, the realization had spread that, if Ivan defeated Lithuania and consolidated his power in Livonia, Muscovy would become a direct threat to Poland. Ivan's increasing grasp on Livonia gave new momentum to the movement towards organic union between the two countries. Finally in June 1569 the Polish and Lithuanian Seyms, meeting in Lublin, agreed to create a union, based on having the King and Seym in common. The King would in future be elected jointly, but law and administration would remain separate, each country retaining its own army, treasury, and high civil and military officers. But in foreign affairs and, under the leadership of the King, in war, the two countries would form a single state.

As anticipated in Moscow, two Lithuanian ambassadors, Jan Krotoshevsky and Nikolai Tavrosh, arrived in 1570 to make yet another attempt to negotiate peace. Their proposals were at first rejected, but then they asked to speak to the Tsar directly. Confronted by Ivan they made an interesting report. The Seym had, they said, discussed the succession and had agreed to elect a new sovereign from among the Slav peoples and, indeed, the choice was the Tsar and his dynasty.

Ivan did not, however, respond with any warmth to this proposal. He had heard earlier reports that some in Lithuania favoured electing him or his son to succeed to the throne, and the thought of being elected by the nobles may have offended him. He was in any case more concerned about Livonia at this time. "If you want us to rule over you, then it is desirable for you to avoid making us angry and to do what we instructed our boyars to propose to you in order that Christendom might be at peace," he exclaimed.[2] He then spoke at great length on the course of relations between Muscovy and Lithuania during his reign, stressing in conclusion that not he but the King was responsible for the fighting between their two countries.[3] Finally an armistice was concluded for three years on the basis of maintaining the existing position in Livonia and in the Polotsk region.

The Muscovite ambassadors, sent to Lithuania to ratify this armistice, also reported on the general wish among Poles and Lithuanians that the Tsar or his son should succeed the King. The Seym, they said, did not want a Moslem Turk or a subject of the Emperor, Maximilian II, who had suppressed the nobles in Bohemia and who would afford them no real leadership against their enemies. In Warsaw the nobles were said to be agreed that the Tsar should be chosen.[4] Poles had even begun wearing Muscovite dress and adopting Muscovite customs in anticipation of their new sovereign.

The ambassadors were undoubtedly misled about the extent and strength of the support for the election of the Tsar, or they may have exaggerated. But there was nevertheless a wave of enthusiasm in some quarters for the election of the Tsar, and this was particularly interesting at this time. Poles and Lithuanians knew about Ivan's severity in dealing with his boyars. They knew also of his massacre in Novgorod, and indeed Ivan had briefed his ambassadors carefully to answer any questions asked in Warsaw about Novgorod. Few Polish and Lithuanian nobles could have failed to have heard either directly or at second hand Kurbsky's horrific accounts of Ivan's barbarities. For all this, a body of Polish and Lithuanian opinion favoured electing Ivan or his son to rule over them. The reason was that Ivan was by far the most outstanding ruler in Eastern Europe at this time, and his personality had made an impact on peoples far beyond his frontiers. The Lithuanians and many Poles saw in him a strong and able leader, and this was the first requirement of every nation in an age when defence, security, and effective government depended on the capacity of the sovereign to rule.

Ivan nevertheless continued to display coolness towards the throne of Lithuania–Poland. The conquest of Livonia remained his first concern. The prospect of the Livonian war dragging on for many years and exhausting his limited manpower and resources continued to disturb him. In an attempt to cut short this wasteful campaigning he adopted a new plan. This was to appoint a King of Livonia who would be his vassal, standing in the same relationship to him as the Duke of Courland stood to the King. Two Livonian prisoners, Taube and Kruse, who had been taken to Muscovy and treated with favour by Ivan, probably proposed this plan. They nominated either Furstenberg or Kettler, the last two Masters of the Teutonic Order, but both declined the Livonian crown. The Tsar's choice then fell on Magnus, Prince of Denmark.

By his father's will, Frederick II of Denmark was bound to concede to his brother, Magnus, certain lands in Holstein. But Frederick had offered Oesel and Pilten in place of the Holstein lands, and Magnus had accepted the exchange. He also accepted Ivan's proposal and, arriving in Moscow in 1570, was proclaimed King of Livonia. The conditions, agreed by Magnus, were far-reaching, but not unreasonable, and the Tsar undertook to give him direct help to conquer any Livonian towns failing to recognise him as King.

A term of Ivan's armistice with Sigismund Augustus had been that the Muscovites would not attack any towns in Lithuanian–Polish possession. Reval was, however, occupied by the Swedes and Ivan's armistice, agreed in 1563 with King Erik, was coming to an end. But war with Sweden also raised difficulties.

Between Erik and Ivan there were certain superficial resemblances. Gustavus Vasa had made Erik heir to the Swedish throne, and to his other sons he had bequeathed dukedoms. Erik succeeded on the death of his father, but he went in fear of his nobles, constantly suspecting them of conspiring against him, and most of all he mistrusted his brothers, especially John, Duke of Finland. War had broken out between Erik and Sigismund Augustus, when the latter had sought to expel the Swedes from Reval, and the Swedes had captured Pernau and Wittenstein. But John of Finland supported the Poles, urging Erik to surrender the two captured towns and to join in alliance with Sigismund Augustus against Muscovy. Erik responded by ordering the Finns to take the field against the Poles in Livonia, and by summoning his brother before a court in Stockholm. Duke John rebelled, but he could not stand against the royal armies and after two months siege he surrendered.

This rebellion had a shattering effect on Erik. He became morose and insanely mistrustful of all but a few low-born favourites. He shut himself away from his nobles and even, it was said, suffered bouts of madness. Executions which had been rare in Sweden became frequent. But, against the advice of those close to him, he refused to order the execution of his brother, whom he kept in prison.

During this period, whether insane, as alleged by his enemies, or not, Erik was active in conducting the affairs of his kingdom. He was at war with Sigismund Augustus and with Frederick of Denmark, and therefore eagerly sought alliance with Ivan. In fact, for some time the two monarchs had been corresponding directly, perhaps finding a bond in their similar suspicions and fears. The terms on which they agreed to an alliance were that the Tsar would aid Sweden against Sigismund Augustus, mediate for a peace with Denmark, and surrender Esthonia to Sweden. In return Erik undertook to hand over to Ivan the wife of his imprisoned brother. This was Catherine Jagellon, the sister of Sigismund Augustus, whose hand Ivan himself had sought. His determination to have Catherine as his prisoner may have arisen from the perverse pride of a rejected suitor, but more probably he regarded her as a hostage, whom he would return to her brother on securing satisfactory terms concerning Livonia.

When Ivan's ambassadors arrived in Stockholm, however, Erik was in a state of confusion. He had on an impulse released his brother from prison, and he now had spells of believing that it was his brother who ruled, while he himself was in prison. Attempts by the Muscovite ambassadors to arrange for Catherine to be handed over to them were unavailing. Finally, on 29 December 1568, a rising against Erik ended in his overthrow and the elevation of Duke John of Finland to the throne.

Incensed by the Swedes' treatment of their rightful monarch, Ivan now regarded Sweden as his enemy, the more so because the new King was bound to form an alliance with Sigismund Augustus. When Magnus, King of Livonia, arrived in Moscow with plans for capturing Reval from the Swedes, Ivan gave his full support.

In August 1570 Magnus with a large German force and 25,000 Russian troops laid siege to Reval. But his hopes of starving the town into submission faded when Swedish ships anchored off the shore and sent in supplies. For thirty weeks Magnus invested Reval and then, acknowledging defeat, he withdrew his army, sending the Russian troops on to Narva.

This failure distressed Magnus all the more, because he would have to render account to the formidable Tsar. Taube and Kruse, whom Magnus blamed for misleading him about conditions in Reval, were also afraid to face the Tsar. They fled to Dorpat and secretly offered to betray Dorpat to Sigismund Augustus. They were successful in persuading the commander of the German troops in the Tsar's service to make a sudden attack on the Russian garrison. The ruse nearly succeeded, but all the Russians in the town rallied and expelled the rebels. Taube and Kruse had already made their escape from Dorpat and were kindly received by the King in Lithuania. Meanwhile Magnus was greatly disturbed that he would not only be blamed for the failure at Reval, but also held responsible for the treachery at Dorpat. He took refuge on the island of Oesel, where he was soon reassured by messages that the Tsar had pardoned him.

Reports of the overthrow of the unfortunate Erik and his subsequent death in prison had undoubtedly disturbed Ivan. This was the fate he had always dreaded for himself. He had avoided it, he believed, because unlike Erik he had acted promptly and had ruthlessly crushed sedition. Indeed the elimination of treachery against himself and the nation had become so great an obsession that he saw treason on occasions where it may not have existed. All the time he felt uneasy and insecure. He had established his own personal estate and court, the Oprichnina, but this, too, had failed to satisfy his need for security. He had even felt himself to be in such danger that he might have to find asylum abroad, and this was one of his purposes in seeking closer relations with Elizabeth of England.

The English merchants had continued to flourish in Muscovy, enjoying increasing privileges and the special protection of Ivan. His goodwill towards the English seemed unbounded. In 1567 he even granted further concessions to the Russia Company, which then gained a monopoly of all trade by way of the White Sea to the exclusion of other merchants, English as well as foreign. He also gave the Company permission to trade freely from Russia to Persia and Cathay. But in making these new concessions he was paving the way for his own demands. Anthony Jenkinson was in Moscow at this time and when he set out on his homeward journey, he carried a formal letter from the Tsar. He took also a secret message that troubled Elizabeth and her ministers.

In this secret message Ivan made new and far-reaching requests. He now asked the Queen to "licence masters to come unto him which can make ships and sail them"[5] and to give permission for him "to have out of England all kinds of artillery and things necessary for war".[6] Then came the request, astonishing to Elizabeth, that she should grant him asylum in England, if any misfortune made it necessary for him to flee his own country, and he would grant her similar refuge, if she ever needed it. Finally he proposed an offensive and defensive alliance between them, so that they might be "joined as one" and she would be "friend to his friends and enemy to his enemies and so per contra". His message closed with the request that she should give her answer to these proposals by 29 June 1568, a date allowing her only a few months.[7]

Elizabeth refused to be rushed. It was not until June that she appointed Thomas Randolph, a professional diplomatist, as her envoy to the Tsar. Randolph was most carefully briefed before his departure. He was to express gratitude for favours bestowed upon the Queen's subjects and to assure the Tsar that he would always find a welcome and a safe refuge in England. For herself, however, Elizabeth directed Randolph to reply that she had no need of such an asylum, for "we have no manner of doubt of the continuance of our peaceable government without danger either of our subjects or of our foreign enemies".[8] As for the proposal for an offensive and defensive alliance, Randolph was to "pass those matters in silence".[9]

Receiving no news of Jenkinson's return by the date suggested, Ivan began to put pressure on the Company by granting privileges to rival merchants. The Company had received under its charter a monopoly of English trade with Muscovy and it had no difficulty in enforcing this monopoly, while trade was restricted to the White Sea. In 1558, however, Ivan had captured Narva on the Baltic, and a group of English merchants, not members of the Company, began trading independently, using Narva as their port.[10] To these interlopers Ivan now granted trading privileges.

Elizabeth hastened to the defence of the Company's monopoly. She sent Lawrence Manley and, some months later, George Middleton, to the Tsar to demand that "those naughty Englishmen", engaged in private trade, should be seized and sent to England.[11] Ivan was, however, most reluctant to seize Glover and Rutter, the two chief offenders, both of whom had rendered him services and won his favour.[12] Furthermore, neither Manley nor Middleton had brought replies from Elizabeth to his urgent proposals, and so he had simply detained both men and ignored the messages they had brought.

Thomas Randolph reached Moscow in October 1568, but on the Tsar's instructions he was kept virtually under house-arrest for four months, awaiting audience. When finally he was received, it was at an early hour in the morning and without any of the respects normally extended to the ambassadors of friendly monarchs.[13]

Ivan was plainly indicating his displeasure. But a few days later he sent for Randolph who, disguised in Russian dress and late at night, was conducted in great secrecy into the Kremlin Palace.[14] Unfortunately no record has survived of what took place at this secret audience. It seems, however, that Randolph kept closely to his instructions. Ivan was to complain later that he would talk only about "boorish . . . affairs of merchandise and would seldom talk with us of our princely affairs".[15] Randolph was nevertheless commanded to follow the Tsar to Vologda and there he was received more graciously.

In spite of his disappointment over Elizabeth's response to his proposals, Ivan had resolved to continue negotiating. In Vologda in June 1569 he informed Randolph of the grant of further privileges which gave the Company the most favourable conditions it was ever to enjoy in Muscovy. In his confirmatory letter to Elizabeth, Ivan also stated that he had withdrawn the privileges granted to Glover, Rutter, and other interlopers. They would be sent back to England, but he specially requested Elizabeth "for our sake to show favour unto them and to take away thy displeasure from them".[16]

Randolph sailed for England in July 1569, accompanied by Ivan's ambassador, Andrei Savin. Ivan was now confident that Elizabeth could no longer evade his requests of an alliance, and he wanted confirmation that he could depend on finding a safe and ready refuge in England in case of need. Savin even carried with him a treaty, dealing with these and other matters. The Queen was apparently expected to approve and ratify it without further discussion.

Ivan's chief demand was again for an alliance against his enemies. The ending of hostilities between Denmark, Poland, and Sweden in 1570 faced him with the possibility of these Baltic powers joining forces to exclude Muscovy from their sea. This threat made him all the more impatient to conclude an alliance with England.

Elizabeth now found herself in a difficult position. Blunt rejection of Ivan's demands might lead to an embargo on supplies essential to her navy, and it would certainly mean the end of the Company's trading monopolies in Muscovy. But she was not prepared to make the Tsar's enemies her own. She therefore worked out a compromise. She agreed to an alliance, but subject to the proviso that, if the Tsar suffered harm from any other monarch, she as his ally, on being convinced of the justice of his cause, would call on the aggressor to desist. If he paid no heed, then she would go to the Tsar's aid. She added that she was ready to grant all his other demands.[17]

Savin returned to Moscow, bearing two letters which contained Elizabeth's reply to Ivan's proposals. One was a "secret letter" in which she promised Ivan and his family refuge in England if "by any casual chance, either of secret conspiracy or outward hostility", they were driven from Muscovy. She would appoint a residence for them, but at their own expense, and "with all offices and courtesies let you, our dear brother Emperor and Great Duke, pass into your own country or elsewhere at your pleasure".[18]

Elizabeth's concessions were far from generous and her requirement that Ivan should meet his own expenses in England was downright niggardly. The alliance, as accepted by her, was of little real effect. But she apparently believed that her reply would satisfy Ivan, at least to the extent of persuading him to continue his generous treatment of the Company. In this she was gravely mistaken.

Ivan was infuriated by her response. He at once revoked the Company's privileges and sequestered its goods. He then wrote an angry outspoken letter, listing his complaints and charging her with having set aside his "great affairs". Further, he bluntly stated that Elizabeth had shown herself to be ruler only in name, for "now we perceive that there be other men that do rule, and not men but boors and merchants, the which seek not the wealth and honour of our Majesties, but they do seek their own profit of merchandise".[19]

This letter must have come as a shock to Elizabeth who was more accustomed to the high-flown compliments of her court. She was nevertheless to reply to it with restraint and dignity. News of the revocation of the Company's rights had, however, reached London before the Tsar's letter, and Elizabeth had at once written to protest. Then the Tsar's irate letter arrived. Prompt action to appease him was necessary. One of Ivan's complaints was that the Queen had failed to send "her great ambassador" with Savin to deliver her reply. Elizabeth at once appointed Anthony Jenkinson, whom Ivan had repeatedly asked for, to handle this difficult situation.

Ivan had written in response to Elizabeth's first protest before he had heard of Jenkinson's appointment. He advised her to read his previous letter again, if she wished "to see the occasion of our anger".[20] He wrote further that she would only assuage his wrath by sending her ambassador to deal with "the angry matters".[21] Before he closed his letter, however, he learnt of Jenkinson's arrival in North Russia, and he added, "And even now have we had tidings that Anthony (Jenkinson) is here arrived and when Anthony cometh unto us we will gladly hear him. . . ."[22]

Jenkinson had reached the White Sea at the end of July (1571). From Kholmogory he had written to Lord Burghley on "the miserable state" of Muscovy. Famine had reduced the people to eating bread made from tree-bark and "in some places they have eaten one another". The Tsar had "by sundry torments put to death a great number of his people". Plague had also carried off some 300,000 of the population. This was indeed a time of fearful sufferings for Ivan and his people. A further catastrophe at this time inflicted even greater tragedy on the nation. This was the successful invasion by the Crimean Khan whose Tatars burned Moscow to the ground and thousands lost their lives in the fires. [23]

While Livonia remained uppermost in his mind, Ivan could never for a moment relax his guard against attacks from the south. He made strenuous efforts to reach agreement with Khan Devlet Girei. The time seemed propitious. The Sultan was exerting pressure on the Crimean Horde to join in campaigns to recover Astrakhan and Kazan, and to make the Crescent dominant again in the Volga lands. The Khan opposed this policy. He knew that his Horde would have to bear the main burden of the campaigning and that this policy would inevitably lead to closer Turkish control over the Tatars who treasured their independence. For these reasons the Khan was disposed to make peace with the Tsar. At this time, however, he received approaches from Sigismund Augustus, who offered him money, far in excess of the Tsar's gifts, if he would renew hostilities against Muscovy. The Khan could never refuse rich presents and had at once launched an invasion into the Ryazan region.

Negotiations between Ivan and Devlet Girei nevertheless continued. Late in 1565, after his troops had hastily withdrawn from their abortive raid, the Khan sent an offer of permanent peace on the condition that Ivan surrendered both Kazan and Astrakhan to him. Ivan replied bluntly that he neither uttered nor wished to hear stupid propositions. [24] He had, in fact, taken extensive precautions to secure his grip on Kazan and the upper Volga region, establishing no less than seven new fortress towns, transferring the Tatar inhabitants to new lands in central Muscovy and even in Novgorod and Pskov, and settling Russian families in their place. He was now strengthening his hold on Astrakhan, and planning to establish a fortress on the Terek river, ostensibly for the protection of Temgruk, the father of his second wife. This stronghold on the Terek disturbed the Khan and cast a further shadow over their relations. To Ivan's ambassador, Nagoi, the Khan said angrily that "If he (the Tsar) will build a town on the Terek, then, even if he give me a mountain of gold, I will not make peace with him . . ." [25]

In 1566 Sultan Suleiman, known as "the Magnificent" and "the Lawgiver", died and his son, Selim, a degenerate whose reign was to begin the decline of the great Ottoman Empire, succeeded. With visions of emulating his father's great reign, Selim at once revived plans to recover Astrakhan, and he sought alliance with Sigismund Augustus against Muscovy. In the spring of 1569 Turkish troops,

17,000 strong, reached Kafa on the Crimean penisula and from there proceeded to Azov and up the river Don to Perevolok, where they were to build a canal linking the Don and Volga rivers. Joined by 50,000 Crimean Tatars the Turks were then to move down the Volga to capture Astrakhan. But the heat of August and shortage of supplies compelled them to give up digging the canal. Moreover, on approaching Astrakhan, they were thrown into a panic by news of a strong Russian force advancing to its defence. The Pasha in command burnt all that he could not carry and beat a hasty retreat to Azov.

This ignominious failure to recover Astrakhan did not blind Ivan to the serious danger to Muscovy involved in the revival of Turkish policy to dominate the Volga. In 1570 he sent Novosiltsev as his special envoy to Constantinople to congratulate Sultan Selim on his accession. Novosiltsev was to remind the Sultan of the former friendly relations between their predecessors and to express hopes for the continuance of such relations. Selim's response was not encouraging. In March 1571 Ivan sent a new ambassador, Kuzminsky, to express his readiness to abandon his stronghold on the Terek river and to make other concessions in the interest of peace. But now the Sultan demanded the surrender of Kazan and Astrakhan, and barely concealed his hostility.

During this period Ivan was also pursuing a conciliatory policy towards the Crimean Khan. He had even agreed to send the Khan gifts and gold many times greater in value than in previous years. Nevertheless, during the summer of 1570, frequent reports of large-scale Tatar invasions kept Russian troops alerted on the Oka river. Twice Ivan himself hastened to the Oka to repel the Khan. But the Tatars did not appear and the Muscovite forces were disbanded for the winter.

In the spring of 1571 alarming reports of a massive Tatar invasion again reached Moscow. The leading military commanders—Prince D. Belsky, Prince Ivan F. Mstislavsky, Prince Mikhail I. Vorotynsky, Prince Ivan A. Shuisky, and Prince Ivan P. Shuisky—took up positions with 50,000 troops on the Oka. Ivan with his Oprichniki waited in Serpukhov.

This time the report was not false. The Khan had assembled on the Muscovite frontier an army of 120,000 men. There a number of Muscovite traitors, demoralized by hardships, fled to him, and Mstislavsky himself was implicated in some treachery at this point. The deserters told the Khan that for two years the towns of central

Muscovy had suffered famine and plague, and that their populations had been seriously decimated. They added that the Tsar had executed many of his most able men and that the remaining Muscovite troops were in Livonia, while the Tsar himself had only a few of his guards with him in Serpukhov. They undertook to show the Khan where to cross the Oka to avoid engaging the Muscovite forces posted there, and then Moscow could be taken without difficulty.

The Khan adopted this advice. His Tatars were led across the Oka at some point, not now known, and made for Moscow. Ivan, finding himself cut off from his main force, hurriedly retired to Alexandrovsk and thence to Rostov. He did not wait to attack the Khan with his hopelessly inferior force of guards. Moreover, he probably suspected, if he did not know, that traitors had helped the Tatars, and with his deeply suspicious outlook he believed the worst and expected a mass revolt. In any case his withdrawal was an act of caution, such as Dmitri Donskoi and others of his predecessors had not hesitated to take in similar circumstances.[26]

The Muscovite commanders, learning that the Khan was north of the Oka, moved their troops with desperate haste to defend the capital. They reached Moscow on 23 May and took up positions on its outskirts. The Tatars arrived on the following day and without engaging the Muscovites began setting fire to the outlying suburbs. It was a fine clear day, but a strong wind began to blow. The fires spread rapidly and soon great clouds of smoke enveloped the burning city. The Muscovite troops in their defensive positions found themselves in a furnace and many were burnt to death. The city was crowded with people who had sought refuge within its walls as the Tatars approached and they perished in their thousands.

The fires raged so fiercely that the Tatars could not plunder and the Khan had to order his men to retreat, but they took with them a great crowd of prisoners, said to number as many as 150,000, to be sold as slaves. Within three hours the proud capital had been reduced to ashes. The Kremlin alone remained standing. The gates had been kept closed, even to the Muscovites who had struggled to find refuge within the high walls which gave protection against fire and the enemy. So many Muscovites, troops and ordinary citizens, were burnt alive as they tried to escape the flames that the Moscow river was choked with bodies. Help had to be brought from towns to the north to clear the corpses so that the river could flow again.

Ivan had always exacted the highest respects for his majesty and to have his capital reduced to ashes was a terrible humiliation. But he remained calm. His first concern was still to hold Livonia, while warding off further attacks by the Khan and the Sultan. But his restraint was sorely tested when on his return to Moscow he was met by two Tatar couriers. The Khan was exulting and his message to the Tsar was couched in a tone of lofty arrogance. "I burn and devastate all before me because of Kazan and Astrakhan . . . I came against you. I burnt your city. I wanted your head and crown, but you did not appear and did not match against us, and still you exalt yourself as the Muscovite monarch!" The message ended with threats that, if Kazan and Astrakhan were not given up, the Tatars would come again. [27]

Ivan made a conciliatory and even humble reply. In it he proposed to surrender Astrakhan and, playing on Tatar greed, he instructed his ambassador to suggest that the Tsar might be persuaded to pay him far more richly than ever before. His immediate purpose was to hold the Khan from launching another massive raid in the following year. But he knew that Devlet Girei, feeling that he had the Muscovites at his mercy, was bound to march.

In the summer of 1572 the Khan advanced to the Oka again with a force of 120,000 men. Ivan himself was in Novgorod, but he had posted a strong army under the command of Prince Mikhail I. Vorotynsky at Serpukhov. The Khan detached 2,000 of his Tatars to engage Vorotynsky while with his main force he crossed the Oka and made for Moscow again. But the Russian commander was not misled by this feint. He overtook the Tatars some thirty-five miles from the capital and in a series of engagements completely defeated them. The Khan was forced to flee with the remnants of his force. When shortly afterwards negotiations were renewed, the Khan wrote without arrogance and with the respect he usually showed the Tsar.

Notes to Chapter XIX

[1] The exception was Chancellor Viskovaty who expressed the independent opinion that an armistice might be made without requiring the surrender of the Livonian towns, but on the condition that the King withdrew his troops and did not hinder the Tsar in taking possession of these towns! Solovyev, Bk. III, Vol. VI, pp. 581–3; Klyuchevsky, II, pp. 384–7.

[2] When Ivan had finished speaking, the ambassadors said that owing to their imperfect Russian they had not understood parts of his speech. Ivan replied that his clerk had been present and would relate all that he had said. At this the unfortunate clerk threw himself before the throne and said,

"Gracious Sovereign! It is impossible to remember such great affairs. Your supreme intelligence, endowed by God, is above ordinary intelligence!" Solovyev, *op. cit.*, p. 587.

[3] It was noteworthy that the Assembly of the Land was not convened again. The delegates had given their advice, urging that war in Livonia should continue until the whole country was in Muscovite hands. But this in no way bound Ivan and he did not hesitate to overrule their advice.

[4] Solovyev, *op. cit.*, p. 588.

[5] E. D. Morgan and C. H. Coote (eds.), *Early Voyages and Travels in Russia and Persia*, Hakluyt Society, (London, 1886), II, pp. 236–8.

[6] *Ibid.*

[7] *Ibid.*

[8] G. Tolstoy, *The First Forty Years of Intercourse between England and Russia 1553–93* (St Petersburg, 1875), pp. 44–6.

[9] *Ibid.*

[10] It was indeed not clear that the Russia Company's monopoly applied to the Baltic trade. The Company claimed that it had the monopoly of all English trade with Muscovy, irrespective of the route used. Nevertheless it required an Act of Parliament, passed in 1566, to confirm this monopoly. T. S. Willan, *The Early History of the Muscovy Company 1553–1603* (Manchester, 1956), pp. 76–7.

[11] *Ibid.*, pp. 102–3.

[12] Tolstoy, *op. cit.*, p. xxi.

[13] E. D. Morgan and C. H. Coote, *op. cit.*, pp. 247–9, 282.

[14] *Ibid.*, pp. 249–50.

[15] *Ibid.*, p. 295.

[16] *Ibid.*, p. 283.

[17] Tolstoy, *op. cit.*, pp. 74–8.

[18] E. D. Morgan and C. H. Coote, *op. cit.*, pp. 290–2.

[19] *Ibid.*, pp. 292–7.

[20] *Ibid.*, p. 302.

[21] *Ibid.*

[22] *Ibid.*

[23] Jenkinson in his letter to Lord Burghley, after listing the sufferings of the Muscovites, concluded with the comment that this was "a just punishment of God for such a wicked nation". *Ibid.*, pp. 336–7.

[24] Solovyev, *op. cit.*, p. 600.

[25] *Ibid.*, p. 601.

[26] *Ibid.*, p. 620.

[27] *Ibid.*, pp. 607–8.

CHAPTER XX

IVAN'S TESTAMENT 1572

WITH the passing years Ivan had become more desperate in his struggle to establish Muscovy as a strong centralized nation. The great task to which he had devoted his reign seemed at times impossible to achieve. He suffered depressions when doubts and fears preyed on him. He did not fear his foreign enemies. By arms and skilful diplomacy he had pursued his policies with success against them, and he had maintained the defences of the Tsardom. The Tatars had once broken through and had set fire to Moscow, but his armies had taken swift revenge. Not his foreign enemies, but the enemies within the Tsardom made him desperate, for the struggle against them seemed unending.

Increasingly, too, Ivan was beset by a sense of doom. It hung over him and his dynasty. The crown of Monomakh which he had received as a sacred trust from his forebears was constantly threatened. In a fury he fought against the persistent treason which he believed to be rooted in the boyar-princely aristocracy. He saw this struggle as a fight for the survival not only of the dynasty but of the nation, and this was the background to his outbursts of savagery and his cruel executions.

Even while fighting the enemies in his midst, however, Ivan regarded their treachery as a punishment from God, and therefore something to be accepted humbly. Like the disastrous plagues and famines and the fires of Moscow, it was visited upon the nation, and his family, and upon him for his sins. Ivan was always deeply conscious of his burden of sin. In his letters to Kurbsky he had acknowledged several times that he was "altogether clothed with frailty by nature".[1] He spent hours every day before the blessed ikons in fervent prayer, imploring the intercession and guidance of the Saviour and the saints. But, although this opposition to his grand design might be a punishment from God, he could not give up the struggle, and a report of treachery would always throw him into a rage, when he would strike out unmercifully. Now, however, he was beginning to feel weary, for the struggle was taking heavy toll of him.

Loneliness aggravated his anguish. He had companions and favourites, like Malyuta Skuratov and Boris Godunov. Malyuta Grigory Lukyanovich Skuratov-Belsky, known as Malyuta Skuratov, was his devoted slave and he served Ivan faithfully until his death in the assault on Wittenstein in 1572. His son-in-law was Boris Godunov, a young courtier, related to the family of the first wife of Grand Prince Vasily, Ivan's father. Launched into favour through the goodwill enjoyed at court by Malyuta Skuratov, Boris Godunov himself had quickly made an impression on Ivan and had become one of his favourites. He had great charm of manner, innate discretion and intelligence, and he managed to avoid making enemies. After the death of Malyuta Skuratov he was to become Ivan's first favourite and to wield considerable influence on him.

Such favourites did not, however, banish loneliness and at this time Ivan's thoughts went back particularly to Anastasia whom he had loved tenderly and who had soothed him with her love and companionship. Probably it was in the hope of finding such a wife again that he began urgently planning to remarry.

Tsaritsa Maria, the Asiatic beauty who had been his second wife, had died suddenly on 1 September 1569. Ivan and his court had gone into mourning and in churches throughout the country prayers had been said for her repose. But Maria had been beloved neither by Ivan nor by the people, and the mourning had been formal without the popular demonstrations of grief which had followed the death of Anastasia. It was rumoured that enemies had poisoned her or worked her death by witchcraft, and those who came under suspicion were executed.

Some eighteen months later Ivan declared his intention to take a third wife. Messages went to all parts of the country, calling on fathers of beautiful and virtuous maidens to submit them for preliminary inspection locally by the Tsar's officers. Finally more than 2,000 virgins from great and insignificant families were assembled in Alexandrovsk.[2] From them Ivan chose twelve maidens, who were handed over to his doctor and to old women of the court for more intimate examination. Beauty, character, and intelligence were the main criteria, but also the chosen maiden had to be without blemish and free from such habits as snoring in bed.

Ivan's choice fell upon Marfa, the beautiful daughter of Vasily Sobakin, a Novgorod merchant. From this final group of maidens, too, Evdokiya Saburova was chosen as the bride for Tsarevich Ivan, the elder son. At once the fathers of the two brides were made boyars, their uncles and brothers were also granted high rank, and all received rich estates. As parents and kinsmen of the Tsaritsa and the wife of the Tsarevich they were brought close to the throne and held positions of influence.

Marfa had hardly been chosen when she went into a decline. A young girl, brought up in the seclusion of the women's quarters, she had probably heard alarming stories, and the prospect of marriage with the dread Tsar may have struck terror in her heart. But many said that witchcraft or slow poison, administered by Ivan's enemies, was at work. Marfa's condition grew worse. Suspicion fixed on the families of Ivan's two first wives. Prince Mikhailo Temgrukovich, brother of Maria, was impaled on a stake. Others were executed or poisoned, but not all of the victims belonged to the families of the first two wives, and some may have been guilty of failing in their duty or of treachery during the Khan's assault on Moscow. One of Ivan's former favourites, Grigory Gryazny, died horribly of poison at this time, but the charges against him are not known.

On 28 October 1571 Ivan married Marfa, and both Boris Godunov and Malyuta Skuratov were prominent at the ceremony. Six days later the Tsarevich married Evdokiya. Marfa was ill at the time of her wedding and Ivan declared his hope that by the influence of love and by God's mercy she would be cured. But she grew worse and after sixteen days of unconsummated marriage, the maiden, chosen from 2,000 for her beauty and character, passed away.[3]

To Ivan this tragic death of his bride must have been a clear mark of God's anger. But he reacted with desperate impatience, as though overwhelmed by the need for a wife and companion. Within two months of the death of Marfa, he married again. His fourth wife was Anna Alexeevna Koltovskaya, a beautiful girl of humble origin. This marriage was sudden and almost furtive, without any of the proclamations or assembling of maidens usual when the Tsar took a wife. The reason for the haste and secrecy was that, as Ivan well knew, to take a fourth wife was forbidden by canon law. After committing the offence he was at once appalled that he had in this way added to his heavy burden of sin, and fearing that the Lord might also dissolve this marriage in tragedy, Ivan made haste to seek the forgiveness and blessing of the church.

Formally summoned to the Uspensky Cathedral, the bishops gathered with Leonid, Archbishop of Novgorod at their head, for Metropolitan Kirill had just died. Ivan spoke of the death of his first Tsaritsa by the witchcraft of his enemies and of his second by poison. "I waited some time," he continued, "and I decided on a third marriage, partly for my bodily need . . . for to live in the world without a wife is full of temptations."[4] He referred movingly to the death of Marfa and went on, "in despair and grief I wanted to dedicate myself to the monkish life, but seeing again the tender youth of my sons and seeing the Tsardom in the midst of disasters, I dared to take a fourth wife".[5] Humbly he submitted himself to the church council, beseeching their blessing.

The bishops considered his appeal and imposed certain penances, but they acknowledged the marriage and undertook to pray for Tsaritsa Anna. At the same time, lest anyone be tempted to follow the Tsar's example, they threatened with the condemnation of the church any man who took to himself a fourth wife. The council then turned to the election of the new Metropolitan and chose Anthony, Archbishop of Polotsk, whom Ivan approved.

Tsaritsa Anna held Ivan's affection only for some three years. This may have been because she failed to conceive within this period and was therefore considered barren, or, as is more likely, Ivan simply tired of her. In 1575 she was sent to the Tikhvinsky nunnery and shorn as a nun, which had the effect of divorce. In the same year Ivan took a fifth wife, named Anna Vassilchikova, but without any church ceremony, and her family did not appear at court as would have happened had it been a formal marriage. Indeed, since a fifth wife was unheard of and would have required the very special dispensation of the church, Ivan took her no doubt merely as a mistress. This applied also to his sixth wife, a most beautiful widow, called Vassilissa Melentievna, who was known as "the woman."[6]

In the summer of 1572, while staying in Novgorod, Ivan also made his final testament. It is a moving document, giving some insight into his heart and mind. It revealed him as a man of courage and determination, and of strong loyalties. Also it gave further evidence of his sense of the insecurity of himself and his dynasty on the throne of Muscovy. Unless he waged his unrelenting struggle against his enemies, he and his family would surely be compelled to flee from their fatherland and be condemned to wander as pitiful exiles in foreign lands. Furthermore he believed that his own death was near at hand.

The testament began with a confession of weariness and decay, both bodily and spiritual, although he was no more than 42 years old at this time.

"My body grows weak [he wrote]. My soul is sick. Sores of the flesh and the spirit multiply, and there is no doctor who can heal me. I waited for someone who would grieve with me—but no one have I found to console me. All have returned me evil for good, hatred for love. . . ." [7]

Ivan's instructions to his sons, which compose most of the testament, began with the words of Christ: "This I command, that you love one another." Ivan added his own injunction that "You yourselves must live in love and in every possible way master military matters." The essence of his message to his two sons was that they should stand together indivisibly in everything, until such time as they had swept treason from the land and Tsarevich Ivan had secured himself on the throne. They should bind their people to them, but should never relax their guard. They should love and favour those who served honestly, and those who were evil they should punish, not hastily or in a fury, as he himself had so often done, but after calm consideration.

The Tsarevichi should keep themselves well informed on all affairs of church and state, on the ways of life of people of all classes, both in Muscovy and in other countries, and on the conduct of policy, especially with foreign governments. "If you do not know these things, then you yourselves will not rule your realm, but other people will rule." [8]

Ivan stressed further the need for his sons to stand together in the face of disasters threatening the Tsardom.

"Because of the multitude of my sins, God has sent down his anger . . . and my sins have brought you many misfortunes, but in God's name do not grow weak in affliction. Until such time as God forgives and frees you from misfortunes, you must be divided in nothing." [9]

In the testament, Ivan then addressed his sons individually. Here he broke from the customary injunctions of his predecessors, who had merely enjoined all sons to obey their eldest brother as standing in their father's place. This had not been enough in the past to prevent challenges to the heir to the throne. Ivan required Tsarevich Feodor to obey his elder brother unto death, never opposing him, and even if harmed by him never bearing arms to vindicate his cause. For the first time the younger son was absolutely subservient to the elder. All pretext for family rivalries was destroyed and in future rebellion against the brother who had succeeded to the throne was treason.

A further innovation, made by this testament, concerned the bequest of the Tsardom. Although the Grand Princes of Muscovy had made it a practice to bequeath the greatest part of the realm to their eldest sons, they had always granted substantial independent principalities to their other sons. Ivan abandoned this custom. He blessed Tsarevich Ivan as his heir and successor to the crown of Monomakh with all the dignities of the title of Tsar and with the whole Tsardom. To Tsarevich Feodor were bequeathed only fourteen towns and no part of Moscow. Thus the power and possessions of the elder son were further confirmed by the denial to the younger of any real independence.

In one of the final clauses of his testament, Ivan referred to the Oprichnina, and his instructions reflected his disappointment in this establishment and in the special guards. The Tsarevichi should, he wrote, retain the Oprichnina or abandon it, whichever they considered more advantageous. But within a few weeks he himself had made this decision for them.

In August 1572 Ivan was in Novgorod when couriers brought news of Vorotynsky's crushing defeats of Devlet Girei's Tatars. Ivan was jubilant, for this victory erased the humiliation of the burning of Moscow. Soon afterwards he learnt of the death on 7 July 1572 of his great enemy, King Sigismund Augustus. He made haste to return to Moscow, where he made a triumphal entry and was hailed by his people.

For the first time in many years the people of Moscow were in a mood to celebrate. The plague had passed; food was sufficient for all once more; and finally their forces had routed the hated Tatars. Joyfully they welcomed the Tsar, their leader and little father. Ivan did not, however, spend his time in celebrations. He was occupied with preparations for the invasion of Esthonia. He was also conducting secret negotiations concerning the accession of himself or of his son to the throne of Sigismund Augustus. During these weeks, too, he disbanded the Oprichnina.[10]

For two years and even longer Ivan's confidence in the Oprichnina had been waning. It had failed to give him the security that he wanted. It had failed to protect Tsaritsa Marfa against witchcraft and she had died. His trust in his special guards, the Oprichniki, had been shaken. Several of the most prominent among them had been implicated with Pimen in the Novgorod sedition and had been executed. The failure to defend Moscow against the Tatars in the previous year had demonstrated that they were not to be trusted with the defence of the nation. This had been further proven by the fact that the Zemshchina, led by its boyars, had repelled the Khan's second invasion and had won a resounding victory.

Two other factors played a part in Ivan's decision to disband the Oprichnina. One was the hatred which it aroused in his people. He had formerly accepted this as desirable, believing that it would ensure the loyalty of these guards to himself. But it had not prevented treachery among them. On the other hand the people had been loyal and had patiently endured hardships and disaster without revolt. The other factor was that the evil reputation of the Oprichniki might alarm the Poles and Lithuanians and imperil the negotiations which he was then conducting.

The Oprichnina was therefore abolished, but it took time to unravel the complex situation to which it had given rise. This applied to the organization and seniority of the serving gentry, some of whom served in the Oprichnina and some in the Zemshchina. But the greatest problem arose from the reallocation of land. Heinrich Staden, a German who had served as an Oprichnik, stated that the *zemsky* gentry who had defeated the Tatars were rewarded with grants of patrimonial estates. Oprichniki were dispossessed and had to accept lands elsewhere on service tenure. A further complication was that landowners returning to the estates which had been taken for the Oprichnina found them in ruin and deserted by their peasants.

Ivan III had settled families from Novgorod on service estates, mainly on his eastern frontier, but he had carried out this resettlement in a firm orderly manner, and he had achieved his purpose of consolidating landholding in the new regions. The disorderly return of the old landowners to their estates after the abolition of the Oprichnina and the resettlement of the Oprichniki, continuing over a long period, disrupted military service, impoverished the land and in some degree weakened the military forces of the country.

Ivan at this time, however, was absorbed by the struggle to secure Livonia, if necessary by accepting the throne of Poland–Lithuania, and he was also disturbed by further threats of sedition by the boyars. Prince Ivan Mstislavsky who in rank and nobility stood high above other princes and boyars, and who with others had been head of the Zemshchina, had in 1571 confessed that he had betrayed his country by giving help to Devlet Girei to cross the river Oka. Ivan had pardoned him on the intercession of the Metropolitan and other churchmen, but had exacted from him a sworn undertaking that he would not flee to the Tsar's enemies. He also required that three boyars should stand surety for him and that 285 others should stand as sureties for these three boyars.[11]

The fact that Mstislavsky could behave with such treachery showed that Ivan's fears and suspicions were more than chimera. In 1574 several boyars, the archimandrite of the Chudov monastery, an archpriest, and several others were beheaded in Moscow, and their heads were thrown into the forecourt of Mstislavsky's palace. The victims had no doubt been involved in his treachery, but had paid the penalty with their lives.

In the following year Ivan ordered the execution of Prince Nikita Odoevsky and Mikhail Morozov with his wife and two sons, and Peter Kurakin, and Boyar I. A. Buturlin, all of whom were charged with aiding the Khan or causing the death of the Tsar's bride, Marfa. A number of former Oprichniki were also executed. Most surprising was the arrest of the great military leader, Prince Mikhail Vorotynsky. He had once been incarcerated in the Kirillo-Belozersky monastery, but Ivan had recalled him, giving him high office in which he had served with great distinction. He was now sent again to the monastery on charges not now known, and on the road he died.[12]

No further executions were recorded during the last eight years of Ivan's reign.[13] He may have wearied of sending traitors and suspects to their deaths, or he may have concluded that execution was not effective in eradicating treachery among his nobles. Mstislavsky's betrayal had perhaps demonstrated to him that execution would never be a sufficient deterrent. Throughout his reign Ivan had raged and struck down all who betrayed him or the nation. But now towards the close of his reign he abandoned severity, and, as he had done with Sylvester, he left the punishment of traitors and other malefactors to the final judgment of Heaven.

Nevertheless the constant fear of sedition and the awful burdens of authority weighed heavily on Ivan. At times he felt a longing to be relieved of responsibility for the nation and for his dynasty. He even enacted a charade, appointing a baptized Tatar, Prince Simeon Bekbulatovich, as Tsar in his place. Ivan crowned him formally, showed him all the respects due to the Tsar, and himself went under the name of Ivan Moskovsky. He lived for a time privately as a boyar in Petrovka Street in Moscow. Documents have even survived which were issued in the name of "Grand Prince Semeon of All Russia". For two years Semeon sat upon the throne and Boyar

Ivan Moskovsky lived quietly, going about the streets of Moscow and at court taking his place among the lesser boyars at a distance from the throne. Suddenly Semeon was dethroned and sent into honourable exile in Tver. Ivan, who had relinquished no more than the trappings of office to him, then resumed his place on the throne. He had, in fact, found that he could not divest himself of responsibility or of the office to which he had been born.

Notes to Chapter XX

[1] Fennell, *Correspondence*, p. 123.
[2] Karamzin, Bk. III, Vol. IX, col. 110.
[3] *Ibid.*, cols. 76–7.
[4] *Ibid.*, col. 114.
[5] *Ibid.*, col. 115.
[6] *Ibid.*, cols. 161–2 and note, p. 494.
[7] Solovyev, *op. cit.*, p. 561.
[8] *Ibid.*, p. 562.
[9] *Ibid.*
[10] Karamzin, Solovyev, and Klyuchevsky have accepted that the name, Oprichnina, was abolished, but that the establishment itself continued. See now, however, S. V. Veselovsky, "The Institution of the Oprichny Establishment in 1565 and its Abolition in 1572" in *Voprosy Istorii*, 1946, No. 1, pp. 86–104.
[11] Solovyev, *op. cit.*, p. 564.
[12] Kurbsky stated that Vorotynsky was interrogated under torture as a result of which he died. Solovyev, *op. cit.*, p. 565.
[13] According to some sources many more executions took place. One such source noted that 2,300 of the troops who had surrendered at Polotsk were executed in Moscow in 1582. But executions on such a scale would have been recorded in official documents and by Russian chroniclers who noted such matters in great detail. In fact, it is beyond reasonable doubt that no executions took place among troops or boyars in these last years of Ivan's life. Karamzin, *op. cit.*, col. 210 and note 617; Solovyev, *op. cit.*, p. 565.

CHAPTER XXI

STEFAN BATORY AND THE END OF THE LIVONIAN WAR 1576–82

On the death of Sigismund Augustus without heir, Poles and Lithuanians prepared urgently for the election of a new king. In the past the monarchy had been hereditary, for the king had always been chosen from the Jagellon dynasty, but this election was to be free. The country was at once divided into factions, each fighting for its own special interests. Protestantism was strong among the Lithuanians, who feared Catholic persecution. The Poles, although Catholic, were tolerant, but the church in Poland was dominated by the militant Jesuit Order and struggled to keep all power in Catholic hands. Poles and Lithuanians were also divided into regional and class factions, and the rivalry between magnates and gentry was especially strong.

Ivan, one of five candidates for the throne, had support mainly from the Orthodox Lithuanians, most of whom were Russians, who saw in him their natural ruler. He had supporters also among the Protestants who believed that he would ensure religious toleration, and among the gentry who considered that he would not only humble the magnates, but would also defend them against the Emperor and the Sultan. Against his election were ranged the Catholics and all the support that they could muster.

Ivan was inclined to hold himself aloof. He had shown no real enthusiasm for the Polish throne when first approached some two years earlier, while Sigismund Augustus was still alive. The throne had then attracted him only as a means of advancing his policy for Muscovy. If elected, he would be able to secure his hold on Livonia and to recover Kiev and the Ukraine and White Russia. The interests of Poland–Lithuania did not concern him.

Late in the summer of 1572 Ivan had returned from Novgorod to Moscow. There he had received the courier, Voropai, who had brought formal notification of the King's death and also a message from the Polish–Lithuanian Seym, expressing support for the election of Tsarevich Feodor to the throne. Ivan spoke at length in reply to this message and he showed a wide appreciation of the many factors affecting his candidature. But his comments also revealed conflict within himself. The prestige and power of being monarch of Poland–Lithuania as well as of Muscovy undoubtedly attracted him. At the same time he recognized the tremendous difficulties which he would have to face, and in particular the opposition of the Poles and of the Catholic church. Ivan was practical and singleminded, and he concentrated on his objective of creating a strong Muscovite nation. But he could not be immune to the attraction of the Polish throne, and his speech to Voropai at first revealed some eagerness to be elected.

Ivan began by assuring Voropai that, if the nobles of Poland and Lithuania chose him as their ruler, they would find in him a strong champion and a defender of Orthodoxy. Further, if their two countries were united, no nation could stand against them. Then, realizing that his personal reputation would militate strongly against his election, he defended himself.

> "In your country [he said], many people say that I am ill-tempered; it is true that I am ill-tempered and given to anger. I take no pride in it, but let them ask me against whom I am ill-tempered. I will answer that it is against those who are malicious towards me, but to those who are loyal I will not grudge this chain of mine or my cloak."[1]

Knowing the love of riches and the corruption of the Polish gentry, he spoke of his wealth, claiming that his treasury and his domains were double the value of those of his father and grandfather, which had been famed among Polish and Lithuanian nobles.

Ivan again defended himself in anticipation of criticisms that he had failed to defend Moscow against the Khan in 1571. Certain of his subjects, he said, had betrayed him to the Crimean Tatars who had numbered 40,000 as against his 6,000 men. He had been kept in ignorance of the position and, when he had realized that his people had betrayed him, he had withdrawn. Moscow had already been on fire before he had learnt that the Tatars had penetrated his defences. But he had punished the guilty men, just as in Lithuania traitors were punished.

> "If it please God that I should be their sovereign [he continued, referring to the Polish and Lithuanian nobles], then I swear to God and to them that I will preserve all their rights and freedoms and, as it prove needful, I will grant them more. I do not wish to speak

of my virtues or my failings. If the Polish and Lithuanian nobles should send their sons to serve me or my children, then they would know whether I am ill-tempered or kindly."[2]

At times Ivan's speech suggested that he had shed his misgivings and become enthusiastic about his election. He urged his case and defended himself convincingly. Referring to Kurbsky who had taken refuge in Lithuania and had maligned him with such violent energy, Ivan explained his case persuasively. But when he came to speak of Livonia he showed that it was still the Baltic seaboard rather than the Polish throne which he was seeking.

"But if it is not desired to take me as your sovereign then send to me your great ambassadors so that we may reach a firm understanding. I do not insist on keeping Polotsk; all its surroundings, including those belonging to Muscovy, I will yield, if only Livonia along the Dvina is ceded to me. Then will we conclude an eternal peace with Lithuania."[3]

Six months passed after Voropai's departure before another mission arrived in Moscow. During this period other monarchs interested in election to the Polish throne sent strong embassies to Poland, and by gifts and plotting were doing everything possible to win support. But Ivan refused to canvas for election and would send no ambassadors or bribes. Indeed, during these months, he seems to have changed his mind again. Mikhail Garaburda, the ambassador who came from the Lithuanian Seym only and did not represent the Poles, at the beginning of 1573 found him in a difficult mood. Garaburda asked Ivan to state definitely whether he wished to be chosen as king or was willing to see his son elected. He added that in the event of the election either of him or of his son the Lithuanian Seym would require him to cede certain towns. Ivan was displeased, especially as the Lithuanian conditions touched the Tsarevich. "Our son is not a maiden for whom it would be necessary to give a dowry!" he exclaimed.[4] In any case he did not favour having either of his sons elected to the Polish throne, for it might lead to rivalry between them. But he now recommended the election of Archduke Ernst, son of the Emperor, whom he said he would regard as favourably as his own son on the Polish throne.

A further alternative appealed strongly to Ivan. "If the Grand Principality of Lithuania were to wish our rule alone, and without the Polish Crown, that would be still more agreeable to us," he said to Garaburda.[5] Poland was to Ivan a distant country, while Lithuania was familiar and largely inhabited by his own people. He pressed this alternative, explaining that he was already old and would have difficulty in ruling Poland and Lithuania as well as Muscovy. But he knew that the new union binding Poland and Lithuania could not be easily dissolved. He added the warning, therefore, that whatever the nobles decided they should not choose a French king, who would be bound to support the interests of the Turks rather than of Christianity.

The reports carried back to Vilno and Warsaw by Garaburda and Voropai on the Tsar's attitude to his election and his changes of mind were hardly calculated to strengthen his case. Moreover, he not only continued to refuse to send ambassadors, but rejected suggestions made by Polish and Lithuanian supporters that he send money for bribes, or march with his armies from Polotsk and thus force a decision in his favour. He had, in fact, recognized by this time that he had no real interest in being elected and that Livonia was what mattered to him.

Of the candidates for the throne Archduke Ernst and Henry of Valois, son of Catherine de Medici, were in the strongest position. The magnates favoured Archduke Ernst, but the gentry bitterly opposed him. They declared that they would never accept a Habsburg, who would deprive them of their rights and independence. The Turkish Sultan even threatened war if a Habsburg were elected.

Henry of Valois, the French candidate, had the full support of the Catholics, as well as of the Turkish Sultan. The French envoy in Poland, Bishop Montluc of Valence, was exceptionally able in advancing Henry's cause. But he met with considerable opposition. The savagery of the massacre of St Bartholomew's Day had profoundly shocked not only the Protestants but also the Catholic Poles. For a time all were united in their fears of Catholic religious persecution and, meeting on 28 January 1573, they signed a compact, known as the Confederation of Warsaw, ensuring complete religious toleration throughout the country. When, owing largely to the efforts of Montluc, Henry of Valois was elected king, he was required formally to sign this Confederation as well as special guarantees that he would respect the Polish constitution and the full rights of the gentry.

On 21 February 1574 Henry was crowned in the Cathedral of Cracow. But he at once showed that no more unfortunate choice could have been made. Irresponsible, spoilt, dissolute, Henry was totally unsuited to the duties of sovereign. He was, moreover, antagonized by the factional strife at his court as well as by the demands of the Polish gentry. He abandoned all thought of taking up his responsibilities and gave himself up to riotous living. When unexpectedly his brother died and his mother summoned him to Paris, he secretly slipped out of Poland and his reign came to an ignominious end.

Ivan and Emperor Maximilian had been brought closer together in their mutual opposition to the election of a Frenchman to the Polish throne. France was the ally and Austria the traditional enemy of the Ottoman Porte, and a French king on the throne of Poland–Lithuania might greatly strengthen the Sultan's hand against both the Emperor and the Tsar. Maximilian had even suggested to Ivan that he should take Lithuania, leaving Poland to Austria, and that they should then form an alliance against Turkey. Both men had been appalled by the Massacre of St Bartholomew's Day, and Ivan was particularly incensed by the savagery of the French king in making "so much blood to flow without reason".[6] To Ivan religious intolerance was never sufficient ground for such bloodshed, but treason, threatening the very existence of a nation, was a justification.

Angry and humiliated by Henry's contemptuous attitude to their crown, many Poles and Lithuanians were ready to declare the throne vacant. On the insistence of the Primate, however, Henry was allowed until 12 May 1575 to return to Poland, if he wished to retain the throne. Meanwhile in Poland embassies and agents had begun canvassing and distributing gifts on behalf of the candidates in the new elections which were expected. The rivalry between the Habsburgs and the Valois revived. The Emperor was now more anxious to have his son, Archduke Ernst, elected, in order to weaken French influence in Eastern Europe and strengthen his hold on Hungary at the expense of the Sultan of Turkey.

In January 1576 the imperial ambassadors, Hans Kobenzl and Daniel Prince, arrived in Muscovy. Ivan himself welcomed them at Mozhaisk, and never before had such efforts been made to pay fullest respects and to impress envoys to the Tsar. Ivan received them, wearing his most magnificent robes and his throne was surrounded by boyars and courtiers in robes of gold. At this and the subsequent receptions, the Muscovite ceremonial, ponderous but unequalled in its splendour, staggered the imperial ambassadors. Reporting to Vienna, Kobenzl wrote:

"I have seen the treasures of Your Imperial Majesty, of the Kings of Spain, France, Hungary, Bohemia, and of the Duke of Tuscany, but I have seen nothing like the riches of Ivan. . . . When we travelled to Russia, the Polish magnates frightened us with stories of the intolerable crudity of the Muscovite court. What have we seen? Neither in Rome nor in Spain would we have found a better reception, for the Tsar knows with whom he is dealing and how to treat us." [7]

While showing every respect to the ambassadors, Ivan did not accept all the proposals they brought from the Emperor. He agreed to support the election of Archduke Ernst to the Polish throne, but the demand that he vacate Livonia which, it was claimed, belonged to the Empire was wholly unacceptable. Kobenzl spoke eloquently on the need for a union of Christian powers, headed by the Tsar and the Emperor, who would expel the Sultan from Constantinople into the deserts of Arabia, whereupon the ancient Greek empire would belong to the Tsar. This was a grandiose conception of the kind which did not appeal to the practical mind of Ivan, which was concentrated not on the Bosphorus and the Hellespont, but on the Baltic. Ivan coldly replied that Lithuania and Kiev must be permanently united with Muscovy and that Livonia was and had always belonged to the Tsar. The imperial ambassadors, while reluctantly conceding the Muscovite claims to Kiev and Livonia, now pointed out the difficulty of separating Lithuania and Poland. Kobenzl then warned Ivan of the intention of many Poles to elect to the throne Stefan Batory, Prince of Transylvania, the vassal of the Sultan, but Ivan, concerned only that the Emperor should formally recognize his possession of Livonia, refused to be disturbed by such rumours. [8]

Stefan Batory had not been mentioned during the first election, but his name had now captured the imagination of the Polish gentry. Of Hungarian birth, Batory was already a national hero in Transylvania and in Hungary as a result of his struggle against the Emperor. To the Polish gentry who feared their own magnates and the Habsburgs, he was an ideal choice. The fact that the Sultan supported him also told strongly in his favour.

On 14 December 1575 the gentry elected Batory to the throne on the condition that he should marry Princess Anna, sister of the late Sigismund Augustus, thereby preserving some link with the Jagellon dynasty. Two days earlier, however, the magnates meeting in the Senate in Warsaw had elected Maximilian II to be King of Poland. The gentry vehemently rejected this election; the magnates refused recognition to Batory. The gentry hurriedly sent envoys to Batory and the magnates sent their envoys to Maximilian. The envoys notified each of his election and stressed the need to hasten to

Cracow for the coronation. It seemed that the confusion would be resolved by the race to Cracow, the winner being crowned king. But Maximilian reacted with great caution, and insisted on waiting for confirmation of the Tsar's support to reach him. He did not in fact signify his acceptance of the Polish crown until 23 March 1576. By that date it was already too late.

Batory had accepted the crown at once and had declared publicly on two occasions that he would honour all the conditions laid down by the Polish nobility. By mid-March he had set out on his journey to Cracow and it became a triumphal progress. He made a magnificent entry into the old city amid enthusiastic greetings from his future subjects. He was crowned on 29 April and then celebrated his marriage with Anna.

Within a few months of his coronation, Poles from all parts of the country had sworn allegiance to Batory. The exception was the powerful city of Danzig, which dominated Poland's Baltic trade. The burghers of Danzig had in the second election supported Emperor Maximilian II, hoping that as King of Poland he would restore to the city its ancient rights and also channel more trade through their hands. They had dismissed Batory as no more than a provincial princeling without knowledge of commerce.

Learning of this defiance, Batory acted so boldly that even the Poles were taken aback. He declared the burghers of Danzig outlaws and placed an embargo on their trade. Still they defied him and in June 1576 he laid siege to the city. But it did not yield readily and not until December 1577, nearly two years after his coronation, was Batory able to wring full allegiance from Danzig.

Ivan had accepted the election of Stefan Batory with apparent indifference. Polish ambassadors had come to Moscow later in 1576 from the new king, bringing proposals for permanent peace, for Batory wanted no trouble with the Muscovites while he was engaged against Danzig. But the Polish note in its deliberate failure to observe such basic protocol as addressing Ivan by his proper title of Tsar and in referring to Batory as King of Livonia merely aroused hostility.

Ivan now decided to complete his conquest of Livonia. Taking advantage of Batory's preoccupation with Danzig, he would conquer the Livonian towns in Swedish and Polish possession and then stand ready to negotiate a permanent peace. Towards the end of 1576 his army of 50,000 troops was ready to move from Novgorod, and on 23 January 1577 the Muscovites began their siege of Reval. But the

Swedish garrison and the people defended their city with spirit and after six weeks the Muscovites were compelled by the winter cold and by illness to raise the siege and retreat.

In the spring of 1577 Ivan himself with his two sons went to Novgorod. He had ordered troops from all parts of the Tsardom to assemble there and in Pskov, and it was one of the strongest armies that Muscovy had ever mustered. All now believed that the Tsar intended this time to crush Reval. But, although an armistice with Poland was still in force, he sent his troops into the southern regions of Livonia which were occupied by the Poles. Completely unprepared for this invasion and demoralized by the approach of the Muscovite force, Polish and German garrisons capitulated and within a few days six important towns were taken.

Magnus, whom Ivan had pardoned for his failure to take Reval in 1570, had at last found the courage to appear before the Tsar in Pskov. He had been received graciously and given orders to use his German troops to capture Wenden. But already Ivan had become suspicious of Magnus and his suspicions increased on receiving reports that he was in league with the Poles. He had further cause for anger when Magnus, ignoring his orders to proceed directly to Wenden, had halted to receive the submission of several Livonian towns. Ivan wrote him a stern and threatening letter, but then he learnt that Magnus had been in communication with the Duke of Courland and was also plotting to hand over to Batory the Livonian towns which had surrendered to him. Ivan now ordered Magnus to appear before him and, after charging him with deceit and ingratitude, he placed him under arrest.

Meanwhile the Russians had entered Wenden without opposition. The citizens of the town were left in peace, but strong guards were posted and accommodation was prepared for the Tsar and his attendants. Order reigned in the town, but then German troops, who had served Magnus, locked themselves with their families and possessions in the fortress within the town. Magnus was brought to persuade them to open the gates and surrender, but they refused and began firing on the Russian troops, killing many men. Ivan now ordered all cannons to fire on the fortress. After three days of ceaseless bombardment, the walls began to collapse and the Germans saw that they could not escape capture. They then packed all their gunpowder in the vaults of the fortress and, while men, women and children knelt in prayer, one of their party threw himself on to the powder, holding a burning brand. The explosion completely destroyed the fortress killing all within it and caused considerable damage in the town. But now the citizens of Wenden, although they had not been involved in this desperate exploit, suffered the full weight of Muscovite fury. Men, women, and children were killed. The whole town was littered with corpses and more than any other incident in the war, this massacre of Wenden earned Ivan and his troops the hatred of the Livonians.[9]

Ivan's triumphant advance through southern Livonia continued. Fortresses and towns submitted on his approach and there were no further massacres. Only Riga and Reval remained to be taken. But Ivan withdrew at this stage to Wolmar to celebrate his victories.[10] He then proceeded to Dorpat and there, to the surprise of his court, he pardoned Magnus, who had been brought under guard and was himself expecting death. Ivan in Duneburg also pardoned Taube and Kruse who had betrayed him to Sigismund Augustus in 1570. He then travelled to Pskov and thence to his retreat in Alexandrovsk. He could well feel satisfied with the results of this campaign, for it had completed his conquest of Livonia, except only for Riga and Reval. He could now concentrate on expanding his trade with Western Europe and by adopting new skills and techniques develop his people and country. But his possession of Livonia was to be shortlived.

While jubilant over the successes of his armies and the fulfilment of his policies, Ivan did not overlook his need for allies. He sent an ambassador to Vienna to convey his greetings to Emperor Rudolph who had succeeded to the throne on the death of Maximilian in 1576. He hoped to win Rudolph's agreement to an alliance with the purpose of overthrowing Batory and separating Lithuania from Poland, after which they would combine with the rest of Christian Europe to conquer the Turkish Empire. But Rudolph was not a man to embrace such bold policies and the negotiations came to nothing.

The King of Denmark, Frederick, had in the meantime sent envoys to propose an alliance with the Tsar, for he mistrusted Sweden and was opposed to Batory. Ivan's attitude towards the Danish king, coloured perhaps by his disappointment in Magnus, was one of arrogant condescension. He rejected an offer of eternal peace and would agree only an armistice for fifteen years, and then on conditions which antagonized Frederick.

Towards the Khan of the Crimea, Ivan behaved very differently. In June 1577 Devlet Girei had died, and Ivan was eager to form a permanent alliance with his son and successor, Mahomet Girei. In the previous century Ivan III, Ivan's grandfather, had by his alliance with Mengli Girei freed himself to concentrate his forces against Lithuania–Poland, and Ivan hoped now to follow the same policy. He was encouraged by the fact that Mahomet Girei, soon after his succession, had embarked on raids, not of Muscovite, but of Lithuanian territory.

Prince Mosalsky, Ivan's envoy to the Khan, conveyed not only friendly greetings, but rich presents exceeding any that the Tsar had yet sent. But in return for the proposed alliance Mahomet Girei demanded the return of Astrakhan and also that the Tsar should remove the Cossacks from the Don and the Dnieper. Ivan replied that the Don Cossacks were vagrants and brigands whom his commanders had orders to kill when captured, while the Cossacks of the Dnieper were the responsibility of the King of Poland. Astrakhan, he insisted, belonged to Russia and was being reinforced as a centre of Christianity. Ivan's plans for alliance advanced no further and Mahomet Girei was to prove an implacable opponent.

Meanwhile in 1577 a party of Swedes reached Narva by sea and, after setting fire to the wooden fortifications, captured a number of Russian troops. Another Swedish party laid waste lands in the Kexholm region. At this time, too, Lithuanian troops captured Duneburg. More serious was the success of German troops in the service of Batory who managed to gain entry into Wenden, which had suffered the blowing up of its fortress and then the Tsar's anger. The Germans killed the Russian garrison troops, most of them in their sleep, and manned the town's defences. Also at this time Magnus committed his final betrayal when he fled to Batory and swore allegiance to him. Magnus then went into hiding in the small town of Pilten in Courland, taking with him his young Muscovite wife, Maria, the daughter of Prince Vladimir Andreevich, whom Ivan had bestowed upon him four years earlier. Although minor, these reverses enraged Ivan, especially the loss of Wenden. He sent his leading commanders, even including Mstislavsky, to recapture the town, but they were repelled and then forced to withdraw by the approach of troops, sent by Batory.

Once he had secured the allegiance of Danzig, Batory turned his attention to Muscovy. He did not, however, plunge headlong into war. Many Poles were, he knew, still suspicious of him and intimidated by the might of the Tsar. He could not therefore assume that the Seym would vote him the necessary funds. He was also disturbed by misunderstandings with Turkey and Sweden. But he himself was impatient to meet the threat of Muscovite power.

In January 1578 Batory's envoys arrived in Moscow to negotiate a further peace. The King was, they said, anxious to live on friendly terms with his neighbours, especially Muscovy and, although the Tsar had by invading Livonia transgressed the existing armistice, they were empowered to negotiate afresh. But then they demanded the cession of the whole of Livonia and all the ancient Russian lands from Kaluga to Chernigov and the Dvina. The Tsar countered by requiring the cession to him of Kiev, Kanev, Vitebsk, and other towns as well as an undertaking that the King would not venture into Livonia or Courland. Such demands were patently unacceptable and, as each side well knew, a permanent peace was impossible between them. The envoys nevertheless agreed a three-year armistice, but on their return to Poland the King refused to ratify it.[11]

While his envoys were in Moscow, Batory appeared before the Seym to ask for subsidies to enable him to mobilize an army and march against Muscovy. He urged the Polish and Lithuanian nobles to recognize that Ivan's possession of Livonia would make Russia mistress of the Baltic, and that from Livonia he would conquer other parts of East Prussia and Lithuania. The Seym was, however, reluctant to authorize a full-scale campaign, and voted subsidies only for a defensive war. But Batory at once began preparations to attack and his objectives were ambitious. He confided to the Papal Nuncio and to his chancellor, Jan Zamojsky, that he had two aims; first to recover Livonia and, second, to conquer Muscovy. His strategy was to begin with the capture of Polotsk, which would enable him to shield both Lithuania and Livonia against further Muscovite attack, and also give him an advance position from which to march on Moscow when he was ready.

Batory had hoped to open his campaign in 1578, but he was unable to mass his army in time. The struggle for Danzig had emptied the treasury, and it took time to gather in the levies to provide the subsidies, voted by the Seym. Many Poles were unenthusiastic and some were opposed to the war against Muscovy, believing that of Poland's two great enemies, the Crimean Tatars and the Muscovites, the former should be dealt with first. But with his great charm, energy, and leadership he successfully overcame these obstacles.

In June 1579 Batory sent Ivan a formal declaration of war, and in the following month he advanced with his army from Svir towards Polotsk. He had 60,000 well-equipped troops and under his leadership their morale was high. But Ivan had not been inactive during these months. He realized that Batory would either attack his garrisons in Livonia or, since he was bold and ambitious, that he might invade Muscovy but he considered the attack on Livonia more likely. Ivan had therefore mobilized his forces earlier in the year. He had placed detachments at strategic points on the banks of the Volga, Don, Oka, and Dnieper rivers to defend the Tsardom against Tatar attacks. He had then moved his main forces to Novgorod and Pskov.

Polotsk was a well fortified city with two strongholds, known as the Streletskaya and the Ostrog, which were surrounded by a natural moat, formed by the Dvina and Polota rivers. Ivan had captured it sixteen years earlier only because the Lithuanian garrison had readily capitulated. But now, expecting Batory to march into Livonia, he had made no special preparations to defend the city. On 11 August Batory began his siege and maintained a heavy bombardment for several weeks. He offered the garrison generous conditions if they would surrender, but they rejected his offer and resisted strongly. Many believed that the Tsar would march to relieve them. Gradually, however, the bombardment and the fires, spreading swiftly through the tinder-dry houses in the heat of August, wore down the garrison, and there was no sign of the Tsar coming to their aid. In one of the two strongholds the troops planned to blow themselves up rather than surrender. But Peter Volynsky, in command of the Ostrog, entered into negotiations with the enemy. Batory finally agreed to allow all commanders and troops to retreat with their families and possessions into Russia. He tried by offering generous terms to induce them to enter his service. But it was noteworthy that, although it meant returning to face the anger of the Tsar and perhaps his punishments, the Russians to a man refused to enter the King's service.[12] The Poles then captured the small town of Sokol, burnt it to the ground, and savagely massacred the inhabitants, sparing no one.

During the siege of Polotsk, Ivan was in Pskov and his main forces were posted in Pskov, Novgorod, and Smolensk. At the beginning of August he sent 20,000 of his Asiatic troops into Courland and detachments to defend Karelia and Izborsk against the Swedes, and he strengthened his garrisons in Livonia. He also sent a small force to relieve Polotsk, but its commander did not dare to attack Batory's siege positions and quickly withdrew.

The question remains, why did Ivan not advance against Batory with his main forces? He might easily have overwhelmed the Poles.

The explanation was probably that he was unwilling to risk everything in a single engagement, particularly while mistrusting his own boyars and expecting attacks by the Swedes and, possibly, the Tatars. Batory might have taken such a risk, but Ivan, cautious by nature and inheriting the attitude of his predecessors, would have regarded it as a reckless gamble.

The Grand Princes had asserted the hegemony of Moscow, not by dashing exploits or by victories won in open battle, but by careful diplomacy, steady expansion, and by taking advantage of the enemy's weaknesses. They had been forced to adopt such tactics under the Tatar yoke, for the Golden Horde had then wielded such power as Moscow could not openly challenge. But even after throwing off the Tatar domination, the Muscovites had had to continue these tactics, because they had found that their western enemies had evolved more effective techniques of war and held corps of regular troops, usually mercenaries, who were more than a match for the hasty levies of untrained men on whom the Grand Princes depended. It was indeed this sense of military inferiority which lay at the root of Muscovite caution and of Ivan's reluctance to meet the Poles in open battle.

Batory returned triumphant to Vilno and from there sent a message to Ivan, blaming him for causing the bloodshed at Polotsk and Sokol. Ivan responded with a note protesting his desire for peace and inviting Polish ambassadors to Moscow to negotiate. This drew an arrogant reply from Batory in March 1580 in which he directed Ivan to send his ambassadors to Poland. He added that he had already mounted his horse and was ready to lead his army wherever God might show the way, but he would await the Tsar's ambassadors for five weeks from 14 June (1580). This was bluff on Batory's part; he was, in fact, playing for time, until his army was ready to march. The Seym, meeting in Warsaw, had voted him subsidies for a second campaign, but the collection of special levies was slow. Moreover, his troops had not been fully mobilized and he had difficulty in recruiting infantrymen.

Ivan, too, was seeking in every possible way to postpone the renewal of hostilities. He sent a courier to Batory, complaining that his ambassadors could not possibly reach Vilno by the time specified. But no extension of the time was allowed and, realizing that Batory would invade as soon as he was ready, Ivan made hurried preparations. He assembled his troops and, as in the previous year, manned all the defence points on his south and south-eastern frontiers against

Tatar attacks. He also posted detachments in the northwest where the Swedes, taking advantage of the Polish campaign against Polotsk, had attacked Narva and Kexholm.

Batory's second campaign had as its objective the capture of Velikie Luki. This would advance his salient more deeply and widely into Muscovy. From this stronghold, too, he would threaten Novgorod, Pskov, and Smolensk, the three main Muscovite defence points in the east, and he would be able more readily to strike at Moscow. Batory conducted this campaign with great skill. He made a feint by sending a detachment of 2,000 men towards Smolensk, and then with his main force of 50,000 troops he marched rapidly to Velikie Luki, where he was least expected. At the Polish camp here the Tsar's ambassadors, who had been travelling for some weeks, were brought before Batory. But it was obviously not his intention to consider peace at this stage, and the ambassadors were treated with insulting discourtesy. They were permitted, however, to send a courier to their Tsar, requesting new instructions.

In the meantime the Poles had begun their bombardment and had succeeded in setting fire to the walls of the fortress. The Muscovite garrison, taken by surprise by this siege, were already demoralized, and soon began negotiating a surrender. But the Hungarian troops, serving under Batory, feared that an agreed surrender would rob them of the chance for plunder. Ignoring their orders, they broke into the town, followed by Polish troops, and began a slaughter of the inhabitants. Velikie Luki was then given over to plunder.

Batory's second campaign concluded with the capture of Velikie Luki, but some military operations continued during the winter of 1580–1. The Poles took a number of small towns both in Muscovy and in Livonia. Moreover, adding to Ivan's anxieties, the Swedes invaded Karelia (November 1580) and captured Kexholm, killing 2,000 Russians. In Esthonia they starved the garrison in Padis, near Reval, into surrender. The Swedes then moved into Livonia and captured Wesenberg. But the Russians, too, were active, and laid waste Lithuanian territory around Dubrovna, Orsha, and Mogilev. They also destroyed the Polish detachment, sent by Batory towards Smolensk.

Ivan was deeply disturbed by the loss of Velikie Luki and the other towns, and afraid that he would be unable to prevent further losses. The Turks and Crimean Tatars were, he knew, engaged against Persia, but at any time they might be free to march into Muscovy, and they would arouse the Tatars along the Volga to attack simultaneously. He would then be struggling for survival against several enemies all of whom he could not hope to repel.

The two ambassadors whom he had sent to Batory early in 1580 were still in attendance at the Polish camp. They suffered privations and insults, for the Poles, arrogant in victory, lost no opportunity to humiliate the Tsar in this way. But Ivan, although always highly sensitive about his dignity and exacting always the fullest observance of protocol, made no issue of this treatment of his ambassadors. Indeed, at this time he appointed two new envoys, Ivan Pushkin and Feodor Pisemsky, and instructed them not to insist on protocol. It was notable that Ivan could exercise restraint when he saw that it was necessary in pursuit of policy.

Pushkin and Pisemsky presented to Batory the new concessions that Ivan was now prepared to offer for the sake of peace. His concessions indicated his desperate mood, for they amounted to nothing less than the surrender of Livonia, except for four towns. But Batory rejected the offer out of hand. He asserted that he could conclude hostilities only on the condition of the surrender of the whole of Livonia, together with the towns of Sebezh, and the payment of 400,000 gold crowns in compensation for his military expenses. Couriers passed between the two monarchs and the wrangling became more drawn out. Batory even taunted Ivan with cowardice in failing to lead his troops and to meet him in battle.[13]

In his mood of high confidence, Batory seemed to consider himself invincible. He appeared before the Seym in Warsaw in February 1581 and proposed that subsidies should be levied for two years to enable him to conquer Muscovy. But the Polish nobles were tired of war and reluctant to levy further contributions. They wanted to negotiate peace while in a position of strength, but again Batory by his force of personality and leadership managed to persuade them to vote money for a third campaign.

The Polish objective this time was the capture of Pskov, the most strongly fortified city in Muscovy, not excluding even the capital. With Pskov in his hands Batory would be able to shield Livonia completely from Muscovite attacks and he would significantly further his conquest of Muscovy. But he gravely overestimated his strength and the quality of his Polish troops and underestimated the Russians in attempting to take this stronghold. Pskov was not only fortified to the point of being nearly impregnable, but also it had a garrison of 50,000 infantry and 7,000 cavalry, commanded by V. F. Skopin Shuisky and Ivan P. Shuisky, and ample supplies.

On 26 August, Batory's army, 100,000 strong, laid siege to Pskov. Cannon made a breach in the walls, but the Polish attempt to take the fortress by storm was, after an initial success, repelled with heavy losses to the Poles. Batory then found that he had expended all his powder, and his troops had to wait until new supplies were brought. Further bombardment and assaults made no impression on the garrison. Autumn was approaching and many Poles urged a retreat, but Batory stubbornly decided to maintain the siege throughout the winter. The Polish troops were constantly on the point of mutiny, because of the cold and hardships and the length of the campaign. Only the stern discipline of Jan Zamojski kept the army under some semblance of discipline. Pskov stood firm and it destroyed completely Batory's grandiose idea of conquering Muscovy.

Military operations were not, however, limited to Pskov. The Lithuanian Hetman, Christopher Radziwill, with a small force advanced eastwards of Velikie Luki to the Volga, but quickly withdrew. The Swedish attacks were more serious. The Swedes took Narva and several smaller Baltic towns, and then carried the war on to Russian soil, capturing Ivangorod, Yam, and Koporie.

Ivan was now desperate to end hostilities, and he warmly welcomed the mediation of the Jesuit priest Antonio Possevino, sent by Pope Gregory XIII. Early in 1580 Ivan had sent an envoy to Vienna, requesting the Emperor's intercession with the Polish King. He reminded Rudolph also of his undertaking to send his ambassadors to Moscow to negotiate an alliance. But Rudolph, indecisive and timorous, was anxious not to become involved against Batory, and pleaded that the ambassadors he had appointed to go to Moscow had died or had fallen ill.

Ivan's appeal to Rome, made later in 1580, had brought prompt results. Shevrigin, his envoy, presented to Pope Gregory XIII the Tsar's strong complaints that Batory had instigated war against Muscovy as an act of revenge, because the Tsar had supported the Habsburg candidate for election to the Polish throne. Further, the Tsar argued that he was fighting for Christianity, since Batory was vassal and ally of the Sultan. He urged the Pope to exercise his great authority immediately in restoring peace between Muscovy and Poland.

Gregory XIII was impressed by Ivan's respectful approach. He saw in it the opportunity first, to draw Muscovy into a league of Christian nations to crusade against the Moslem Turks, and, second, to revive the union of the Eastern and Western Churches under the

Pope, as had been agreed at Florence in 1439. Over a hundred years earlier Pope Paul II had pursued exactly the same purpose when he had offered to Ivan III the hand of his ward, Zoe Palaeologa, who had become Ivan's grandmother.

Pope Gregory at once appointed the Jesuit, Antonio Possevino, to lead an embassy to the King and the Tsar to bring peace between them. Possevino went first to Vilno where Batory, on the point of departing for Pskov, had told him bluntly that the Tsar was deceiving the Holy Father, and that Poland would win a satisfactory peace by force of arms, not by papal mediation.

Possevino proceeded to Muscovy and on 18 August 1581 he was received by the Tsar at Staritsa. An active man, eager to further the glory of Rome and of his Jesuit Order by bringing about the union of the churches, he attached great importance to his meeting with the Tsar. For his part Ivan, while he had no thought of agreeing to the union or of acknowledging the supremacy of the Pope, was depending on Possevino to bring him a respite from Polish aggression. He therefore received the Jesuit mission with even greater magnificence and respect than he had shown to the imperial ambassadors five years earlier. He was punctilious in demonstrating his reverence for the Pope and examined with special care the printed volume on the Union of Florence, richly bound and brought as a personal gift from the Pope himself.

Possevino, his hopes of achieving his goal raised by the grand reception, spoke of Batory's conditions for peace and then of the great Christian alliance against the Turk, and of the glorious union of the churches. He asked also that Venetian merchants should be allowed to trade freely and to build Catholic churches in Muscovy. Ivan expressed warm appreciation of the Pope's blessings and gifts, and praised his great enterprise against the Sultan. He did not reject the proposed union of the churches, but undertook to give his answer after peace with Poland had been signed. He gave permission for Venetian merchants to trade freely in Muscovy, bringing their own priests and praying to God in their own fashion, but that they should be allowed to build their own Catholic churches was unacceptable, "for we have not had Roman churches in the past, nor will we have them in future".[14]

Ivan made it clear that peace with Poland was the first consideration and he explained his position in detail. The terms which he asked Possevino to convey to Batory conceded less than he had authorized Pushkin and Pisemsky to offer in the previous year. The new conditions were that the Tsar would cede to Poland 66 towns in Livonia together with Velikie Luki, Zavolochie, Nevel, Velizh, and Kholm, but Muscovy would retain 35 towns in Livonia and also Dorpat, Narva, and certain other Esthonian towns.

Possevino had probably realized by this time that Ivan was unlikely to agree to the union of the churches and his zeal in urging the Muscovite cause to Batory, who was at least a Catholic, had certainly dimmed. Arriving in the Polish camp he had a meeting with Batory after which he sent the message to Ivan that the King was ready to negotiate, but on the terms already stated. Batory threatened further war, but in the meantime he awaited the arrival of the Tsar's ambassadors.

Dmitri Eletsky and Roman Olferiev were appointed to carry out this humiliating mission of negotiating the peace. They met the Polish representatives with Possevino in attendance in a devastated village ten miles from Zapolsky Yam. Batory had departed for Warsaw, leaving instructions that the negotiations were to be concluded in three days, but they were to drag on for five weeks. The Poles tried at once to impose their terms and to force immediate agreement; the Muscovites acted with measured dignity, examining every point raised and causing delays.

Not far distant from the village, the siege of Pskov continued. The Poles were by this time mutinous and their morale was low. The Muscovite garrison was making bold sallies in which they inflicted severe casualties on the Poles. Batory was in Warsaw, but he knew that he was unlikely to be able to persuade the Seym to vote further subsidies for war, and in any case his army was exhausted. He needed peace more than Ivan, whose ambassadors seemed to realize the growing strength of their position as the siege of Pskov continued. They argued and prevaricated over the conditions demanded by the Poles and appealed to Possevino to use his good offices, but the Jesuit was now firmly supporting the Polish cause.

The Muscovite ambassadors nevertheless had specific instructions to conclude a peace and they did not dare disobey or gamble on the exhaustion of Batory's army. On 6 January 1582 they concluded an armistice for ten years on conditions which, while humiliating to Ivan, nevertheless involved important concessions by the Poles. Muscovy ceded the whole of Livonia together with Polotsk and Velizh to Poland. But Batory was obliged to forgo his claim for 400,000 gold crowns compensation and to omit Sweden from the treaty, thus leaving Ivan free to decide with the King of Sweden the future of the Esthonian ports. Batory also agreed to return all the Russian lands which he had captured. The ambassadors of both sides wrangled for some days about the titles of their monarchs, but there was general relief that hostilities had come to an end, and the relief was especially noticeable among the Poles at Pskov.

Ivan had thus lost the Baltic seaboard which he had struggled to win for Muscovy. To him it was a great disaster, for it meant that the Baltic nations would again shut Muscovy off from intercourse with Western Europe. The policy of the Swedes, Poles, and Germans of defending themselves by retarding Russian growth filled him with bitterness. But he could do nothing further at this stage, and Russia had to wait nearly 150 years before Peter the Great achieved what Ivan had won and then lost.

Notes to Chapter XXI

[1] Solovyev, Bk. III, Vol. VI, p. 620.
[2] *Ibid.*, p. 621.
[3] *Ibid.*
[4] *Ibid.*, p. 624.
[5] *Ibid.*, p. 626.
[6] Karamzin, Bk. III, Vol. IX, col. 139.
[7] *Ibid.*, cols. 142–3.
[8] *Ibid.*, col. 142.
[9] *Ibid.*, col. 153.
[10] At this time in Wolmar Ivan wrote his second letter to Kurbsky. See p. 158.
[11] Apparently one reason why King Stephen Batory refused to ratify this agreement was that the Russian version contained a condition that the King would not invade Livonia, and this condition was absent from the Polish text. But it is clear that Batory had decided on war and it is unlikely that such discrepancies between the two versions played any real part in his decision to reject the armistice. Karamzin, *op. cit.*, col. 166.
[12] *Ibid.*, col. 176.
[13] Solovyev, *op. cit.*, p. 663.
[14] Karamzin, *op. cit.*, col. 194.

CHAPTER XXII

THE LAST YEARS 1581–3

TOWARDS the end of 1581 Ivan was experiencing the full bitterness of defeat. The loss of Polotsk and Velikie Luki, and the threat to Pskov, then under siege, had forced on him the terrible decision to surrender Livonia. It meant the total destruction of the westward policy which he had laboured for twenty-eight years to achieve. But the Tsardom was in danger and it was essential to negotiate peace with Poland. At the time of greatest stress when he had despatched his ambassadors and anxiously awaited the outcome of their negotiations with the Poles, he was suddenly overwhelmed by personal tragedy.

Tsarevich Ivan, the eldest son of Ivan by Anastasia, his beloved first wife, was now twenty-seven years of age. He had his father's high intelligence and gave promise of being a strong and able ruler. For some years he had been his father's constant companion, and Ivan's testament bore witness to the bonds of trust and affection existing between father and son. They were seldom separated, not solely because Ivan probably craved his son's company, but also because he was introducing him to the duties of the autocrat. At formal court audiences, when troops were mustered and commanders briefed, and when traitors and criminals were executed, the Tsarevich was at his father's side. He was present throughout the Novgorod massacres, and he apparently did not quail on these savage occasions. In fact, there is no evidence to suggest that he did not fully support his father in everything, and their companionship was evidently based on understanding and affection.

In November 1581, as he waited impatiently for news from Pskov and from his ambassadors, Ivan was under great strain. He had always been extremely irascible by temperament, and the smallest incident could throw him into a towering rage. In Alexandrovsk at this time the Tsarevich said something concerning the relief of Pskov or on some domestic matter[1] which made Ivan suddenly explode in anger. Raising the iron-tipped staff which he always carried he struck at his son. Boris Godunov was present and, trying to ward off the blow, he was hurt. Infuriated by this interference Ivan lunged again at his son, this time striking him on the head. The Tsarevich sank slowly to the ground and blood began to flow from the wound.

Horrified by his impulsive action, Ivan knelt and took his son in his arms, trying with his fingers to staunch the wound. He was now beside himself with horror. He wept convulsively. He called for doctors, shouted that he had killed his son. He uttered prayers that the Tsarevich might be spared, and then kissed him and implored his forgiveness.

The son was dazed and weak, but had not lost consciousness. He kissed his father's hand and begged him not to give way to grief and despair. Doctors came and the Tsarevich received every care. But slowly life was ebbing from him and four days later, on 19 November, he died.[2]

Ivan was inconsolable. The death of his son was a matter for grief, but to have killed him with his own hand was a tragedy too great for grief. For three days Ivan sat beside the open coffin in which the body lay. On 22 November, boyars and priests, clad in deep mourning, aroused him. They bore away the coffin to Moscow, escorted on foot through the snow by priests and monks chanting. Immersed in silence Ivan followed the bier all the way to the Cathedral of St Mikhail the Archangel, where a place had been made ready between the tombs of forbears. Ivan now wore a simple mourning robe without any insignia of rank or dignity. He was still silent while the boyars and people present wept and prayed for the soul of the Tsarevich. But, as the coffin was lowered into the ground, he threw himself upon it and uttered a cry which echoed through the cathedral.

For some time Ivan grieved. He could not sleep and wandered about his palace, sometimes crying out to heaven that his sorrows were beyond endurance. He did not seek to pass his guilt to others and did not call his son's death an accident. The Tsarevich had died by his hand, because he had sinned and this was God's punishment. Unsleeping, Ivan padded through the palace, without even stopping to pray before the ikons, lit dimly by oil lamps, in the corners of every room, for his sin and his grief were beyond the intercession of saints. Finally he would sink to the floor in the sleep of physical exhaustion. Then his personal servants, who had kept out of his sight, came to put pillows under his head and feet and covers on him against the winter cold. Awakening, he would resume his wanderings, a lonely man who could find no rest and no comfort.

Slowly Ivan came to himself again, but he remained a stricken figure, bearing the marks of grief. He summoned before him the leading men of church and state. To them he formally declared that, thus punished by God, it only remained for him to end his days, praying in solitude in some distant monastery. Tsarevich Feodor was not capable of ruling and it was therefore the duty of the boyars to choose a sovereign to whom he would at once surrender power. Boyars and churchmen alike were astonished to hear such an instruction from his lips, and some even suspected a trap to catch those whose loyalty was infirm. But most saw that he had spoken sincerely, and all replied, "Do not leave us! We do not want a Tsar other than him given to us by God—you and your son!"[3] Ivan bowed to the general will. At the time he undoubtedly desired to withdraw to a monastery. But he was a man too dedicated to his high office and to the Tsardom to be able to lay them aside for long, and he was soon throwing all his energies into affairs of state.

Boris Godunov had absented himself from court during these weeks. It was assumed that he was recovering from the wounds, received as he tried to protect the Tsarevich. Ivan heard, however, that not his wounds but anger and sorrow were keeping him away. Bereft of companionship and missing his favourite, Ivan called unexpectedly on Godunov to learn the truth about his absence. He found that Godunov was indeed still recovering from his wounds which had been stitched by the merchant, Anika Stroganov, who was adept in such matters.[4] Ivan embraced Godunov and showed him the greatest favour, as though in acknowledgment of his efforts to save the Tsarevich and also, perhaps, because, Godunov's sister, Irina, having married Tsarevich Feodor in the previous year, he cherished in his favourite someone who would help in his younger son's reign to bear the responsibilities of the throne.

Some three months after the death of the Tsarevich, Possevino returned to Moscow from the negotiations between the Muscovite and Polish ambassadors. He brought from Stefan Batory messages of goodwill and proposals for co-operation. The King was eager to encourage commerce between Muscovy and Poland–Lithuania and offered reciprocal trading rights. He also proposed that the two nations should wage joint campaigns against the Crimean Tatars. But Ivan was not ready for further military operations, least of all in combination with Batory. "It is not possible for us," he said to Possevino, "to send our army to Perekop, for our troops are exhausted from the war against King Stefan." He added that he had just received reports that his ambassador had agreed conditions for a peace with the Khan.[5]

Possevino then came to the main purpose of his mission, the union of the churches. He asked that he might speak alone with the Tsar. "We are ready to talk with you, but not alone," Ivan replied. "How could we be without our closest advisers at such a time?" He was in fact reluctant to allow this discussion at all. He pointed out that Possevino had rendered him a service in bringing peace between Muscovy and Poland. "But," he added, "if we start to talk about religion, then each being jealous for his own faith, will praise it above the others. Quarrels will ensue and we fear that hostility will arise between us."[6]

Possevino insisted, however, that no quarrels could arise. He then spoke of the Pope's desire that there should be but one church, and he developed the arguments for the union of the Greek and Roman churches. But Ivan remained unconvinced. "You say that your Roman faith is one with the Greek faith: we hold not to the Greek, but to the one true Christian faith." Possevino pressed his arguments, but made no headway. It became even clearer that Ivan would never accept the supremacy of the Pope. "The Pope is not Christ," he asserted. "The throne on which he is borne is not a cloud, and those who carry him are not angels. Nor is it right for Pope Gregory to liken himself to Christ. . . ."[7]

The Jesuit resigned himself to the failure of his great mission. But then he tried to obtain two concessions which would advance the Catholic cause among Russian Orthodox believers, and facilitate the union of the churches in years to come. He asked Ivan to permit the building of Catholic churches in Muscovy and also to allow parties of young Russians to go to Rome to study Latin. But Ivan was not deceived. He stressed that all were free to worship in Muscovy according to their own faith and even to have their own priests. But he would not allow Catholic churches to be erected in his realm or permit young Russians to be seduced from their faith in Rome. Possevino departed from Moscow, a disappointed man, bearing messages of goodwill from the Tsar to the Pope.

By this time Ivan had begun to rule again. His great natural energy and his lively concern in all matters affecting the Tsardom asserted themselves so strongly that he was saved from the inaction of brooding over grief and defeat. At this time, too, he was gratified by news of conquests beyond the Urals. The powerful Stroganov family, whom he had encouraged and controlled during the past twenty-five years, had colonized new lands and now had extended the Tsardom eastwards. Nothing could compensate Ivan for the loss of Livonia and the Baltic seaboard, and he can hardly have appreciated the full significance of this vast new acquisition. But he was a man of vision and this bold expansion impressed and gratified him.

The Stroganovs were a family of pioneers, colonizers, and adventurers who had come originally from Novgorod. They had prospered by colonization and astute commercial enterprise. In the 15th century they had settled at Solvychegodsk, where they mined salt, traded in furs, extended their estates, and were renowned for their shrewdness. Their riches were such that at one time they alone were able to pay the enormous ransom, said to have been 200,000 rubles in gold, for the release of Grand Prince Vasily Temny, captured by the Kazan Tatars. The Stroganovs always took care to cultivate good relations with the Grand Princes of Moscow. Luka Stroganov and then his son, Anika, were familiar and respected men at court and accepted as general contractors to the throne.[8]

The river routes into Siberia were already known, but it was the capture of Kazan and Astrakhan that opened the way to colonization.[9] At first it had seemed necessary only to declare it to be part of the Tsardom. In January 1555 the Siberian Khan had petitioned to become a vassal of the Tsar. Ivan had received his loyal messages and had fixed the amount of tribute to be paid. But it had soon become clear that the Tatars and other peoples of Siberia were riven by feuds and that their protestations of loyalty were merely attempts to obtain the Tsar's protection against rivals.

Ivan was determined to impose his rule and to restore order in Siberia, but he could not spare troops for the purpose. At this point in 1558 Grigory Stroganov, possibly on the initiative of Ivan himself, petitioned to be allowed to settle the virgin lands along the banks of the Kama river and its tributaries, south of the Perm region. Ivan readily granted the petition and his charter described in detail the rights conferred on the Stroganovs for the term of twenty years. They were authorized to build towns, maintain their own army and to make weapons; they could cultivate the land, mine salt, fish the rivers, and enjoy complete exemption from taxes and customs dues on trade. They could prospect for ores, but had to report all finds of copper, tin, or silver to the Tsar who retained the right to mine them himself. The charter expressly forbad the employment of runaway peasants, criminals, and deserters from the Tsar's armies. In short they were authorized to establish their own independent principality, not under the jurisdiction of the Tsar's governor in the Perm region, but governed, administered, and defended by themselves alone.

The Stroganovs—Anika, the father, a grand patriarchal figure, then in his seventies, but robust and active as ever, and his three sons, Grigory, Yakov, and Semeon—rapidly brought the virgin lands under cultivation. They built the town of Kankor and, six years later, after a second petition to the Tsar, the town of Kergedan. They were undaunted by the engulfing immensity of this new land, which seemed to lure them onwards with its fertile soil, and abundance of game and fur-bearing animals. Several times they petitioned to settle farther to the east and the Tsar did not hesitate to grant their requests.[10]

During the first fourteen years the Russian colonists were untroubled by the Ostyak, Cheremis, Mordva, Tatar, and other peoples of the Kama and Ural regions. But in 1572 reports reached Moscow of attacks on Russian settlements in the Perm region. Ivan at once sent orders to the Stroganovs to suppress the rebellious tribesmen, but taking care to deal kindly with all who were loyal. They promptly carried out their orders, but they foresaw that more serious troubles were coming. Kuchum, the new Siberian Khan, was hostile to the Russians and had already attacked several of the Siberian tribes who paid tribute to Moscow. In July 1573 Mametkul, Kuchum's son, invaded the Stroganov's territories, causing considerable damage, but he turned back on reaching the towns.

Reporting this invasion to Moscow, the Stroganovs now petitioned the Tsar for permission to extend their authority beyond the Urals. They claimed that they would then be able to maintain effective defences against the Siberian Khan and take under their protection those tribes which were ready to swear allegiance to the Tsar and to pay tribute. Moreover they undertook this defence of the new territories at their own expense. Again Ivan granted their petition without question. His charter conferred on them rights to develop lands and establish industries beyond the Urals on the banks of the Irtysh, Ob, and Tobol rivers. But he also authorized them to establish strongholds at suitable points and to pursue aggressive as well as defensive tactics against the Siberian Khanate.

The Stroganovs already had troops in their service, but for this ambitious expansion they had to raise a new private army. The various peoples of Siberia, whom they might have enlisted, were unreliable and unsuitable, and they continued, therefore, to rely on Cossacks. Freebooters, hunters, and robbers, the Cossacks of the

Don, Dnieper, and Volga served the Tsar when it suited them. They could be useful in raiding and opposing the Turks and Tatars, but they were lawless and often troublesome, especially when they took to plundering Moscow's trade routes. In the 1570s Ivan was forced to send troops to disperse the bands of Cossacks who were disorganizing trade along the Volga by their raids. One band of Cossacks, 540 strong and led by their Ataman, Ermak Timofeev, fled northwards to escape the Tsar's troops, and in the spring of 1579 reached the territories of the Stroganovs, who at once took them into their service.

For over two years Ermak and his Cossacks quietly manned defences. But in July 1581 tribesmen from the Urals made a surprise attack on the Russian settlements and before they were repelled they had burnt villages and taken a number of prisoners. Further surprise attacks were clearly to be expected and in the dense forests of the Kama region it was difficult to guard effectively against them. In any case the Stroganovs were not men to wait to be attacked. At once they decided on action and they equipped Ermak and his Cossacks, together with 300 additional troops, comprising Lithuanians, Germans, Tatars, and Russians in their pay, for a campaign against the Siberian Khanate.

Ermak's expedition set out on 1 September 1581, and on that same day bands of Asiatic tribesmen, coming from a different direction, attacked settlements belonging to the Stroganovs and in the Perm region. Semeon and Maxim Stroganov, reporting to Moscow, requested troops and arms and Ivan ordered the governor of the Perm region to provide 200 men to help in their defences. But in the following year Ivan received a denunciation of the Stroganovs, alleging that instead of maintaining their forces to defend themselves and the Tsar's frontier, they had sent them to the east to conquer the Siberian Khan for their own gain.

Since he had granted the first charter to the Stroganovs nearly twenty-five years earlier, Ivan's interest in Siberia had become keener. He had even set up a special Siberian ministry in Moscow. It may have been that Boris Godunov who was of Tatar origin and who showed a lively concern in this eastward colonization had influenced him. But from the early years of his reign Ivan had devoted himself to the expansion of the Tsardom and he had begun to look beyond the Urals as soon as Kazan and Astrakhan had been captured. At first he had been concerned primarily with securing his eastern frontier against predatory Tatar attacks. But reports from the

Stroganovs and others had stirred him and he had felt the challenge of the vastness and the riches of Siberia. In this age of colonization, when other European nations were expanding across the seas, he found virgin lands on his frontier awaiting colonization.

On receiving the denunciation, Ivan wrote angrily to the Stroganovs. He accused them of putting their interests above those of the Tsardom by sending Ermak into Siberia instead of holding his Cossacks to defend the Russian settlements. He was angry, too, that they had engaged fugitive Cossacks without his approval.[11] His anger was, however, moderate. He knew that the Stroganovs were not traitors, but hardy enterprising colonizers who merited the respect and fullest support that he had always shown them. He accepted their independent spirit as necessary in men who colonized unexplored lands beyond the frontiers and among hostile peoples. But on this occasion they had ignored his orders, and he exacted obedience from his subjects.

Meanwhile Ermak and his small force had moved eastwards along the Tura river, capturing a number of Tatar camps. The Siberian country with its thick coniferous forests, teeming with wild life and especially fur-bearing animals, and the network of mighty rivers with their tributaries and streams, all abounding with fish, made their progress fairly swift, but the cruel cold of winter was coming and they had to be on their guard against ambush and sudden attack. Their expedition was in fact spreading alarm among the nomadic Tatars. Khan Kuchum was gravely disturbed by stories that Ermak and his men were invincible and armed with weapons which spat fire and were more deadly than arrows. But the Khan had no thought of surrender. He reinforced his defences at Isker (Sibir) on the Irtysh river and called on all his subject tribes to send their fighting men to help repel this invader. Meanwhile Mametkul, his son, with the main Tatar forces advanced to engage Ermak. Tatars and Cossacks met in battle at Babasan, a settlement near the junction of the Tobol with the Irtysh. The Cossacks were greatly outnumbered, but they fought with spirit and their muskets finally won them victory over the Tatars, armed with bows. On the banks of the Irtysh Ermak engaged another Tatar force and was again victorious. Several Cossacks were killed, however, and few escaped wounds of some kind.

Ermak fully realized how dangerous his position was now that he had advanced so far into Siberia. He could not retreat; his force, already small, was dwindling as a result of the constant fighting;

winter with its savage cold was approaching and his supplies of food and ammunition were low. But he knew that he had to advance.

Near the confluence of the Tobol and Irtysh rivers, Kuchum had established his army in a strongly fortified camp. This became Ermak's objective. At dawn on 23 October he launched his Cossacks against the Tatars, who resisted strongly. But the spirited fighting of the Cossacks and their musket fire won them success. The Tatars fled and in growing numbers they began to desert Kuchum. Ermak and his Cossacks had crowned their reputation for being invincible. Three days later they entered Isker, the capital of the Siberian Khan, which they found deserted Kuchum had fled and Ermak had conquered Siberia.

Ataman Ivan Koltso with a small group of Cossacks returned to inform the Stroganovs and to report to the Tsar on their expedition. Koltso and his comrades appeared before the Tsar not without misgiving, for they were still fugitive Cossacks who had not been brought to justice. But they received a hearty welcome in the Kremlin. Ivan listened intently to their report and received their priceless gifts of sable, black fox, and beaver furs. He pardoned them and rewarded them with his favour and with rich presents. He also acknowledged the services of the Stroganovs and bestowed on them new estates. He then appointed Prince Semeon D. Bolkhovsky to proceed with 500 musketeers to Isker to receive formally from Ermak on his behalf the new Tsardom of Siberia.[12]

In Moscow the bells rang and in every church services of thanksgiving celebrated this great event. The people gathered in the Kremlin squares, saying to each other, "God has bestowed a new Tsardom on Russia!"[13] The excitement recalled the popular mood on the conquest of Kazan. But then the Tsar had led all his troops against a strong enemy. The conquest of Siberia was the fruit of the vision and enterprise of the Stroganovs and of the courage and fortitude of a small band of Cossacks. It was a brave exploit which became at once a cherished legend among the Russians and an inspiration to generations to come.

A further demonstration of Ivan's active rule and of his tenacity was his revival in 1582 of his negotiations for an alliance with Elizabeth of England. He could never really abandon his westward policy and this was an attempt to save something of it after the armistice with Poland.

Ten years earlier when Elizabeth had virtually rejected his proposals for an alliance Ivan had in a fury revoked all the privileges of the Russia Company. She had then sent Anthony Jenkinson to calm his anger. Ivan had a genuine fondness for "Anthony" as he called him, and indeed towards all the Englishmen who appeared at his court he showed special affection. It was something more than diplomatic tact. He was always capable of sincere and spontaneous affection for those whom he liked and respected. His disfavour and harsh punishments were reserved for those whom he mistrusted.

Jenkinson had had most satisfactory audiences with Ivan who was in a benign mood. Now that Jenkinson had come with Elizabeth's "loving letters and full mind", he expressed himself content and undertook to restore all privileges to the Company.[14] He had previously made strong complaints against certain merchants, but when pressed by Jenkinson he refused to specify the offences or to name the guilty men. "It was not princely," he said, "to forgive and after accuse the parties, whereupon Her Majesty's displeasure might fall upon them at home."[15]

In further audiences Jenkinson obtained most, but not all, that he requested. His mission had proved unexpectedly successful, but this was primarily because Ivan had for some reason decided not to press for an alliance, although he made it clear that his demands were merely in abeyance.

During these years Elizabeth was constantly importuning Ivan on behalf of the Company and he always responded helpfully. But suddenly in August 1574 he wrote angrily about the misbehaviour of certain merchants. He alleged, too, that Englishmen had aided Sweden against Muscovy, and then he revived the question of an alliance.

Fearing that the Company's privileges were about to be revoked again, Elizabeth had in May 1575 appointed Daniel Sylvester to go to Moscow. Sylvester had two stormy meetings with the Tsar who complained bitterly of the Queen's tergiversations. He emphasized his liberality towards the Company and swore that, if he did not receive similar treatment, he would give all trade to the Venetians and Germans.

Sylvester returned to England and soon afterwards sailed again for Muscovy, bearing Elizabeth's reply, but it was destined never to reach Ivan. Sylvester arrived in Kholmogory where, while trying on

> "a new yellow satin jacket or jepone in an upper room of his lodgings in the English house, and the tailor gone scarcely down the stairs a thunderbolt came and struck him dead. A flash of lightning killed also his boy and dog by him, burnt his desk, letters, house all at instant."[16]

Ivan, learning of this incident, muttered only "God's will be done!" But he was a superstitious man and this act of fate may well have influenced him to relinquish his threatened reprisals against the Company. Moreover, the war against Poland had then absorbed his attention and for five years he apparently exchanged no letters or messages with Elizabeth.

In 1582 Ivan renewed his proposals and they took almost exactly the same form as the proposals first presented some twelve years earlier. But there was one curious additional request: Ivan now wanted an English bride and his choice had fallen on Lady Mary Hastings, the Queen's cousin. It was a curious request because Ivan had only recently married for a seventh time. His new wife, whom he took without any ceremony or blessing of the church, was Maria Feodorovna, daughter of Feodor Nagoi, and she was to bear him a son, named Dmitri.[17] But the fact of taking a new wife did not inhibit Ivan in asking for the hand of Lady Mary. Like Elizabeth's father, he apparently had no scruples in disposing of his wives.[18]

Ivan's ambassador, Feodor Pisemsky, arrived in England in September 1582 with instructions to negotiate an alliance and to inspect Lady Mary. The negotiations proved slow and difficult. Elizabeth held firmly to her refusal to agree the alliance as proposed and insisted on the provisos which he had rejected some time earlier. At the same time she boldly pressed her demands for confirmation of the Company's monopoly of the White Sea trade.

Elizabeth was also most reluctant to agree to the proposed marriage. Reports from her ambassadors and from English merchants had painted Ivan in black colours. The torture and execution of many of his boyars and the facts that he had married so often, that his latest wife was alive, and that he was said to be attended always by a retinue of concubines made Elizabeth unwilling to surrender her cousin. Apparently Lady Mary herself was so terrified by the tales of Ivan's ferocity that she begged the Queen to free her from such a "dangerous honour" as this marriage.[19]

Intent on avoiding a blunt refusal, Elizabeth did everything to discourage the Tsar's suit. Pisemsky received only adverse reports on Lady Mary. Elizabeth herself told him that, while gratified by Ivan's wish to become "nearer" to her, she did not think Lady Mary, whose only ornaments were her moral qualities, would please such a "well-known admirer and appreciator of beauty" as the Tsar.[20] Lady Mary had recently had smallpox and Elizabeth would not allow Pisemsky to see her until the ugly scars had healed. His instructions were, however, to inspect the young Lady and, after long insistence, he finally saw her in May, 1583, some five months after his first request.

The interview took place in the Lord Chancellor's garden. Lady Mary approached the ambassador, bowed slightly and then stood motionless, while he stared intently at her. For some minutes he studied her and then, saying "It is enough," he walked away. In the report which he made to the Tsar, he wrote that "Mary Hastings is tall, slender, pale-faced, has grey eyes, fair hair, a straight nose, and long taper fingers."[21] He did not mention any ravages of smallpox, nor did he refer to her beauty, but he received a portrait of her to take back to Moscow with him.

In June Pisemsky sailed from England, accompanied by Elizabeth's ambassador, Sir Jerome Bowes, a rough, high-tempered man, and a braggart. His task was undoubtedly difficult. He was instructed to be adamant on Elizabeth's terms for the alliance. Further he was to do all in his power to discourage Ivan from pressing for marriage with Lady Mary, especially on the grounds of her poor health and the reluctance of her family to part with her. He could, however, confirm the Queen's promise of refuge in England, a request which Ivan reiterated, although it had already been conceded more than once. In spite of this negative response to two of Ivan's three proposals, Bowes was to press urgently for confirmation of the Company's monopoly of the White Sea trade, especially as the Dutch were seeking to share in it.[22]

Bowes had a number of interviews with Ivan, some of them stormy and several times he was angrily dismissed. Without doubt he was on occasion insolent, but his outspoken manner, although unlike the firm but courteous bearing of Jenkinson, Randolph, and others, apparently impressed Ivan, who even came to like this bluff Englishman. In one typical passage, Bowes flared up in anger because he thought that the Tsar had referred slightingly to the Queen. Ivan ordered him to leave the palace, but then suddenly had him recalled, praising him for his zealous defence of his sovereign, and adding, "Would to God that I had such a faithful servant!"[23] But his liking for the Queen's ambassador did not make her answers to his requests any more acceptable, and the stormy audiences continued.

Fearing that he would fail in his mission, Bowes became more persuasive, even holding out hopes that the Queen might reconsider her policy. He claimed in his reports to London that Ivan had decided to send a new embassy to the Queen, and that he had promised confirmation of certain of the Company's privileges. But on 18 March 1584, before Bowes had received any written confirmation and before a new envoy could be appointed, he received from the Muscovite chancellor a message, reflecting Ivan's anglophile reputation among his own subjects, that "the English Emperor was dead".[24]

Notes to Chapter XXII

[1] According to Karamzin's account the Tsarevich approached his father and demanded to be allowed to lead troops to the relief of Pskov and thus to save the honour of the nation. But another account relates that the Tsarevich was struck down because he spoke up for his wife whom Ivan had chided. Karamzin, *op. cit.*, col. 208; Solovyev, *op. cit.*, p. 703.

[2] Karamzin, *loc. cit.*

[3] *Ibid.*, col. 210.

[4] It is said that Feodor Nagoi, for having informed falsely and maliciously against Godunov, was subjected to the same stitching as Godunov as a punishment. Karamzin, *op. cit.*, col. 210.

[5] Solovyev, *op. cit.*, p. 671.

[6] *Ibid.*

[7] *Ibid.*, p. 672.

[8] *Ibid.*

[9] M. N. Tikhomirov, *Russia in the 16th Century* (Moscow, 1962), pp. 464-6.

[10] Kergedan is the present-day town of Orel. In 1566 Yakov Stroganov petitioned the Tsar to take their towns of Kankor and Kergedan with all their industries and trade into the Oprichnina, so that they would be protected from the plunder and persecution of the Oprichniki. The Tsar granted the request. Solovyev, *op. cit.*, p. 691; Tikhomirov, *op. cit.*, pp. 460-2.

[11] Solovyev, *op. cit.*, pp. 398-9.

[12] Fact and legend concerning the conquest of Siberia by the Stroganovs and Ermak are so intertwined that it is almost impossible to differentiate. The account given here is based on that of Karamzin, but there are variations on this story, as Solovyev [*op. cit.*, pp. 715-23] points out. See also Tikhomirov, *op. cit.*, pp. 464-6. Karamzin, *op. cit.*, cols. 219-42.

[13] Karamzin, *op. cit.*, col. 235.

[14] T. S. Willan, *op. cit.*, p. 120.

[15] *Ibid.*

[16] *Ibid.*, p. 128; E. A. Bond [ed.], *Russia at the Close of the 16th Century* (London, Hakluyt Society, 1856), p. 184.

[17] On Ivan's death his son, Feodor, succeeded to the throne and Tsarevich Dmitri with his mother and relatives was removed to the small town of Uglich on the Volga to the north of Moscow. Dmitri is said to have died in 1591, and the disputes surrounding his death were to prove disastrous for Boris Godunov personally and for Russia, for they were the immediate

cause of the period of anarchy, known in Russian history as "The Time of Troubles" which ended in 1613 with the election of Mikhail, the first of the Romanovs, to the throne.

[18] The background to Ivan's sudden desire for an English bride is obscure. He may have discussed it as early as 1568 with Jenkinson, but this is improbable. Robert Jacob, who was Ivan's English physician, or Eliseus Bomelius, a Westphalian physician and astrologer who had gone to Russia from England, may have aroused his interest in an English bride. Whatever the origin of the request, it is clear that Ivan had no thought of seeking the hand of Elizabeth herself, but he certainly required that his English bride should be related to the Queen. E. D. Morgan and C. H. Coote [eds.], *op. cit.*, p. 257; Willan, *op. cit.*, p. 161; E. A. Bond [ed.], *op. cit.*, pp. xlvii–xlviii.

[19] N. Casimir, "Historical Notes Relating to Czar John the Terrible of Russia and Queen Elizabeth of England" in *The Reliquary*, Vol. xvi, 1875–6, p. 13.

[20] *Ibid.*, p. 11.

[21] *Ibid.*, pp. 12–13.

[22] G. Tolstoy, *op. cit.*, p. 205.

[23] N. Casimir, *op. cit.*, p. 17.

[24] R. Hakluyt, *op. cit.*, II, p. 262.

CHAPTER XXIII

THE DEATH OF IVAN 1584

FOR some years Ivan had complained of feeling old and near to death. But his great energies, physical and mental, had remained unimpaired. He possessed a strong constitution, which seemed unaffected by the long tension of fear, by his furies, and by the bouts of debauchery of which he was so often accused. Apart from one major illness, he had always enjoyed good health, often under conditions of strain which would have broken most men. But in the winter of 1584 he began to show symptoms of the illness which was to prove fatal.

Like his birth, his death was heralded by portents. Early in 1584 Ivan observed between the golden domes and crosses of the Uspensky and Blagoveshchensky Cathedrals a comet in the sky, and its tail formed a nebulous cross, an illusion aided perhaps by the Northern Lights. Struck by this phenomenon, Ivan went out on to the Red Staircase, the formal entrance to the palace, and gazed at it intently for a long time. Then his face became overcast and turning he said to his suite, "That is the sign of my death."[1]

This portent began to prey on his mind. He summoned astrologers from all parts of Russia and even from Lapland. Sixty of these wise men were brought to Moscow and housed together in a separate building. Daily he sent Belsky to consult with them. They consistently spoke of his death as near at hand and even agreed on 18 March as the day. Ivan sent orders that they were to be silent and to make no more predictions. At the beginning of March, however, a message went out to all monasteries that the Tsar in his suffering implored all monks to pray for him that his sins might be forgiven and his health restored.[2]

By this time Ivan had begun to suffer seriously. His body became horribly swollen and, according to contemporary reports, he showed signs of internal putrefaction. The news of his illness spread through Moscow and into most of the country. The people crowded into the churches to pray for his recovery. They acted not from any kind of compulsion, but because they revered their Tsar and because he was their protector without whom they would be lost.

Ivan now made a new testament. He declared Tsarevich Feodor his heir and successor to the throne. Since Feodor was physically weak and backward, he appointed a special council to guide him and to ease the weight of his responsibilities. The leading men of this council were Prince Ivan Petrovich Shuisky, who had distinguished himself in the defence of Pskov, Ivan Feodorovich Mstislavsky, a close relative of Prince Vasily Mstislavsky, Nikita Romanovich Yuriev, the brother of Anastasia, the first Tsaritsa, Boris Godunov, and Belsky. To the young Tsarevich Dmitri, born to his last wife, he bequeathed the town of Uglich and its environs, and entrusted his upbringing to Belsky.[3] He counselled Feodor, his heir, to rule with love and kindness, avoiding wars against Christian powers, and giving thought to the relief of his people so that they did not suffer the burdensome taxes and the hardships which they had endured during his reign. Finally he ordered that criminals and prisoners of war from Lithuania and Germany should be freed.

On 15 March, Ivan felt some relief from his sufferings. He spent some time with the Englishman, Jerome Horsey, showing him his priceless collection of diamonds, rubies, sapphires, and other stones. It was said that later in the day, when the young wife of his son, Feodor, called to see him, he gazed on her so lustfully that she fled in terror.[4] But soon afterwards he became delirious and began calling anxiously for Tsarevich Ivan, the son whom he had killed. He imagined that he saw him and began speaking affectionately to him.

Two days later Ivan felt better. Warm baths had brought him great relief. He gave orders that the Lithuanian ambassador, who had been halted at Mozhaisk because of his illness, should come to Moscow where he would be received in audience. According to Horsey, he felt so much better that he believed he had proved the predictions to be false, and he even ordered the execution of the "lying astrologers".[5]

On 18 March Ivan lay for three hours in a warm bath and again felt great benefit. He rested on his bed and then called for the chessboard. He was setting up the chessmen to play with Belsky when suddenly he collapsed. Doctors tried to revive him and the Metropolitan, following the custom whereby the monarch was shorn as a monk before death, pronounced over Ivan the prayers for his dedication to God.

The people of Moscow were stunned by the death of Ivan. To them he was not "the Terrible" but their Tsar, appointed by God to rule over them.¹ They had respected him as a strong and able monarch, who had identified himself completely with the nation. He had been severe to traitors and to the boyars and princes who had opposed him, but the people of all other classes had been loyal, serving him faithfully and without question." They had seen in him their defender against the boyars and princes and against the enemies of the nation. The conquest of Kazan and of Astrakhan had invested him in their minds with an aura of greatness and they had cherished their faith in him as the great Tsar. They had endured hardships and in the last years of the reign defeats, but these were punishments from God, not to be blamed on their Tsar. Perhaps, too, they were moved by some premonition of the horrors they were to endure during the coming years, known in Russian history as the Time of Troubles, when their lives were harrowed by calamities, and they were to long for the strength of Ivan's rule and the stability of his reign.

For two days the body lay in its open coffin and the people crowded to take their last leave of him. Then on the third day, attended by the grief of the whole nation, he was buried in the Cathedral of St Mikhail the Archangel in the Kremlin.

Notes to Chapter XXIII

¹ Karamzin, Bk. III, Vol. IX, col. 256.
² Solovyev, Bk. III, Vol. VI, p. 704.
³ R. Hakluyt, *op. cit.* (London, 1809), pp. 525–6.
⁴ Karamzin, *op. cit.*, col. 257.
⁵ *Ibid.*
⁶ The nature of Ivan's fatal illness is obscure. Certain physicians have, however, ventured to diagnose that it was "diffuse cerebral syphilis and syphilis of the aortic valve" which might explain Ivan's violent irascibility and his immorality. This diagnosis is, however, vitiated by the fact that it is based on the most lurid and false legends and tales which have attached to Ivan; it is at best no more than wildest guessing, and not deserving of credence. C. MacLaurin, *Mere Mortals* (New York, 1925); W. W. Ireland, *The Blot upon the Brain* (Edinburgh, 1893).
⁷ In the course of structural renovations to the Arkhangelsky Cathedral in the Kremlin, the graves of Ivan and of his two sons, Tsarevich Ivan and Tsar Feodor, were opened. Some information has been published in the Soviet Press concerning the contents of these tombs. The inner tombstone of Ivan's grave confirms that he died on 18 March, not 19 March as is sometimes stated. The remains were found to be clad in the simple robes of a

monk, and he had been shaven and blessed under the name of Iona as he lay dying or, as seems more probable, immediately after death. Also in his grave was found a magnificent drinking goblet of Venetian glass, which contained the residue of the chrism or sacramental unguent. M. N. Tikhomirov, "The Last of the Kalita Dynasty" in *Izvestiya* (Moscow, 21 July 1963).

POSTSCRIPT

After the opening of the tomb of Ivan the Terrible in late summer of 1963, the remains were taken to Moscow University for examination and also for reconstruction of his head and face by the Soviet anthropologist and sculptor, M. M. Gerasimov. Information concerning this work has appeared from time to time in the Soviet press, the most complete account of the findings being published in an article in *Ogonyok* [No. 12, March, 1964] from which the following details are taken.

Ivan had a strong face with prominent aquiline nose, high forehead, large heavy-lidded eyes, and a small mouth. His teeth were strong and even, and might have belonged to a man twenty years younger. Owing to the shape and crowding of his mouth, however, he may possibly have had a defect of speech. In physique he was a massive man, nearly six feet tall, powerfully built and muscular.

In his tomb Ivan lay not with his hands crossed on his chest in the customary Christian burial position, but with his right arm bent and raised as though to shield his face. It may be that he believed himself about to be attacked and raised his arm in self-defence. A far more likely explanation, however, is that he had convulsions during which his arm was raised, and that, while he was always awesome in appearance, his expression and position in death were so frightening that no one dared to force his arm to his chest.

Chemical analysis of the remains revealed the presence of an excessive amount of mercury. For this reason the possibility that he was poisoned cannot be wholly ruled out. This hypothesis is, however, highly improbable. Mercury was commonly used by doctors at this time, especially in ointments which were applied liberally to swellings and to painful areas. It was not then known that mercury was poisonous and that even its fumes were dangerous. It is, then, most probable that Ivan absorbed excessive quantities of mercury from ointments and inhalation, and that this inadvertent poisoning was one of the causes of the pain he suffered.

One corner of the sarcophagus was found to have been broken, and the left foot of Ivan was damaged. Analysis showed, however, that this damage was done early in the 20th century when the floor of the cathedral was repaved. Possibly one of the workmen, ignorant of the fact that the Tsars were customarily buried in the simple robes of a monk and without regalia or jewels, had the idea of plundering the tomb but did not persevere with his attempt.

Photographs of the reconstructed bust of Ivan, made by M. M. Gerasimov using a cast of the skull taken from the tomb, show a likeness remarkably similar to the portrait in the contemporary "Book of Titles," which is reproduced as the frontispiece to this study.

20 April 1964
London

BIBLIOGRAPHY

The following list contains the main sources which I have studied or consulted. It is by no means exhaustive. Other authorities are given in the notes to chapters.

Bakrushin, S. V., and others, *History of Moscow*, Vol. 1, *Period of Feudalism*, Moscow, 1952.

"The Chosen Council of Ivan the Terrible" in *Istoricheskie Zapiski*, Moscow, 1945, Vol. 15.

Ivan the Terrible, Moscow, 1945.

Bartenev, S. P., *The Moscow Kremlin in Ancient Times and Now*, Moscow, 1912.

Baynes, N., and Moss, H. St L. B. (eds.), *Byzantium*, Oxford, 1948.

Bazilievich, K. V., *External Policy of the Russian Centralized State in the Second Half of the 15th century*, Moscow, 1952.

Blum, J., *Lord and Peasant in Russia from the 9th to the 19th Century*, Princeton, 1961.

Bobrinskoy, A. A., *The Gipsholm Cannon*, St Petersburg, 1914.

Bond, E. A. (ed.), *Russia at the Close of the 16th Century*, London, Hakluyt Society, 1856.

Chronicles, The Full Collection of Russian, 26 vols., Moscow 1841–1930, resumed 1949.

Contarini, A., *Travels to Tana and Persia*, London, Hakluyt Society, 1873.

Eckhardt, H., *Ivan the Terrible*, trans. from German, New York, 1949.

Fennell, J. L. I. (ed. and trans.), *The Correspondence between Prince A. M. Kurbsky and Tsar Ivan IV of Russia 1564–79*, Cambridge, 1955.

Ivan the Great of Moscow, London, 1961.

Hakluyt, R., *The Principall Navigations, Voiages and Discoveries of the English Nation*, London, Hakluyt Society, 1903.

Hamel, J. V., *Russia and England*, London, 1854.

Herberstein, Sigismund von, *Notes upon Russia*, trans. and ed. by Major, R. H., London, Hakluyt Society, 1851–2.

Karamzin, N. M., *History of the Russian State*, St Petersburg, 1842–3, 5th edition.

Kashtanov, S. M., "Feudal Immunity in the years of the Boyar Rule 1538–48" in *Istoricheskie Zapiski*, Vol. 66, 1960.

Klyuchevsky, V. O., *Course of Russian History*, Moscow, 1956–9.

Koraiev, A. I., "The Population of the Russian State in the 16th Century" in *Istoricheskie Zapiski*, Vol. 64, 1959.

Korotkov, I. A., *Ivan the Terrible; his Military Activity*, Moscow, 1952.

Likhachev, D. S., and Lur'ye, Ya. S., *Letters of Ivan the Terrible*, Moscow, 1951.

Likhachev, D. S., *The National Consciousness of Ancient Rus*, Moscow–Leningrad, 1945.

Lubimenko, I., *Les Relations Commerciales et Politique de L'Angleterre avec la Russie avant Pierre le Grand*, Paris, 1932.

Morgan, E. D., and Coote, C. H. (eds.), *Early Voyages and Travels in Russia and Persia*, London, Hakluyt Society, 1886.

Nolde, B., *La Formation de L'Empire Russe*, Paris, 1952.

Olearius, Adam, *The Voyages and Travels of the Ambassadors sent by Frederick, Duke of Holstein, to the Great Duke of Muscovy and the King of Persia, begun in the year 1633 and finished in 1639*, London, 1662.

Oman, C., *The English Silver in the Kremlin 1557–1663*, London, 1961.

Pember, A., *Ivan the Terrible*, London, 1895.

Pierling, LeP., *La Russie et le Saint-Siège*, Paris, 1896.

Platonov, S. F., *Ivan the Terrible*, Berlin, 1924.

Boris Godunov, Prague, 1924.

Essays on the History of the Troubled Times in the Muscovite State in the 16th and 17th Centuries, Moscow, 1937.

Reddaway, W. F., and others [eds.], *The Cambridge History of Poland*, Cambridge, 1950.

Romanov, B. A., "The Sudebnik of Ivan the Terrible" in *Istoricheskie Zapiski*, Vol. 29, Moscow, 1949.

Skrynnikov, R. T., "The Oprichnaya Land Reform of Ivan the Terrible 1565" in *Istoricheskie Zapiski*, Vol. 70, Moscow, 1961.

Smirnov, I. I., "The Revolt of Andrei Staritsky, 1537" in *Istoricheskie Zapiski*, Vol. 50, Moscow, 1955.

Solovyev, S. M., *History of Russia from Earliest Times*, Moscow, 1960.

Staden, H., *Concerning the Moscow of Ivan the Terrible. Notes of a German Oprichnik*, Trans. by I. Polosin, Moscow, 1925.

Suslov, V. V., *The Church of St Basil in Moscow*, St Petersburg, 1912.

Tikhomirov, M. N., *Russia in the 16th Century*, Moscow, 1962.

Tolstoy, G., *The First Forty Years of Intercourse between England and Russia 1553–93*, St Petersburg, 1875.

Ustryalov, N. (ed.), *The Statements of Prince Kurbsky*, St Petersburg, 1833.

Vernadsky, G., *Kievan Russia*, Yale, 1948.

The Mongols and Russia, Yale, 1953.

Russia at the Dawn of the Modern Age, Yale, 1959.

A History of Russia, 5th ed., Yale, 1961.

Veselovsky, S., "The Institution of the Oprichny Court in 1565 and its Abolition in 1572" in *Voprosy Istorii*, 1946, No. 1.

"The First Experience of Reform of the Central Power in the Reign of Ivan the Terrible" in *Istoricheskie Zapiski*, Vol. 15, Moscow, 1945.

Waliszewski, K., *Ivan the Terrible*, trans. by Lady Mary Lloyd, London, 1904.

Willan, T. S., *The Early History of the Muscovy Company 1553–1603*, Manchester, 1956.

Wipper, R., *Ivan Grozny*, trans. by J. Fineberg, Moscow, 1947.

Zabelin, I. E., *History of the City of Moscow*, Moscow, 1905.

The Domestic Life of the Russian Tsars and Tsaritsas, Moscow, 1862–9.

Zernov, N., *The Russians and their Church*, London, 1945.

Eastern Christendom, London, 1961.

Zimin, A. A., "Towards the History of the Military Reforms of the 50s of the 16th Century", in *Istoricheskie Zapiski*, Vol. 55, Moscow, 1956.

"On the Court Institutions of the Russian State at the end of the 15th and in the 16th Centuries" in *Istoricheskie Zapiski*, Vol. 63, Moscow, 1958.

I. S. Peresvetov and his Contemporaries, Moscow, 1958.

Reforms of Ivan the Terrible, Moscow, 1962.

With D. S. Likhachev (eds.), *The Works of I. S. Peresvetov*, Moscow and Leningrad, 1956.

(ed.), *Anthology of the History of the U.S.S.R. in the 16th and 17th Centuries*, Moscow, 1962.

INDEX

253

Index

Index